THE BEST TOEFL TEST BOOK

AF327443

THE BEST TOEFL TEST BOOK

Nancy Stanley

ADDISON-WESLEY PUBLISHING COMPANY

Reading, Massachusetts • Menlo Park, California • New York
Don Mills, Ontario • Amsterdam • Workingham, England • Bonn
Sydney • Singapore • Tokyo • Madrid • Bogata • Santiago • San Juan

A publication of the World Language Division

Also available as: package (book + 1 cassette) 15421-8
            cassette 1 16472-8
            cassette 2 16473-6

ISBN: 0-201-15422-6
  BCDEFGHIJ-AL-898

For Violet and her dad.

WHY THIS BOOK WILL HELP YOU

You will find everything you need in this book to focus your attention and energies on your primary goal—to pass the TOEFL and pass it with the highest possible score you can.

The Forty Focused Exercises will help you

- concentrate on the kinds of structural items that often cause problems for the test-taker
- recognize and reject the typical wrong answers that appear on the TOEFL
- understand *why* these answers are wrong
- recognize similar ''tricky'' items as you take the TOEFL

The Preview to the Six Practice Tests will help you

- understand the nature of the three different sections
- build and *change* strategies from one section to another
- budget your time

The Six Practice Tests and the *Answer Keys* will help you

- get comfortable with items that are as close as possible in length, style, and type to those on the TOEFL itself
- avoid choosing the same kinds of wrong answers that you will find on the TOEFL
- learn from your mistakes *and* your correct answers

    There is no unnecessary or irrelevant material; each section has been carefully designed to do just one thing—sharpen your skills and your self-confidence as a TOEFL test-taker.

The Ten Stages for Essay Planning and Writing will help you

- familiarize yourself with the essay format
- develop appropriate strategies for writing different kinds of essays
- make the best use of the time available
- take full advantage of the English you know

What to Expect on the TOEFL Examination

The multiple-choice part of the test is divided into three distinct sections: *Listening Comprehension, Structure and Written Expression,* and *Reading Comprehension and Vocabulary.* There are specified time periods allotted to each section, and you cannot work on one section in the time allowed for another one. However, each of the three sections is further broken down into a number of parts, and within Sections 2 and 3 it is possible to allow yourself more time on some parts than on others. Because Section 1, Listening Comprehension, depends upon the speed of the tape, you must answer each question within the specific time allotted for it on the tape. This section usually takes about 40 minutes. On the 150-question tests, you will be given 25 minutes to work on Section 2 and 45 minutes to work on Section 3. (Some tests have 200 questions, and you will be allowed more time to complete the longer tests.)

Section 4, the Writing Question, is the only section which requires you to produce English. You have 30 minutes to plan and write an essay (about 300 words) in response to a detailed and specific question. Your score will depend heavily on how well you organize and develop your ideas.

The TOEFL will seem like a long, difficult exam—which it is. Be sure to get enough sleep the night before. Allow yourself enough time to eat or do anything else you need to do *before* entering the examination room. You will not be permitted to leave the room for any reason during the actual examination. If you do, the test administration will declare your test invalid. Be sure to bring at least two sharpened pencils (#2 type) and a good eraser to complete the test.

Precautions for the Day You Take the TOEFL

You must be careful to avoid the following behavior, or the test administration may refuse to grade your answer sheet:

- taking the test for someone else
- bringing books or notes of any kind into the testing room
- not following the supervisor's instructions
- reading or working on a part of the test in the time designated for a different part
- helping someone else or accepting help
- marking the test booklet or making notes on the answer sheet (except for the essay section)
- copying out test questions or answers
- removing test materials from the testing room
- cheating in any way, or appearing to cheat

Strategies**

In order to get a high score on the TOEFL, you need a good understanding of English and the nature of the test. But that's not enough. What *will* help you raise your score is learning when and how to apply specific strategies for each part of the test.

Section 1: Listening Comprehension

STRATEGY for Part A: look at all the answer choices before you hear the question.

STRATEGY for Part B: aim for a more general understanding than in Part A but more specific than in Part C.

STRATEGY for Part C: aim for a general understanding of what you hear.

Section 2: Structure and Written Expression

GENERAL STRATEGY: work at a steady pace and read each possible answer very carefully.

STRATEGY for Part A: read carefully and choose the one correct sentence completion.

STRATEGY for Part B: choose the one incorrect part.

Section 3: Reading Comprehension and Vocabulary

GENERAL STRATEGY: do Part A quickly to allow yourself more time for Part B.

STRATEGY for Part A: work quickly; if you do not know the meaning, guess and continue on to the next item.

STRATEGY for Part B: think about the items and recheck them with the information given.

Section 4: Essay Practice

GENERAL STRATEGY: Plan your essay before starting to write.

STRATEGY for Planning: Focus on a step-by-step plan.

STRATEGY for Writing: Let the logic of your argument dictate the structure, and control the level of English.

Now you are ready to do the Focused Exercises. Go through these carefully before you do any of the practice tests. You will probably find that once you have done the exercises, you will be able to complete the tests more easily. And when you have completed all six practice tests, you should be ready to take the TOEFL with increased skill and confidence!

**See the Preview to the Practice Tests (pp. 42-45) for more specific strategies and tactics for raising your TOEFL score.

CONTENTS

THE FOCUSED EXERCISES

These exercises concentrate on the kinds of structural items that often cause problems for test-takers. They do not cover the broad field of English structure as a whole, and are NOT intended to replace regular study and reference to a good English grammar. *The focus of these exercises is on preparing you for Section 2 of the TOEFL.*

Section 2 has forty questions and is divided into two parts. You will be free to use your time as you wish, so long as you complete the forty questions in 25 minutes. The two parts, however, call for different strategies.

a. In Part 1 (questions 1-15), you will choose the *correct* answer from four options. Obviously, the other three options are wrong in some way.

b. In Part 2 (questions 16-40), you will choose the one underlined part of the sentence (from four underlined parts) which is *incorrect*.

The Focused Exercises are set up in the same way. The Answer Key to Exercises 1-15 tells you *why* one answer is correct and the others are wrong. The Answer Key to Exercises 16-40 tells you only the correct answer, but you should be able to recognize why that is the appropriate choice from the exercise itself.

How can you get the most out of these Focused Exercises?

a. Go through them *before* you try any of the Practice Tests.

b. Check your answers. Concentrate on the explanations as to *why* the three wrong answers are wrong—especially if you have made mistakes. Do this even if you have made few or no mistakes. Knowing *why* the wrong answers are wrong will help you during the test. (If you have made quite a few mistakes on any exercise, you probably need to review the structural focus of that exercise.)

c. Both the exercises and Practice Tests are cross-referenced. Before each exercise there are references to relevant examples in Section 2 of the Tests, while references to the appropriate Focused Exercise appear in the Test Answer Keys. If you don't do well on Section 2 of any test, go back to the appropriate exercise for help.

FOCUSED EXERCISES 1-15

Focused Exercise 1: The Subject

> Every main clause must have a subject and one main (finite) verb. This is true for complete dependent clauses as well.

Probable Distractors (wrong answers)

In this section the TOEFL test will include four possible answers for you to choose from. Three of these will be wrong. You should be prepared for the following types of wrong answers.

If the main verb is given but the subject is missing:

- **The subject is repeated.** The weather it is warm.
- **There is an anticipatory _it_ + verb.** It is a book is on the table.
- **There is an expletive _there_ + verb.** There is a book is on the table.

If the _main_ clause subject is missing:

- **A subordinating element is included.** Convinced he was right, which made him argue longer.

(See Practice Tests II:12; III:ex.1; III:14)

Exercise

Write the letter of the correct answer.

1. _______ united effort is needed if the problem of the "underground economy" is to be resolved.

   (A) It is a

   (B) A

   (C) There is a

   (D) An

2. _______, which certainly look wise, are not thought to be among the most intelligent of animals.

   (A) They are owls

   (B) Owls are

   (C) Owls

   (D) There are owls

3. _______ took its name from the nearby Muskingum River.

   (A) Muskingum College

   (B) Because Muskingum College

   (C) It was Muskingum College

   (D) Muskingum College, which

4. _______ unsuccessful attempts were made to sail through the northwest passage.

   (A) There were several

   (B) Several valiant but

   (C) Although several

   (D) They were several

5. Located in Florida, _______ is the oldest city in the United States.

   (A) is St. Augustine

   (B) the city of St. Augustine

   (C) St. Augustine it

   (D) where St. Augustine

Focused Exercise 2: Noun Clause as Subject

> A noun or noun clause may be the subject of a sentence. On the TOEFL noun clauses are often preceded by an introductory word or expression such as _That_ or _The fact that_. This construction is always followed by a singular verb. It is generally used only in formal written English (*That the problems are immense _is_ obvious*). In spoken English it is more common to find an anticipatory _it_ construction (*_It_ is obvious that the problems are immense*).

Probable Distractors (wrong answers)

- **The introductory expression is not exactly as given above.** It is a fact that rain may fall in deserts is true.
- **The introductory expression is omitted.** Corn needs a lot of sun is accepted by farmers.
- **The noun clause has no verb.** That Einstein a great scientist is undeniable.
- **The noun clause is followed by a plural verb.** That the problems are immense are obvious.

(See Practice Tests I:15; IV:8)

Exercise

1. _______ a tenth planet may exist is suggested by discrepancies in the motions of Uranus and Neptune.

   (A) It is the fact that   **(C)** That
   (B) In fact   **(D)** The fact

2. _______ the predicted "W" particles do exist was proved in the CERN particle accelerator.

   (A) The fact is   **(C)** That is
   (B) In fact   **(D)** The fact that

3. _______ is sometimes disputed.

   (A) Columbus was an Italian   **(C)** An Italian that was Columbus
   (B) That Columbus was an Italian   **(D)** That Columbus an Italian

4. _______ was attributable partly to psychological factors.

   (A) That a depression   **(C)** The fact that a depression occurred
   (B) What a depression occurred   **(D)** A depression occurred

5. _______ frequently escapes comment.

   (A) The fact that   **(C)** The fact that the computer revolution
   (B) That the computer revolution is in its infancy   **(D)** Although the computer revolution is in its infancy

Focused Exercise 3: Non-repetition of Subject

> Every full clause needs a subject. Although the subject may include more than one noun (*Men, women, and children were left homeless by the attack*), the subject must *not* be repeated (*Men, women, and children they were left homeless by the attack*).

Probable Distractors (wrong answers)

If the subject already appears in the sentence given:

- **The subject is repeated.** The children they were left homeless.
- **An alternative, non-complementary subject is given.** Those two boys, there should be no fighting.
- **The subject of a dependent clause is included, resulting in the absence of a main clause or in an incomplete main clause.** To modernize their economies which has been a goal of many African countries.
- **Two main (finite) verbs are included in the same clause.** There are many problems are to be solved.

If as the subject of an adjective clause that is missing, the introductory relative pronoun, *who, which,* or *that*, is necessary, but:

- **The required relative pronoun is missing.** All drive cars must have licenses.
- **The relative pronoun is followed by another subject.** The girl who she lives here is a graduate student.

(See Practice Tests I:ex.2(D); I:13(B); II:1(C); IV:9(A,D); VI:11(B,D))

Exercise

1. _______, being in the public eye appears to be eminently desirable.

   (A) For many Californians
   (B) They are many Californians
   (C) Many Californians
   (D) There are many Californians

2. To achieve independence _______ the goal of many nations since the end of the Second World War.

   (A) it has been
   (B) which has been
   (C) has been
   (D) is

3. _______, Margaret Mead was able to confirm her beliefs regarding cultural determinism.

   (A) The Samoans
   (B) Among the Samoans
   (C) She
   (D) That she

4. Any person _______ to leave the country must first obtain a passport.

   (A) who decides
   (B) who he or she decides
   (C) who they decide
   (D) he or she decided

5. The horse _______ the triple crown in 1973 was named Secretariat.

   (A) which it won
   (B) it won
   (C) which it was the winner of
   (D) which won

Focused Exercise 4: Impersonal or Anticipatory *It*

> Impersonal *it* occurs with
> (a) a predicate adjective + adverbial (*It is usually warm* in Austin.)
> (b) predicates relating to identification, time, weather, and distance (*It is 12 o'clock now.*)

Probable Distractors (wrong answers)

- **_There is_ appears instead of _it is_.** There is generally cold in the winter.
- **The impersonal _it_ is omitted.** Is often rainy in England.
- **An introductory word is present which would result in a dependent clause without a main clause.** Although it was an adventure story.

> Anticipatory *it* anticipates the real subject which occurs in the predicate. It is always possible to move up this subject to the initial position to replace *it* (*It was in June that the war ended*).

Probable Distractors: Those mentioned above.

(See Practice Tests II:9; III:6; IV:9; V:2; VI:13)

Exercise

1. _______ from San Diego to the Mexican border.

   (A) Few miles

   (B) It's not far

   (C) Not far

   (D) There is not far

2. _______ people in Scotland and Wales to be called English.

   (A) It offends

   (B) There offends

   (C) They offend

   (D) Offends

3. _______, the match had to be postponed.

   (A) Because snowing

   (B) Because was snowing

   (C) Because there was snowing

   (D) Because it was snowing

4. _______ in Florida in the winter.

   (A) There is usually warm

   (B) Is usually warm

   (C) It is usually warm

   (D) Though it is usually warm

5. _______ in the 1970's that America's steel industry was suffering from a number of structural disadvantages.

   (A) It became obvious

   (B) There was obvious

   (C) Became it was obvious

   (D) An obvious problem

Focused Exercise 5: Expletive *There*

> *There* is used as an expletive in the following constructions, usually with the linking verb *to be*, though certain other verbs are possible. The verb may be in any tense and is singular or plural according to the following subject.
>
> (a) *there* + *be* (etc.) + subject + prepositional phrase (*There is a tree in front of the house.*)
>
> (b) *there* + *be* + subject + adjective modifier (*There are many flowers blooming now.*)

Probable Distractors (wrong answers)

- **The required *there* + *be* is omitted.** A bee in the garden.
- ***There* is replaced by *it*.** It was enough gas in my car this morning.
- **There is no agreement between the verb following *there* and its subject.** There is seven days in a week.
- **An inappropriate verb (e.g., *have*) is used with expletive *there*.** There have swallows here in the summer.

(See Practice Tests I:ex.1; II:ex.1; III:3)

Exercise

1. ________ no type of plant immune to attack by insects.

   (A) It exists
   (B) There exist
   (C) Because there exists
   (D) There exists

2. Because ________ of severely harmful effects from chemical dumps, the government has implemented tougher clean-up measures.

   (A) evidence
   (B) is evidence
   (C) there is evidence
   (D) evidence there is

3. ________ salmon in vast numbers readily available to the Kwakiutl Indians.

   (A) Nutritious
   (B) There was
   (C) It was
   (D) There were

4. ________ penguins in the Arctic.

   (A) There are no
   (B) No
   (C) There are not
   (D) Are not

5. Probably ________ little oil left under the North Sea by the year 2000.

   (A) will be
   (B) there will be
   (C) it will be
   (D) there will have

Focused Exercise 6: Main Verb Requirement

> Frequently sentences appear on the TOEFL which have a single main clause containing all the required elements except the main verb.

Probable Distractors (wrong answers)

- **There is an introductory word, creating a subordinate clause with a non-existent or incomplete main clause.** A box which contains 12 oranges.
- **The subject is repeated in addition to the main verb.** Einstein he discovered the theory of relativity.
- **No finite form of the verb is given.** Paper being made from trees.
- **The subject and verb do not agree or the verb is in the inappropriate tense or form.** It often is raining in April.

(See Practice Tests I:ex.2; I:7; I:10; II:1; III:1; IV:1; IV:3; V:5; VI:1; VI:9)

Exercise

1. A laser beam ________ a concentration of pure light.

   (A) consists of
   (B) which consists of
   (C) it consists of
   (D) consisting of

2. Eli Whitney, a northerner, ________ the cotton gin that revolutionized the economy of the South.

   (A) who invented
   (B) when he invented
   (C) invented
   (D) he invented

3. Diamonds ________ an unstable form of carbon.

   (A) which are
   (B) being
   (C) although they are
   (D) are

4. Lightning rarely ________ twice in the same place.

   (A) is striking
   (B) strikes
   (C) does it strike
   (D) it strikes

5. The regular major league baseball season ________ each team to play 162 games.

   (A) which requires
   (B) requiring
   (C) it requires
   (D) requires

Focused Exercise 7: Active-Passive Distinction

> It is important to check whether the required main verb should be in the active or the passive voice.

Probable Distractors (wrong answers)

In addition to those listed in Exercise 6:

- **The verb is otherwise correct, but is in the active voice where the passive is required.** Penicillin makes from mold.
- **The combination of _to be_ + participle is incorrect.** It has being established that ice takes up more volume than water.

(See Practice Tests I:1; II:4; III:2; V:1; VI:ex.1)

Exercise

1. Many doctors believe cures for many forms of cancer _________ soon.

    (A) will discover
    (B) they will be discovered
    (C) will be discovered
    (D) have been discovered

2. Aspirin _________ from the bark of willow trees.

    (A) was first extracted
    (B) it was first extracted
    (C) extracted
    (D) first extracted

3. _________ that India's annual harvest takes 18.5 million tons of nutrients from the soil.

    (A) It has estimated
    (B) It has been estimated
    (C) Has been estimated
    (D) It has being estimated

4. A scientific process _________ to turn natural gas into animal feed.

    (A) have been developed
    (B) it has been developed
    (C) have developed
    (D) has been developed

5. While the East prospered in the early nineteenth century, much of the western part of the United States _________ by the trail blazers.

    (A) was been opened up
    (B) was opening up
    (C) was being opened up
    (D) was being opening up

Focused Exercise 8: Subject-Verb Inversion

> If certain words or expressions appear in the initial position in a clause, the subject and verb are inverted as they are in questions. Expressions requiring such inversion include: negative conjunctions (_not only_, _neither_, _no sooner_, etc.); adverbials of negation or semi-negation (_in no case_, _never_, _rarely_, _hardly_); adverbial expressions with _only_ and _so_.

Probable Distractors (wrong answers)

If an expression of the type described is given in the sentence, or if the entire clause must be chosen:

- **The subject and verb are not inverted.** Rarely I have heard such nonsense.

- **Inversion is present but not in correct interrogative order.** No sooner came she in, than she created a scene.

If what is given in the sentence is the inversion:

- **Expressions given are not of the type described above.** If does it snow before December.

- **Expressions given are of the type described but inappropriate in meaning.** Not only warm sunshine, did we have, since it was pleasant.

(See Practice Tests I:14; II:13; III:7; V:13; VI:5)

Exercise

1. Not only ________, but he also owned a movie studio.
   - **(A)** Hughes owned Las Vegas hotels
   - **(B)** did Hughes own Las Vegas hotels
   - **(C)** owned Hughes Las Vegas hotels
   - **(D)** Las Vegas hotels owned Hughes

2. ________ great was the destruction that the South took decades to recover.
   - **(A)** Very
   - **(B)** Too
   - **(C)** Such
   - **(D)** So

3. ________, when the Chargers found themselves 7-0 down.
   - **(A)** Hardly had the game begun
   - **(B)** Hardly the game had begun
   - **(C)** The game hardly begun
   - **(D)** Hardly had begun the game

4. ________ does an individual find himself sought by both parties as their presidential candidate, as did General Eisenhower.
   - **(A)** Not only
   - **(B)** Sometimes
   - **(C)** Rarely
   - **(D)** If

5. Only when in danger ________ human beings.
   - **(A)** snakes will most attack
   - **(B)** will most snakes attack
   - **(C)** most snakes will attack
   - **(D)** will attack most snakes

Focused Exercise 9: Noun or Noun Phrase in Apposition

> A second noun or noun phrase may be used to define or explain the first in any position in the sentence. In this case, the second noun or noun phrase is always separated off by commas. This construction may be replaced by a relative clause.
>
> Check to be sure the noun or noun phrase (adjective + noun; noun + prepositional phrase) redefines the previous one.

Probable Distractors (wrong answers)

- **Incomplete clauses or phrases are given (but more than noun/noun phrases).** The tallest building, the Empire State building is, used to be located in New York City.

- **The relative clause is also a redefining main clause.** Digitalis, it is a cardiac drug, was used in Pre-Columbian America.

(See Practice Tests III:9; V:6)

Exercise

1. The world's highest peak, _______, is in the Himalayas.

   (A) Mount Everest
   (B) this is Mount Everest
   (C) it is Mount Everest
   (D) being Mount Everest

2. Hannibal chose an unlikely mode of transportation, _______, for crossing the Alps.

   (A) were African elephants
   (B) they were African elephants
   (C) African elephants
   (D) African elephants they were

3. The Great Bear, _______, is probably the most recognized constellation in the northern hemisphere.

   (A) in the shape of a plow seven stars
   (B) it is seven stars in the shape of a plow
   (C) seven stars in the shape of a plow
   (D) they are seven stars in the shape of a plow

4. Canada has two official languages, _______.

   (A) they are French and English
   (B) French and English
   (C) which they are French and English
   (D) French and English they are

5. The duck-billed platypus, _______, has been described as the world's strangest animal.

   (A) is an Australian marsupial
   (B) which an Australian marsupial
   (C) Australian marsupial
   (D) an Australian marsupial

Focused Exercise 10: Dependent Clauses

A dependent clause cannot exist alone. It must be attached to a main clause. Dependent adverbial clauses contain an introductory word (*Before* the show began, the performers were introduced to the audience). Dependent adjectival clauses contain an introductory relative pronoun (He bought a machine *which* could carry out a variety of operations).

Full dependent clauses, like main clauses, must contain both a subject and a main verb. In the case of adjectival clauses, the relative pronoun itself constitutes the subject.

Quite frequently, items in Section 2 (questions 1-15) test main clause-dependent clause relationships and components.

- **The dependent clause has no subject.** Although are famous, not many people have actually seen the northern lights.

- **There is no main (finite) verb.** Despite their injuries, they winning the game.

- **An adverbial dependent clause has no introductory word.** It is sent express, the package will get there sooner.

- **An adverbial dependent clause has an inappropriate introductory word.** Sometimes strawberries are easy to grow, you must watch them for mold.

- **The subject of an adjectival clause is repeated.** They live in Boston, which it is in New England.

- **Adjectival clause has no subject.** Amsterdam has many canals were once important for shipping.

- **Dependent clause has no attached main clause.** Because so many people depend on railroads as well as on highways.

(See Practice Tests I:2; I:13; II:14; III:8; IV:2; VI:11; VI:12)

Exercise

1. _______ there, the southwest desert contains a remarkable variety of flora and fauna.

   (**A**) Although rarely rains
   (**B**) It rarely rains
   (**C**) Although it rarely rains
   (**D**) Sometimes it rains

2. Because morels are both rare and highly prized, _______.

   (**A**) they are very expensive
   (**B**) very expensive
   (**C**) are very expensive
   (**D**) as well as very expensive

3. _______, litmus paper turns blue.

   (**A**) If in an alkali it is dipped
   (**B**) If is dipped in an alkali
   (**C**) Is dipped in an alkali
   (**D**) If it is dipped in an alkali

4. East Liverpool, _______, is located in a spot where potter's clay was discovered.

   (**A**) which was founded in 1798
   (**B**) was founded in 1798
   (**C**) in 1798 was founded
   (**D**) which it was founded in 1798

5. Peas _______ lose much of their flavor.

   (**A**) which overcooked
   (**B**) have been overcooked
   (**C**) which they have been overcooked
   (**D**) which have been overcooked

Focused Exercise 11: Abridged Dependent Clauses

> Some dependent adverbial clauses are incomplete and leave out *both* subject and main verb. The subject of the main clause then becomes the subject of the dependent clause as well, with some meaning of the verb *to be* understood (*When buying a computer, you should seek professional advice* = *When you are buying a computer, you should seek professional advice*). An abridged dependent clause is not possible if the subject of the main clause cannot logically function as the subject of the dependent clause (*Though twenty-one, John's work is that of an eight year old. John's work* is the subject of the main clause and cannot logically be the subject of the abridged clause).

Probable Distractors (wrong answers)

- **The subject is present but the finite verb is missing.** When they hungry, children cry.
- **The finite verb is present but the subject is missing.** While is very easy to drive a car, you must be careful.
- **There is no introductory subordinating word.** It is very expensive, well-made furniture will last a long time.

(See Practice Tests III:ex.2; V:12; V:15; VI:7)

Exercise

1. The 55-mile per hour speed limit must be observed ________.

   (A) where applicable

   (B) where it applicable

   (C) where is applicable

   (D) where application

2. ________, *Alice in Wonderland* appeals to many adult readers, too.

   (A) Though it written for children

   (B) Though for children written

   (C) Though written for children

   (D) It was written for children

3. Armadillos seek protection from nearby undergrowth ________.

   (A) when are they threatened

   (B) when they threatened

   (C) when are threatened

   (D) when threatened

4. ________, nitroglycerine is extremely volatile.

   (A) It is highly effective

   (B) Highly effective it is

   (C) While highly effective

   (D) Highly while effective

5. ________ the ancient and honored style of wrestling, the professional version of the sport is largely amateur theatrics.

   (A) Compare it to

   (B) If compared to

   (C) It compared to

   (D) Comparing

Focused Exercise 12: Participial Phrases

> Participial phrases are verbal constructions which do not function as verbs. Those functioning as adverbs or adjectives are dealt with here. Like abridged dependent clauses, they contain neither subject nor verb. But unlike an abridged clause, they do not necessarily imply the verb *to be*. The subject of the participial phrase is the same as the subject in the main clause. These phrases may contain a present participle or a past participle. The negative form contains *not* in the initial position.

Probable Distractors (wrong answers)

- **The participle is not in the initial position in the phrase (it follows a word other than *not* or an adverb).** About the accident hearing, the family rushed to the hospital.
- **A subject and/or finite verb is included.** She believing the worst, Jane called the doctor.
- **The choice of participle (present or past) is logically inconsistent with the subject of the main clause.** Melted quickly, the snow disappeared the same day.

(See Practice Tests I:6; IV:4; IV:10; V:4; VI:15)

Exercise

1. The doctor, ________, apologized.
   - **(A)** his mistake realizing
   - **(B)** he realized his mistake
   - **(C)** realizing his mistake
   - **(D)** realized his mistake

2. ________, the Greeks resorted to a trick.
   - **(A)** They finding the walls impregnable
   - **(B)** Finding the walls impregnable
   - **(C)** Finding they the walls impregnable
   - **(D)** Finding impregnable the walls

3. ________ the law of the time, Margaret Sanger opened the country's first birth-control clinic in Brooklyn in 1916.
   - **(A)** Disregarded
   - **(B)** She disregarded
   - **(C)** It was disregarded
   - **(D)** Disregarding

4. ________ mainly along the eastern seaboard and once used as legal tender, tobacco became America's most important export in colonial times.
   - **(A)** Grown
   - **(B)** Grew
   - **(C)** To grow
   - **(D)** It grew

5. ________, London Bridge was then rebuilt as part of a tourist attraction.
   - **(A)** It was sold to an Arizona entrepreneur
   - **(B)** To an Arizona entrepeneur selling
   - **(C)** Sold to an Arizona entrepreneur
   - **(D)** Selling to an Arizona entrepreneur

Focused Exercise 13: Word Order

> There is a wide range of possible mistakes in this category. The main thing to remember is that the normal word order in an English clause is SUBJECT—VERB—REST OF PREDICATE.

NOTE: This exercise excludes subject-verb inversion, which is dealt with in Focused Exercise 8.

Probable Distractors (wrong answers)

The issues dealt with here are:

i. Relative clauses

- **The relative is followed by the question word order.** Houses made of wood, when do they need painting, must first be properly prepared.

- **The clause contains some other variation on standard word order indicated above.** Gardens, which planted have been in shade, do not grow well.

ii. Position of object

- **The object appears between the subject and the verb.** When the ruler the two kingdoms unified, he used the symbols of both in his crown.

iii. Position of prepositional phrases

- **The prepositional phrase appears between the verb and the object.** Grape growers need for picking their crops much seasonal labor.

iv. Phrases with fixed word order (e.g., *however* + adjective + determiner + noun; *whatever* + determiner + noun)

- **The fixed word order is ignored.** Whatever is the problem, I am sure a solution can be found.

(See Practice Tests III:10; III:13; IV:15)

Exercise

1. Medicare provided the first federally-funded hospital insurance for the over sixty-fives ________ in 1965.

   (A) when it was introduced
   (B) when was it introduced
   (C) was when it introduced
   (D) it was when introduced

2. ________, there can be no avoiding it.

   (A) However the decision is difficult
   (B) However difficult the decision
   (C) The decision however difficult
   (D) However the difficult decision

3. The famous Concord Coach of the Wild West was named after the New Hampshire town _______.

(A) where was it manufactured

(B) it was manufactured

(C) where it manufactured

(D) where it was manufactured

4. When Robert Beamon _______, hardly anyone present could believe it.

(A) made his incredible jump in 1968

(B) made in 1968 his incredible jump

(C) his incredible jump in 1968 made

(D) his incredible jump made in 1968

5. The ancient Greeks _______.

(A) crowned with laurel leaves their champions

(B) with laurel leaves crowned their champions

(C) crowned their champions with laurel leaves

(D) their champions crowned with laurel leaves

Focused Exercise 14: Parallelism

> Items joined by coordinate conjunctions (*and* or *or*) should have the same grammatical form. This issue may be tested in either questions 1-15 or questions 16-40.
>
> In questions 1-15 the wrong answers will have a different grammatical form from the other item(s) in the sentence. Frequently, the missing part (questions 1-15) or the underlined item (questions 16-40) will be part of a series of three when parallelism is the issue.

(See Practice Tests II:6(B); II:12; III:13)

Exercise

1. Presbyterian minister, college professor, and _______, James Naismith is best remembered as the inventor of basketball.

(A) he was athletic director

(B) directing athletics

(C) athletic director

(D) directed athletics

2. With its 151-mile long reservoir, the Grand Coulee Dam provides hydro-electric power, _______, and water for irrigation.

(A) in addition flood control

(B) offers flood control

(C) it controls floods

(D) flood control

3. Exceeding speed limits and _______ safety belts are two common causes of automobile death.

(A) not to wear

(B) failing to wear

(C) don't wear

(D) not having worn

4. In recent times, the invention which has most changed the face of the world, most influenced the industrial development of the world, and _______ is the automobile.

(A) most affected its culture

(B) most affecting its culture

(C) with most effect on its culture

(D) most to affect its culture

5. While not lacking in presence, _________ poise, this actor is simply not suited to leading roles.

(A) he is charming and   (C) charm, or

(B) charming   (D) he has charm or

Focused Exercise 15: Comparisons

> The issue of correct comparison form appears both in questions 1-15 and questions 16-40. However, in questions 1-15, the comparative expressions are less common and often link up with issues of word order and parallelism.
>
> No probable incorrect answers are given since the issues dealt with are so varied.

(See Practice Tests I:3; II:3; II:7; III:14; IV:12; V:ex.2; V:7; V:8)

Exercise

1. _________ a person wears eyeglasses, the more dependent on them he or she tends to become.

(A) When   (C) The longer

(B) The longest   (D) If

2. A radiologist deals with objective reproducible evidence _________ with patients' subjective descriptions.

(A) rather than   (C) than

(B) instead than   (D) than rather

3. _________ powerful member of the entire cat family is the tiger.

(A) Most   (C) More

(B) The most   (D) The more

4. The problems facing engineers in Yakutia, the coldest inhabited place on earth, are _________ anywhere else.

(A) alike those   (C) unlike to

(B) those unlike   (D) unlike those

5. The Florida panther is _________ as well as most striking of America's native wild-life species.

(A) among the rarest   (C) exceedingly rare

(B) ferocious and rare   (D) among the rarer

Answer Key/
Focused Exercises 1-15

Focused Exercise 1: The Subject

Remember: PROBABLE DISTRACTOR (PD) = a wrong answer. The probable distractors identified in the introduction to each Focused Exercise are listed again here for you to check and understand your answers.

PD 1. **repeats the subject**
2. **has an anticipatory *it* and main verb**
3. **has an expletive *there* and main verb**
4. **includes a subordinating element when the main clause is missing**

1. A PD-2
   B Correct
   C PD-3
   D The *u* in *united* has a consonant sound, and *an* should only be used before a vowel sound.

2. A Two main (finite) verbs in the same clause (are . . . are)
   B Two main (finite) verbs in the same clause (are . . . are)
   C Correct
   D PD-3

3. A Correct
   B PD-4
   C PD-2
   D PD-4

4. A PD-3
   B Correct
   C PD-4
   D Two main (finite) verbs in the same clause (were . . . were)

5. A Two main (finite) verbs in the same clause (is . . . is)
   B Correct
   C PD-1
   D PD-4

Focused Exercise 2: Noun Clause as Subject

PD 1. **introductory expression is not exactly as given (That/The fact that . . .)**
2. **introductory expression is omitted**
3. **noun clause has no verb**
4. **noun clause is followed by a plural verb**

1. A PD-1
   B PD-1
   C Correct
   D PD-1

2. A PD-1
   B PD-1
   C PD-1
   D Correct

3. A PD-1
   B Correct
   C PD-2
   D PD-3

4. A PD-3
   B PD-1
   C Correct
   D PD-2

Focused Exercise 3: Non-repetition of Subject

In numbers 1-3, the explanations begin by identifying the subject of the main clause. In 4 and 5, the correct answer is needed to complete the subjects.

PD 1. **subject is repeated**
   2. **alternative, non-complementary subject is given**
   3. **subject of a dependent clause is included, resulting in no or incomplete main clause**
   4. **two main verbs included in same clause**
   5. **required relative pronoun is missing**
   6. **relative pronoun is followed by another subject**

1. Subject: being in the public eye
   A Correct
   B PD-4
   C PD-2
   D PD-4

2. Subject: to achieve independence
   A PD-1
   B PD-3
   C Correct
   D Wrong tense with *since*

3. Subject: Margaret Mead
   A PD-2
   B Correct
   C PD-1
   D PD-3 (creates noun clause subject)

5. A Missing predicate in noun clause
   B Correct
   C PD-3
   D Adverb clause (cannot function as subject)

4. A Correct
   B PD-6
   C PD-6
   D PD-1, 5

5. A PD-6
   B PD-5
   C PD-6
   D Correct

Focused Exercise 4: Impersonal or Anticipatory *It*

PD 1. ***there is*** appears instead of *it is*
    2. **impersonal** *it* **is omitted**
    3. **contains an introductory word resulting in dependent clauses without a main clause**

1. A PD-3
  B Correct
  C PD-3
  D PD-1

2. A Correct
  B PD-1
  C *They* subject cannot relate to *to be called*
  D PD-2

3. A PD-2 (and main verb omitted)
  B PD-2
  C PD-1
  D Correct

4. A PD-1
  B PD-2
  C Correct
  D PD-3

5. A Correct
  B PD-1
  C PD-3
  D Needs linking verb *was* before *that*

Focused Exercise 5: Expletive *There*

PD 1. **required** *there* **+** *be* **is omitted**
    2. ***there*** **replaced by** *it*
    3. **no agreement between verb following** *there* **and its subject**
    4. **inappropriate verb used with expletive** *there*

1. A PD-2
  B PD-3
  C Dependent clause (Focused Exercise 10)
  D Correct

2. A PD-1
  B PD-1
  C Correct
  D Wrong word order

3. A Creates subject with no predicate
  B PD-3
  C PD-2
  D Correct

4. A Correct
  B PD-1
  C *Not* requires quantifier (*any, many*) or determiner before noun
  D PD-1

5. A PD-1
  B Correct
  C PD-2
  D PD-4

Focused Exercise 6: Main Verb Requirement

PD 1. **introductory word creating subordinate clause with non-existent or incomplete main clause**
   2. **repetition of subject in addition to main verb**
   3. **no finite form of verb**
   4. **no agreement between subject and verb, or verb has wrong tense or form**

1. A Correct
   B PD-1
   C PD-2
   D PD-3

2. A PD-1
   B PD-1
   C Correct
   D PD-2

3. A PD-1
   B PD-3
   C PD-1
   D Correct

4. A PD-4
   B Correct
   C Inversion only correct if *rarely* begins clause (Focused Exercise 8)
   D PD-2

5. A PD-1
   B PD-3
   C PD-2
   D Correct

Focused Exercise 7: Active-Passive Distinction

PD 1-4 **(above)**
   5. **verb is otherwise correct, but is in the active rather than passive voice**
   6. **combination of *to be* + participle is incorrect**

1. A PD-5
   B PD-2
   C Correct
   D PD-4

2. A Correct
   B PD-2
   C PD-5
   D PD-5

3. A PD-5
   B Correct
   C Needs anticipatory *it* (Focused Exercise 4)
   D PD-6

4. A PD-4
   B PD-2
   C PD-4, 5
   D Correct

5. A PD-6
   B PD-5
   C Correct
   D PD-6

Focused Exercise 8: Subject-Verb Inversion

If an expression like _not only_, _neither_, _no sooner_, etc. is already given, or the entire clause must be chosen:

PD 1. **subject and verb are not inverted**
2. **inversion given but not in correct interrogative order**
3. **inversion given but no expressions like those above**
4. **inversion given with expressions like those above, but inappropriate in meaning**

1. A PD-1
   B Correct
   C PD-2
   D PD-2

2. A PD-3
   B PD-3
   C _Such_ must be followed by noun
   D Correct

3. A Correct
   B PD-1
   C _Had_ omitted
   D PD-2

4. A _Not only_ would require a corresponding _but also_ clause (PD-4)
   B PD-3
   C Correct
   D PD-3

5. A PD-1
   B Correct
   C PD-1
   D PD-2

Focused Exercise 9: Noun or Noun Phrase in Apposition

PD 1. **a relative clause that is incomplete, but more than noun/noun phrase**
2. **a relative clause that is a redefining main clause**

1. A Correct
   B PD-2
   C PD-2
   D PD-1

2. A PD-1
   B PD-2
   C Correct
   D PD-2; unnecessary inversion

3. A Adjective phrase must follow noun subject
   B PD-2
   C Correct
   D PD-2

4. A PD-2
   B Correct
   C _They_ repeats subject _which_ (Focused Exercise 3)
   D PD-2; unnecessary inversion

5. A PD-1
   B PD-1
   C _Platypus_ is an example of the class _marsupial_; therefore, requires article
   D Correct

Focused Exercise 10: Dependent Clauses

PD 1. **dependent clause has no subject**
   2. **no main verb**
   3. **adverbial dependent clause has no introductory word**
   4. **adverbial dependent clause has inappropriate introductory word**
   5. **subject of an adjectival clause is repeated**
   6. **adjectival clause has no subject**
   7. **dependent clause has no attached main clause**

1. A PD-1
   B PD-3
   C Correct
   D PD-4

2. A Correct
   B PD-1 and 2; main clause
   C PD-1; main clause
   D PD-7

3. A Wrong word order (Focused Exercise 13)
   B PD-1
   C PD-3 and 1
   D Correct

4. A Correct
   B PD-6
   C PD-6; word order (Focused Exercise 13)
   D PD-5

5. A PD-2
   B PD-6
   C PD-5
   D Correct

Focused Exercise 11: Abridged Dependent Clauses

PD 1. **in a dependent adverbial clause the subject is present but the main verb is missing.**
   2. **the main verb is present but the subject is missing.**
   3. **there is no introductory subordinating word.**

1. A Correct
   B PD-1
   C PD-2
   D *Application* is a noun; adjective is needed to modify *speed limit*

2. A PD-1
   B Word order (Focused Exercise 13)
   C Correct
   D PD-3

3. A Inappropriate (question) order
   B PD-1
   C PD-2
   D Correct

4. A PD-3
   B PD-3; unnecessary inversion
   C Correct
   D *While* not in introductory position

5. A Imperative form does not give a dependent element as required
   B Correct
   C PD-3 and 1
   D Makes first phrase the subject; would need to be followed by a finite verb

Focused Exercise 12: Participial Phrases

PD 1. participle is not in initial position in the phrase (except if the initial word is _not_ or an adverb)
   2. a subject and/or main verb is included in participial phrase
   3. participle (present/past) is logically inconsistent with subject of main clause

1. A PD-1
   B PD-2
   C Correct
   D PD-3

2. A PD-2
   B Correct
   C PD-2
   D Object must follow participle

3. A PD-3
   B PD-2
   C PD-2 and 3
   D Correct

4. A Correct
   B No participle
   C No participle
   D PD-2

5. A PD-2
   B PD-1 and 3
   C Correct
   D PD-3

Focused Exercise 13: Word Order

PD i. **Relative clauses**
   1. relative is followed by question word order
   2. clause contains a variation from standard word order
   ii. **Position of object**
   3. object is between subject and verb
   iii. **Position of prepositional phrases**
   4. prepositional phrase is between verb and object
   iv. **Phrases with fixed word order**
   5. fixed word order is ignored

1. A Correct
   B PD-1
   C PD-2
   D PD-2

2. A PD-5
   B Correct
   C PD-5
   D PD-5

3. A PD-1
   B Two inappropriately linked main clauses
   C PD-2
   D Correct

4. A Correct
   B PD-4
   C PD-3
   D PD-3

5. A PD-4
   B Misplaced prepositional phrase
   C Correct
   D PD-4

Focused Exercise 14: Parallelism

For each item the explanation begins by identifying the grammatical structure which requires parallel form.

1. Nouns
   A Clause
   B -ing form
   C Correct (noun)
   D Verb

2. Nouns
   A Would require preceding *and*, no subsequent comma
   B Verb
   C Clause
   D Correct (noun)

3. Gerunds
   A Infinitive
   B Correct
   C Imperative
   D Perfect form

4. Dependent clause + abridged dependent clause with past participle
   A Correct
   B Present participle
   C Prepositional phrase
   D Infinitive

5. Nouns
   A Clause
   B Adjective
   C Correct (coordinate conjunction is required)
   D Clause

Focused Exercise 15: Comparisons

1. A No link with *the more dependent*
   B See 1-A
   C Correct
   D See 1-A

2. A Correct
   B Adverbial *instead* cannot be used with conjunction of comparison *than*
   C Conjunction *than* needs preceding comparative form
   D Wrong order; *than* links with following prepositional phrase not *rather*

3. A *The* necessary with superlative
   B Correct
   C *More* would need different sentence structure
   D *The more* only possible when comparing two things; does not function with *entire*

4. A *Alike* is adjective which cannot be followed by anything else
   B *Unlike* modifies "problems ... Yakutia," not *anywhere else*
   C *To* cannot follow *unlike*
   D Correct

5. A Correct
   B Simple forms of adjective fail to pro-
      vide the *the* needed to complete
      most striking (Focused Exercise 14)
   C See 5-B
   D Possible if *the* were included in sec-
      ond part of sentence; *the* would
      need repetition here because the
      two adjectives *rare* and *striking*
      would be used distinctly—one in
      comparative, the other superlative.

FOCUSED EXERCISES 16-40 ▬▬▬

Each item in this section consists of a single sentence with four underlined parts. Three of the underlined parts are correct; one is incorrect. Here
you must choose the underlined part that is incorrect.

Focused Exercise 16: Subject-Verb Agreement

> Check that the verb agrees in number with its subject (both singular or
> both plural). It is possible that the verb may be widely separated from
> the subject in the sentence.

(See Practice Tests III:30; IV:23; V:23; VI:22; VI:39)

1. The recession, which has been attributed to a variety of factors, have resulted in the
           A   B   C   D
   highest unemployment levels since the Great Depression.

2. In the early 1980's, major league baseball, in spite of public opposition to players' sala-
                                                         A
   ries, were more popular than ever before and attracted record crowds.
         B   C   D

3. Binary stars are twin stars which forms close enough together for their mutual gravita-
                                  A   B
   tion to set them orbiting each other.
         C   D

4. Mount Rushmore National Memorial, with its four presidential heads, were authorized
                                          A   B
   by the two houses of Congress during the 1925 session.
       C   D

5. One of the requirements for foreign students whose native language is not English and
                                                                A
   who wish to enter American universities are to take the TOEFL.
         B   C   D

Focused Exercise 17: Noun-Pronoun (and Quantifier) Agreement

> Check that pronouns and quantifiers are appropriate to the nouns to which they refer, particularly in terms of number.

(See Practice Tests I:26; II:30; IV:35; IV:40; V :16; VI:16)

1. Producers of basic chemicals and <u>their</u> derivatives for industrial use <u>find</u> <u>its</u> fortunes
                             A   B   C
   <u>tied</u> closely to the business cycle.
   D

2. Considering <u>their</u> vast numbers <u>in</u> the <u>seventeenth</u> century, not <u>much</u> sheep are raised
             A   B   C   D
   in Spain today.

3. With <u>their</u> country's citizens suffering <u>from</u> the <u>effects</u> of the Great Depression, Presi-
        A   B   C
   dent Franklin D. Roosevelt introduced <u>his</u> "New Deal."
                                     D

4. The seeds of Darwin's *The Origin of Species* <u>were</u> sown during <u>their</u> <u>five-year</u> voyage <u>on</u>
                                   A   B   C   D
   the "Beagle."

5. <u>Many</u> people consider Stieglitz to be one of the greatest of American <u>photographers</u>,
    A   B
   and there can be <u>few</u> disagreement as to <u>his</u> seminal influence.
                C   D

Focused Exercise 18: Repeated Subject

> Check that a subject is not repeated within the same clause or following the relative *which*.

(See Practice Tests I:30; II:38; III:ex.1; III:36; IV:39; V:18)

1. Gabriel García Márquez, after <u>receiving</u> <u>his</u> 1982 Nobel Prize for literature, <u>he</u> <u>appeared</u>
                                    A   B   C   D
   on the cover of *Time* magazine.

2. Maine, New Hampshire, and Vermont <u>they</u> are all in New England, and <u>their</u> inhabi-
                                          A   B
   tants are renowned <u>for</u> <u>their</u> independent spirit.
                      C   D

3. In spite of the recent surge in stock-market prices, <u>these</u> have still failed <u>to keep pace</u>
                                                   A   B
   with inflation, <u>which</u> <u>it</u> rose sharply throughout the late seventies.
                    C   D

4. When <u>they</u> are in danger, Acanthomyops, <u>which</u> are common North American ants,
          A   B
   <u>they</u> give off a citronella-like odor <u>they</u> use as an alarm substance.
    C   D

5. <u>Some</u> industrial plants <u>they</u> help <u>to create</u> acid rain with the sulphur dioxide which
   A   B   C
<u>they</u> emit.
D

Focused Exercise 19: Personal Pronoun Forms

> Check that personal pronouns are in the correct form (do they function
> as subject, object, or possessive pronouns?) and that reflexive pronouns
> are spelled correctly.

(See Practice Tests II:19; IV:33; V:35; VI:ex.1; VI:21; VI:25)

1. While shields obviously enabled medieval kings and <u>their</u> knights to protect <u>theirselves</u>,
                                                A   B
the device on the shield eventually became more important for <u>its</u> bearer than the
                                                   C
shield <u>itself</u>.
      D
2. After leaving the beach where <u>it</u> was born and swimming hundreds of miles in the
                              A
ocean, the green turtle can find <u>it</u> way back to dig <u>its</u> own nest in virtually the same
                                 B   C
spot <u>it</u> was born in.
    D
3. Although <u>hers</u> early films were extremely successful, Sandra Dee failed to make the
            A
transition to adult star since <u>hers</u> was a quality which depended on <u>her</u> being the
                           B   C
teenager <u>she</u> originally portrayed.
        D
4. Howard Hughes not only financed <u>his</u> "Spruce Goose" but also piloted <u>it</u> <u>hisself</u> on <u>its</u>
                                 A   B   C   D
only flight.

5. When <u>he</u> returned to England, Neville Chamberlain was convinced that the meeting
       A
between <u>he</u> and Hitler offered proof of <u>their</u> shared desire for peace between <u>their</u>
         B   C   D
countries.

Focused Exercise 20: Relative Pronouns

> Check that the appropriate relative pronoun has been used (especially
> *what/which* and *who/which*) and that *where* has not been used after a
> preposition.

(See Practice Tests I:28; I:38; II:34; IV:20; VI:30)

1. Calcium channel blockers are agents <u>which</u> act on the chemical substance <u>what</u> <u>most</u>
                                            A   B C
   affects the <u>heart's</u> functioning: calcium.
                 D

2. One area of the United States <u>which</u> has grown enormously in importance <u>is</u> "Silicon
                                    A   B
   Valley" in California <u>at where</u> many developments <u>in</u> computer technology have taken
                                        C   D
   place.

3. The Chief Justice of the United States Supreme Court is the person <u>which</u> administers
                                                                    A
   the oath of office and from <u>whom</u> the new president <u>receives</u> <u>his</u> first congratulations.
                                        B   C D

4. <u>What</u> Hemingway called "grace under pressure" is a quality <u>what</u> bullfighters fre-
   A   B
   quently show and is <u>one</u> <u>for which</u> professional athletes in many sports strive.
                        C   D

5. Excellent examples of the English monarchy, <u>who</u> dates back more than a thousand
                                                       A
   years, are to be found in certain queens <u>who</u> ruled for long periods and <u>whose</u> popu-
                                                 B   C
   larity among <u>their</u> subjects was unrivalled.
                   D

Focused Exercise 21: Articles

> Check that the appropriate article (*the/a*) has been used and that the form of the indefinite article (*a/an*) is correct.

(See Practice Tests III:34; IV:16; V:38)

1. A soccer match starts with <u>the</u> ball being kicked forwards from a spot in <u>a</u> center of <u>the</u>
  <u>A</u>   B   C   D
   field.

2. <u>The</u> sperm whale is <u>an</u> unique organism in that it is <u>the</u> largest mammal <u>on earth</u>.
   <u>A</u>   <u>B</u>   <u>C</u>   <u>D</u>

3. Dizzy Dean was never as good <u>a</u> pitcher again after <u>the</u> toe was injured as <u>a</u> result of
                                    A   B   C
   being hit by <u>a</u> batted ball.
                D

4. <u>The</u> trend towards attaching <u>the</u> designer's name to <u>a</u> whole range of products peaked
   <u>A</u>   B   C
   in <u>a</u> summer of 1982 with a famous film star's salad dressing.
      <u>D</u>

5. A sixty-two-year-old man was <u>the</u> participant in <u>a</u> hotly-contested triathlon race in Ha-
   <u>A</u>   <u>B</u>   <u>C</u>
   waii involving a 2½-mile ocean swim, a 112-mile bicycle ride, and a 26-mile run all on
   the same day.
   <u>D</u>

Focused Exercise 22: Adjectives and Nouns

> Check that an adjective has not been used where a noun is required and vice versa.

(See Practice Tests II:27; III:26; IV:37; V:31; VI:36)

1. The <u>deep</u> of the <u>ocean</u> is measured using <u>sophisticated</u> sonar <u>equipment</u>.
      A   B   C   D

2. <u>Competitors</u> in the luge <u>events</u> usually claim to be motivated by a <u>spirit</u> of <u>adventurous</u>.
     A   B   C   D

3. The unicorn, a <u>fabled</u> <u>one-horned</u> <u>beast</u> of the Middle Ages, was actually a
            A   B   C

   <u>non-existence</u> animal.
       D

4. It is of course the <u>fact</u> that <u>the</u> ball used in American football is an oblate spheroid
               A   B

   rather than truly <u>sphere</u> in <u>shape</u> that makes it difficult to catch.
             C   D

5. When Krakatoa erupted in the <u>nineteenth</u> <u>century</u>, the <u>noisy</u> was heard <u>hundreds</u> of
                            A   B   C   D

   miles away.

Focused Exercise 23: Adjectives and Adverbs

> Check that an adjective has not been used where an adverb is required and vice versa.

(See Practice Tests I:25; II:26; IV:ex.1; V:ex.2; V:37; VI:32)

1. Ships can only reach Antarctica during a <u>relatively</u> <u>short</u> period because of the <u>extreme</u>
                                        A   B   C

   <u>cold</u> conditions.
    D

2. The popularity of "E.T." grew so <u>fast</u> and <u>unexpected</u> that stores <u>swiftly</u> <u>ran out</u> of E.T.
                                   A   B   C   D

   dolls.

3. <u>Initially</u> the natives behaved <u>friendly</u> towards Magellan and his crew, but
    A   B

   <u>subsequently</u> their attitude changed <u>drastically</u>.
      C   D

4. Breaking the sound barrier seemed <u>extraordinarily</u> in 1947, but it has <u>since</u> become
                                  A   B

   <u>commonplace</u> thanks to <u>swiftly-developing</u> technology.
      C   D

5. Having served <u>effectively</u> as vice-president, Walter Mondale was <u>subsequently</u> a <u>likely</u>
   $\quad\quad\quad\quad\quad\,$ A $\quad\quad\quad\quad\quad\quad\quad\quad\quad\quad\quad\quad\quad\quad\quad$ B $\quad\quad\quad\quad$ C
   and <u>popularly</u> candidate for the presidency.
   $\quad\quad$ D

Focused Exercise 24: Comparisons (Form of Adjective or Adverb)

> Check the following: (1) superlative form after *the*; (2) comparative form with *than*; (3) no redundant comparative form (*more* + *-er*).

(See Practice Tests I:34; II:18; III:19; III:40; IV:18; V:29; VI:18)

1. For a number of years, electronic games were the <u>faster-growing</u> Christmas items of all,
   $\quad$ A $\quad\quad\quad\quad\quad\quad\quad\quad\quad\quad\quad\quad\quad\quad\quad\quad\quad\quad$ B
   as well as being among the <u>most expensive</u>.
   $\quad\quad\quad$ C $\quad\quad\quad\quad\quad\quad\quad\quad$ D
2. Though ostriches can run <u>quickest</u> than any other bird, <u>they</u> are not <u>as fast as</u> the
   $\quad\quad\quad\quad\quad\quad\quad\quad\quad\quad$ A $\quad\quad\quad\quad\quad\quad\quad\quad$ B $\quad\quad\quad$ C
   <u>swiftest</u> mammal, the cheetah.
   $\quad$ D
3. Nowadays the <u>most sophisticated</u> chess computers are <u>as better as</u> <u>all</u> but
   $\quad\quad\quad\quad\quad\quad$ A $\quad\quad\quad\quad\quad\quad\quad\quad\quad\quad$ B $\quad\quad$ C
   <u>the best</u> human players in the world.
   $\quad$ D
4. Even <u>more significant</u> than the fact that <u>the majority</u> of the energy from sunlight is lost
   $\quad\quad\quad$ A $\quad\quad\quad\quad\quad\quad\quad\quad\quad\quad$ B
   in the atmosphere, and perhaps the <u>difficultest</u> problem for scientists to solve, is
   $\quad\quad\quad\quad\quad\quad\quad\quad\quad\quad\quad\quad\quad$ C
   silicon's failure to use <u>more than</u> 14% of the solar energy it receives.
   $\quad\quad\quad\quad\quad\quad\quad$ D
5. Although the British Isles are <u>farther</u> north <u>than</u> New York City, winters are <u>more mild</u>
   $\quad\quad\quad\quad\quad\quad\quad\quad\quad\quad$ A $\quad\quad\quad$ B $\quad\quad\quad\quad\quad\quad\quad\quad\quad\quad\quad$ C
   because the waters of the Gulf Stream are <u>warmer</u> than those of the North Atlantic.
   $\quad\quad\quad\quad\quad\quad\quad\quad\quad\quad\quad\quad\quad\quad\quad$ D

Focused Exercise 25: Comparisons (Form of Conjunctions)

> Check particularly for *than/that*; *too/very*; and *so/too* mistakes.

(See Practice Tests I:40; III:23; III:38; IV:19; V:39; VI:29; VI:34; VI:37)

1. The quality control standards for space equipment are <u>very</u> high <u>indeed</u> and some
   $\quad\quad\quad\quad\quad\quad\quad\quad\quad\quad\quad\quad\quad\quad\quad\quad\quad\quad\quad\quad$ A $\quad\quad\quad$ B
   items have been rejected <u>as</u> being <u>very</u> unreliable to be acceptable.
   $\quad\quad\quad\quad\quad\quad\quad\quad$ C $\quad\quad\quad$ D
2. Some educators claim <u>that</u> more of the money <u>that</u> is spent on education should be
   $\quad\quad\quad\quad\quad\quad\quad\quad$ A $\quad\quad\quad\quad\quad\quad\quad\quad$ B
   earmarked <u>for</u> mathematics and science <u>that</u> is spent now.
   $\quad\quad\quad$ C $\quad\quad\quad\quad\quad\quad\quad\quad\quad\quad$ D

3. When <u>they</u> have switched from typewriters to the new word-processors <u>that</u> have re-
A   B
cently been developed, some writers have become <u>too</u> enthusiastic that their output
C
has <u>more than</u> doubled.
D

4. The royal yacht Britannia, <u>which</u> visited California during <u>the worst</u> storms <u>that</u> had
A   B   C
struck that state in decades, is longer <u>that</u> a football field.
D

5. A survey has shown <u>that</u> Americans believe Kansas, <u>alike to</u> Alaska, is <u>less visited</u> by
A   B   C
foreign tourists <u>than</u> other states of the Union.
D

Focused Exercise 26: Coordinate or Split Conjunctions

> Check that the two parts of a coordinate or split conjunction (*neither/nor*; *either/or*) are consistent with each other.

(See Practice Tests I:16; II:ex.2; II:16)

1. Though both cats <u>and</u> dogs existed before man, <u>without</u> man neither one group <u>and</u>
A   B   C
the other would have developed <u>so</u> many varieties.
D

2. Not only oil <u>and also</u> cattle are symbols <u>of</u> the great wealth <u>of</u> both Texas <u>and</u> Okla-
A   B   C   D
homa.

3. Women clearly play an important role <u>in</u> influencing the size of the gross domestic
A
product if both their household <u>also</u> their child-rearing work is included, though econ-
B
omists usually take account of <u>neither</u> one <u>nor</u> the other.
C   D

4. Hepatitis is <u>an</u> illness so debilitating <u>than</u> for a period of several weeks <u>both</u> work <u>and</u>
A   B   C   D
exercise are out of the question.

5. Fruit <u>and</u> vegetables should be <u>carefully</u> washed whether <u>eaten</u> fresh <u>and</u> cooked.
A   B   C   D

Focused Exercise 27: Time Prepositions

> Check particularly for mistakes with *on/in* and *from/since*.

(See Practice Tests I:35; I:39; II:22; II:32; V:19)

1. Babe Ruth played <u>for</u> the New York Yankees <u>since</u> 1920 <u>to</u> 1934 and won the home-run
A   B   C
title <u>in</u> most of those years.
D

2. Rhode Island, located <u>in</u> New England and the <u>smallest</u> state <u>in</u> the United States,

       A   B   C
achieved statehood <u>in</u> May 29, 1790.
D

3. Thanksgiving, celebrated <u>on</u> the fourth Thursday <u>on</u> November, commemorates the
A   B
first Thanksgiving, held <u>in</u> 1620.
C   D

4. The game starts precisely <u>by</u> three o'clock, but most spectators arrive <u>at</u> the stadium <u>in</u>
A   B   C
time <u>for</u> the pre-game festivities.
D

5. The 1930's was probably America's worst period <u>from</u> the beginning of the century, the
A
Great Depression lasting <u>from</u> the early thirties <u>to</u> the beginning <u>of</u> the Second World
B   C   D
War.

Focused Exercise 28: Other Prepositions

> Check the following: (1) that the correct preposition has been used; (2) that the preposition is complete (*according to*, NOT *according*); (3) that a preposition, usually *to*, has not been used where none is required (NOT *He watched to the man*).

(See Practice Tests II:25; III:31; III:32; IV:29; V:32; VI:20)

1. When President Kennedy spoke <u>in</u> Berlin <u>on behalf</u> the American people, he was re-
A   B
ceived <u>with</u> a show <u>of</u> enormous enthusiasm.
C   D

2. Oscar Wilde lived out his final days <u>in</u> obscurity <u>in</u> France <u>in spite</u> the extraordinary
A   B   C
brilliance <u>of</u> his early career.
D

3. The Federal Government provides considerable funds <u>in order to</u> help <u>to</u> the universi-
A   B
ties remain <u>in</u> the forefront <u>of</u> scientific research.
C   D

4. The New York Stock Market, located <u>in</u> Manhattan <u>on</u> Wall Street <u>is</u> the largest stock
A   B   C
market <u>of</u> the world.
D

5. "Invisibles" are some <u>from</u> the most important exports made <u>by</u> the industrialized na-
A   B
tions <u>to</u> countries <u>in</u> the "Third World."
C   D

Focused Exercise 29: Tense Usage

> Check for correct use of past, present perfect, and past perfect tenses.

(See Practice Tests I:27; II:40; III:27; IV:30)

1. The Elgin Marbles, which <u>have been taken</u> <u>to</u> England in the nineteenth century,
   A B
   <u>have recently been</u> <u>the</u> subject of considerable controversy.
   C D

2. When Alaska <u>became</u> the forty-ninth state, the <u>forty-eighth</u>, Arizona, <u>was</u> a state <u>for</u>
   A B C D
   forty-seven years.

3. If England <u>had won</u> the Revolutionary War, <u>the</u> whole history of the <u>English-speaking</u>
   A B C
   world <u>had been</u> different.
   D

4. Genetic engineering <u>has already made</u> vast progress <u>even though</u> Crick and Watson
   A B C
   <u>had discovered</u> DNA's "double helix" conformation only a relatively short time ago.
   D

5. The Olympic Games, <u>first celebrated</u> in Athens in 1896, <u>were held</u> <u>every four years</u> so
   A B C
   far this century, except <u>during</u> the two world wars.
   D

Focused Exercise 30: Past Tense and Past Participle Forms

> Check that the form of the verb used is correct and that an irregular verb has not been given a regular form.

(See Practice Tests I:22; I:24; II:31; III:24)

1. Before <u>the eighteenth century</u> <u>was ushered in</u>, very <u>few</u> Europeans <u>had drank</u> coffee.
   A B C D

2. When Henry Aaron <u>hitted</u> <u>his</u> seven-hundred-and-fifteenth home run, the ball
   A B
   <u>was caught</u> by <u>an</u> Atlanta Braves pitcher.
   C D

3. More people <u>seen</u> at least one episode of "The Winds of War" <u>than</u> <u>had seen</u> any previ-
   A B C D
   ous television mini-series.

4. In some English <u>villages</u> <u>in</u> the Middle Ages, the entire population <u>catched</u> bubonic
   A B C
   plague and <u>died</u>.
   D

5. When <u>they were first introduced</u>, electronic calculators were less powerful and <u>costed</u>
     A   B   C

much more than they <u>do</u> today.
                    D

Focused Exercise 31: Passive Voice Form

> Check the following: (1) that the participle form is correct; (2) that an appropriate form of the verb *to be* is present

(See Practice Tests I:31; II:17; III:16; V:21; V:40)

1. "Twelfth Night" <u>was wrote</u> by Shakespeare <u>in</u> ten days after he <u>was invited</u> <u>to write</u> a
                A   B   C   D
play for Queen Elizabeth I.

2. Pioneer 10 <u>programmed</u> to pass Jupiter and <u>was involved</u> in <u>man's</u> first organized at-
               A   B   C
tempt <u>to communicate</u> with extraterrestrial civilizations.
        D

3. Evidence <u>has been put</u> forward <u>showing</u> that astronauts <u>exposed</u> to long periods of
                A   B   C
weightlessness <u>have affected</u> quite severely.
            D

4. Cochineal <u>made</u> from <u>the</u> blood of insects and <u>was formerly used</u> very <u>widely</u>.
         A   B   C   D

5. Scientists <u>have found</u> the remains of corn cobs, <u>proving</u> that corn <u>was cultivated</u> and
           A   B   C
<u>ate</u> by inhabitants of Mesoamerica about 10,000 years ago.
 D

Focused Exercise 32: Non-finite Verb Forms

> Check particularly the following: (1) *-ing* form after prepositions; (2) that *for to* does NOT occur; (3) the *to + infinitive complement* of certain expressions (*It is difficult to ...*); (4) that *to* is not used after a modal, except for *ought*; (5) that the form of the second verb is appropriate where two verbs occur together (*He dislikes swimming; He wants to eat*) where the first is not a modal.

(See Practice Tests I:ex.2; II:24; II:35; III:18; III:33; IV:31; V:25; VI:17)

1. Because <u>many</u> athletes were not used <u>to run</u> at high altitudes, <u>their</u> performances at
           A   B   C
the Mexico City Olympics <u>were affected</u>.
                        D

2. <u>It</u> is unlawful <u>in</u> the United States <u>driving</u> without <u>having</u> a license.
   A   B   C   D

3. It was <u>for to</u> warn <u>of</u> an attack by the British <u>that</u> Paul Revere made <u>his</u> famous ride.
      A   B   C   D

4. In certain circumstances Congress can <u>to do</u> nothing <u>to prevent</u> the president from
   A   B   C
<u>taking</u> action.
  D

5. <u>It</u> is not always possible <u>making</u> <u>oneself</u> <u>understood</u> in a foreign country.
  A   B   C   D

6. Herschel Walker was invited <u>to become</u> <u>a</u> professional football player before
                               A   B
<u>to complete</u> his college <u>career</u>.
    C   D

7. Children may not enjoy <u>to eat</u> sweets after a meal <u>so much as</u> <u>at</u> other times, but it is
                       A   B   C
healthier for them <u>to do so</u>.
              D

8. Some people decided <u>staying</u> in <u>their</u> homes when these <u>were threatened</u> by Mount St.
                 A   B   C
Helens, in spite of <u>warnings</u> by scientists.
                  D

9. In many countries, people <u>holding</u> dual nationality must <u>to choose</u> which nationality
                          A   B
they wish <u>to retain</u> when they cease <u>to be</u> minors.
        C   D

10. The indigenous inhabitants of Pennsylvania <u>had used</u> the local oil <u>for its</u> medicinal
                                            A   B
properties in <u>relieving</u> stomach disorders long before it was used <u>for</u> to provide fuels
                C   D
and lubricants.

Focused Exercise 33: Parallelism

> Check that items joined by a conjunction (especially *and*) are grammatically equivalent.

(See Practice Tests I:29; II:33; III:39; IV:27; IV:34; V:24; VI:24)

1. Drinking, <u>cigarettes</u>, and <u>staying out late</u> are activities which are intrinsically undesir-
           A   B
able and <u>punishable</u> <u>according to</u> school rules.
          C   D

2. <u>Preparing</u> lectures and <u>keeping</u> abreast of recent research are <u>involved in</u> this position,
  A   B   C
as is <u>to write</u> articles for scholarly journals.
        D

3. The judge described the attack and <u>subsequent kidnapping</u> as vicious,
                                         A
not to be tolerated, <u>unscrupulous</u>, and <u>inexcusable</u>.
      B   C   D

4. The popularity of TV <u>game shows and quiz shows</u> is partly attributable to the fact that
                               A

participants can win cash, <u>merchandise</u>, and <u>go</u> to exotic <u>American and foreign</u> holiday
B   C   D
resorts.

5. Theories involving <u>plate tectonics and terranes</u> have successively encountered
A
<u>growing, if reluctant</u> acceptance on the part of geologists and <u>dealing</u> with ancient
B   C
earth <u>movements and collisions</u>.
D

Focused Exercise 34: Word Order

> Check particularly the following: (1) adjective-noun order (especially
> when a noun is used as an adjective); (2) modifying adverb-adjective
> order; (3) subject-verb order in embedded questions.

(See Practice Tests I:19; III:28; IV:28; V:33)

1. <u>Lamp desks</u> and other <u>office equipment</u> should be chosen with an eye to
   A   B
   <u>design efficiency</u> and <u>worker comfort</u>.
   C   D

2. When choosing a major, college students <u>should consider</u> how good <u>are they</u> at differ-
   A   B
   ent subjects as well as what the <u>job market</u> <u>will be</u> when they graduate.
   C   D

3. Among the <u>asked commonly</u> questions by prospective <u>condominium buyers</u> are ones
   A   B
   related to <u>interest rates</u> and <u>down payments</u>.
   C   D

4. One of the <u>favorite pastimes</u> of both <u>economic analysts</u> and computer manufacturers
   A   B
   seems to be guessing how many <u>home computers</u> <u>will there be</u> in 1990.
   C   D

5. Almost 2,000 <u>exercise books</u> were published following the <u>fitness revolution</u> of the
   A   B
   1970's but most <u>methods current</u> concentrate on <u>certain parts</u> of the body only.
   C   D

Focused Exercise 35: Compound Adjectives (and Adjectives as Nouns)

> Check that the noun in a compound adjective is in the singular form.
> An adjective used as a noun is always singular in form but plural in
> meaning; it always takes a plural verb.

(See Practice Tests II:23; II:28; II:39; III:ex.2; V:27)

1. When Richard Nixon became president, he was quite <u>familiar</u> with <u>the White House</u>,
   A   B
   having served an <u>eight-years</u> term as <u>vice-president</u> under Eisenhower.
   C   D

2. A <u>down-to-earth</u> way of describing a nano-second is with <u>an</u> <u>eleven-inches</u> piece of
      A   B   C
wire, which represents the distance light <u>will travel</u> in that time.
                                          D

3. If the <u>poors</u> are taken to mean people below the official <u>poverty</u> level in the United
       A   B
States, some of <u>those</u> included would be regarded as <u>well-off</u> in some countries.
                 C   D

4. About <u>one inch long</u>, a <u>two-days-old</u> kangaroo is <u>blind</u> and virtually <u>invisible</u> against its
            A   B   C   D
mother.

5. The president <u>set up</u> a <u>five-men</u> commission <u>to</u> investigate the <u>charges</u> of corruption.
                A   B   C   D

Focused Exercise 36: Plural Nouns in Certain Expressions

> Check that a count noun is plural after such expressions as *one of* and *a number/group/variety of.*

(See Practice Tests II:37; III:17; IV:17; V:17)

1. Large <u>quantities</u> of corn and <u>tomato</u> <u>are</u> <u>grown</u> in Indiana.
          A   B   C   D

2. Of <u>all</u> the <u>mammal</u> in the world, perhaps <u>none</u> is stranger than <u>the narwahl.</u>
     A   B   C   D

3. "Gone with the Wind" was <u>undoubtedly</u> one of <u>Victor Fleming's</u> <u>most famous</u> <u>film.</u>
                              A   B   C   D

4. <u>Providing</u> relief after the disaster necessitated the mobilization of vast amounts of <u>food,</u>
   A   B
<u>medical</u> <u>supply</u>, and <u>people.</u>
       C   D

5. Laborde, one of <u>the foreigner</u> captured by Queen Ranavalona of Madagascar, later
                       A
became one of the most influential <u>men</u> at <u>her</u> court.
   B   C   D

Focused Exercise 37: Place Names and Compass Points

> Check that the definite article *(the)* is present where required with place names, especially those in the plural, and nouns deriving from points of the compass.

(See Practice Tests I:21; IV:22; V:26; VI:27)

1. <u>Pyrenees</u> <u>form</u> a natural frontier between <u>France</u> and <u>the Italian peninsula.</u>
   A   B   C   D

2. After <u>leaving</u> Acapulco <u>in</u> 1521, Magellan sailed to <u>west</u> and discovered <u>the Philippines.</u>
      A   B   C   D

3. The Mount McKinley is the highest mountain in the United States.
   A   B   C   D

4. Hundreds of miles away is El Paso, located in southwest of Texas.
       A   B   C   D

5. Westbound travelers found Rocky Mountains the last great barrier before reaching
     A   B   C

the west coast.
  D

Focused Exercise 38: (Vocabulary) Confusing Verbs

> Check that the correct verb form pairs of commonly confused verbs (*remind/remember*) has been used.

(See Practice Tests II:36; III:25; IV:36; V:20; VI:38)

1. The picture was so valuable that a corps of guards was hired to see it twenty-four
    A   B   C   D

hours a day.

2. The Congressional Medal of Honor is awarded for exceptional service beyond merely
                               A   B   C

making one's duty.
  D

3. Temperature inversion, which may result in smoggy conditions, occurs when hot air
                           A   B

raises and meets cold air above it.
  C   D

4. When athletes are suffering from dizziness, it is preferable for them to lay down for a
                                   A   B

few minutes rather than try to run it off.
          C   D

5. In examinations set by some testing authorities students are required to set in as-
            A   B   C

signed seats.
  D

Focused Exercise 39: Confusing Adjectives and Nouns

> Check that the correct form has been used where two adjectives or two nouns may be derived from the same root form (*interesting/interested*).

(See Practice Tests I:17; IV:38; VI:23; VI:36)

1. Though many were scornful of the project, all were delightful to be invited to partici-
             A   B   C   D

pate.

2. The static was so bad that the broadcaster's words were barely intelligent.
               A   B   C   D

3. Amber is a <u>substantive</u> derived from the resin of <u>certain</u> trees as a result of a <u>specific</u>
          A   B   C

   <u>combination</u> of circumstances.
      D

4. After twelve hard <u>rounds</u> of boxing, it would have been natural for Leonard to be
               A

   exhausted, but he <u>came out</u> for the fourteenth round with <u>renovated</u> vigor.
     B   C   D

5. Ford's <u>application</u> of the assembly-line to auto-making was a crucial step in the
        A

   <u>development</u> of <u>manufactured</u> <u>processes</u>.
      B   C   D

Focused Exercise 40: Redundancy

> Check that two words or expressions have not been combined (usually by *and*) as though they mean something different when they actually mean the same thing.

(See Practice Tests I:37; II:20; III:20; VI:28; VI:33; VI:40)

1. The possibility that <u>skirmishes, and even full-scale war</u>, might break out between
                                A

   the <u>North and South</u> was a <u>source</u> of <u>concern and worry</u> to all.
        B   C   D

2. Horowitz gave an <u>extremely excellent</u> concert <u>performance</u> of Rachmaninov's third pi-
                    A   B

   ano concerto on the <u>fiftieth anniversary</u> of his <u>concert debut</u> in the United States.
                         C   D

3. Huge computers are needed to <u>absorb and process</u> the millions of pieces of
                             A

   meteorological information <u>collected and gathered</u> throughout the world so that
                             B

   <u>short and long-range</u> weather forecasts may be made more <u>quickly and accurately</u>.
        C   D

4. <u>Drinks and beverages</u> are sold at most <u>little league and high school</u> ball games as
         A   B

   <u>a means</u> of defraying the costs of <u>uniforms and equipment</u>.
      C   D

5. <u>Bands and drill teams</u>, together with <u>floats and giant figures</u>, make the Macy's
         A   B

   Thanksgiving Day Parade a <u>yearly annual</u> event which appeals to <u>children and adults</u>
                               C   D

   alike.

ANSWER KEY/ FOCUSED EXERCISES 16-40

FE-16

1 D
2 B
3 A
4 B
5 C

FE-17

1 C
2 D
3 A
4 B
5 C

FE-18

1 C
2 A
3 D
4 C
5 B

FE-19

1 B
2 B
3 A
4 C
5 B

FE-20

1 B
2 C
3 A
4 B
5 A

FE-21

1 C
2 B
3 B
4 D
5 B

FE-22

1 A
2 D
3 D
4 C
5 C

FE-23

1 C
2 B
3 B
4 A
5 D

FE-24

1 B
2 A
3 B
4 C
5 C

FE-25

1 D
2 D
3 C
4 D
5 B

FE-26

1 C
2 A
3 B
4 B
5 D

FE-27

1 B
2 D
3 B
4 A
5 A

FE-28

1 B
2 C
3 B
4 D
5 A

FE-29

1 A
2 C
3 D
4 D
5 B

FE-30

1 D
2 A
3 B
4 C
5 C

FE-31

1 A
2 A
3 D
4 A
5 D

FE-32

1 B
2 C
3 A
4 B
5 B
6 C
7 A
8 A
9 B
10 D

FE-33

1 A
2 D
3 B
4 C
5 C

FE-34

1 A
2 B
3 A
4 D
5 C

FE-35

1 C
2 C
3 A
4 B
5 B

FE-36

1 C
2 B
3 D
4 C
5 A

FE-37

1 A
2 C
3 A
4 D
5 B

FE-38

1 D
2 D
3 C
4 B
5 C

FE-39

1 C
2 D
3 A
4 D
5 C

FE-40

1 D
2 A
3 B
4 A
5 C

PREVIEW: THE SIX TOEFL PRACTICE TESTS

Strategies for Taking the TOEFL

Section 1: Listening Comprehension

Strategy: look at all the answer choices before you hear the sentence.

Throughout this section you will *hear* sentences, dialogues, or passages *only once*. You will hear the questions *only once* as well. The time available for answering the taped questions is completely controlled by the tape. The amount of time for answering each question is usually about 13 seconds. In your test booklet you will have the possible answers to each question. Try to pace yourself so that you have time to glance at each of these before you hear the question.

Part A: 20 items.

Each item consists of a single sentence. You are asked to choose the answer which best reflects the sentence you heard. (No question is asked on the tape in this section.) Many of the answers *restate* the original sentence, but some require you to make *inferences* about the general meaning.

Part B: 15 items. BE READY TO CHANGE STRATEGY!

Strategy: aim for a more general understanding than in Part A but more specific than Part C.

Each item consists of a dialogue between two people—very occasionally three. One of the voices is usually male and the other female, but sometimes both voices are either male or female. The dialogue is followed by a third voice asking a question about it.

Part B calls for a more general understanding. There are virtually no questions testing specific details as such, but you will be expected to recognize comments referring to what you have heard, to make deductions, and to demonstrate some insight into the situations. Thus, questions are commonly, "Where did this exchange take place?" "What does the woman mean?" "What can best be said about the man?" "What is the woman's occupation?" This is quite *different* from the restatement of meaning usually asked for in Part A.

Part C: 15 questions. BE READY TO CHANGE STRATEGY AGAIN!

Strategy: aim for a general understanding of what you hear.

In this part more than one question is attached to each item. The items
are talks or dialogues containing factual information. The questions are not
asked until the *end* of the talk or dialogue. Again, a general understanding is
most important, for the questions tend *not* to be a test of memory. The information required to answer the questions is usually given more than once in
the talk or dialogue. However, your attention span must be longer than in
Parts A or B.

Section 2: Structure and Written Expression

General Strategy: work at a steady pace and read each possible answer very
carefully.

In the two parts of this section, you control the speed at which you complete individual answers. However, you must answer 40 questions in 25 minutes. You have an average of only a little over 35 seconds for each item. You
may do the two parts in either order, but BE READY TO CHANGE STRATEGY
between one part and the other.

Part A: 15 items.

Strategy: read carefully and choose the one correct sentence completion.

Each item consists of a single sentence with one part missing. (This may
be at the beginning, in the middle, or at the end.) Four possible completions
are offered, but only one of these is correct. The items involve structural
points rather than vocabulary.

Part B: 25 items. BE READY TO CHANGE STRATEGY!

Strategy: choose the one incorrect part.

Each item consists of a single sentence with four parts underlined. Three
of the underlined parts are correct; you must choose the one *incorrect* part.
Most of the items deal with structural points, but a few involve vocabulary.

General Strategy: do Part A quickly to allow yourself more time for Part B.

As in Section 2, you control the speed at which you complete the individual answers in the two parts of Section 3. You must complete 60 items in 45 minutes, but there is a big difference between the two parts: questions 1-30 test your *knowledge* of vocabulary, while questions 31-60 test your *understanding* of written English. Try to spend no more than 20-25 seconds on each of questions 1-30 (10-12 minutes in all), in order to leave yourself as much time as possible for questions 31-60.

Part A: 30 items.

Strategy: work quickly; if you do not know the meaning, guess and continue on to the next item.

Each item consists of a single sentence with one word or expression underlined. You must choose the option that best reflects the meaning of the underlined part. Generally speaking, you will either know the correct answer immediately or you will not know it at all. *Do not* waste time looking for contextual clues. Almost all the options offered will fit structurally into the sentence given. Furthermore, you will not be able to find the meaning of the underlined word or expression from the content of the sentence. If you do *not* know the meaning, *guess* and go on to the next question. One exception to this advice is if you know the underlined word or expression has more than one meaning, you will be able to tell which meaning fits that particular sentence by looking at the context.

Part B: 30 items. BE READY TO CHANGE STRATEGY!

Strategy: think about the items and recheck them with the information given.

In this section you have to read five or six different passages of varying length and subject matter. The number of questions following each passage may be as few as two or as many as ten. It is important to remember that you do not need any prior knowledge of the subject matter to answer the questions. These questions are always based on information *given in the passage*.

Some of the questions require you to identify *restatements* of specific information given in the passage; some require you to decide what is the *main idea* of the passage. Such questions may include choosing a title that reflects the main idea. Some questions require you to make *inferences or draw conclusions* on the basis of what is stated; some may require *prediction* of what subsequent paragraphs might be about.

It *is* worth spending time thinking about the items in questions 31-60, and you may well need to go back and check the information given in order to be confident of your answers. This is why it is important not to spend too much time on questions 1-30. If you spend 10-12 minutes on those, you should have approximately 35 minutes for the 30 questions in this part. Remember, however, that a significant part of that time will be used in actually reading the passages.

Usually the final questions in this section require you to identify the best restatement of a given sentence. Rather than being asked questions about the sentence, you must choose which option is most nearly the same as the sentence given.

Budgeting Your Time

You must budget your time very carefully on the TOEFL. In Section 1 (Listening Comprehension), you must make decisions very quickly—the tape will go on whether you are ready or not. In Section 2 (Structure and Written Expression), you must move from one question to the next as quickly as possible—especially when you are either sure of the answer, or have no idea at all. In Section 3 (Reading Comprehension and Vocabulary), you must adopt very different strategies for its two parts. You must move quickly through the part on vocabulary in order to leave yourself enough time for the reading comprehension questions.

It is very important for you, therefore, to *practice* budgeting your time on the practice tests which follow. If possible, you should do a complete test in one sitting. This will help you to practice maintaining your concentration for the period required on the actual TOEFL. It will also enable you to practice changing strategies quickly as you move from one part of the test to the next.

Adapting to Style and Content Changes

Be ready to adapt to the changes in style and content that occur as you go through a TOEFL from the Listening Comprehension to the end of the Reading Comprehension.

<u>Section 1</u>

Listening Comprehension, Part A. The style is fairly informal and conversational; the content, everyday topics that might come up in the home, the office, a university, a store, etc. The sentence is out of context.

Listening Comprehension, Part B. The topics that come up are similar to those in Part A, as is the style of language, but context is established by the exchange. You must also remember *who* said what, as many of the questions are of the type "What does the man/woman mean?"

Listening Comprehension, Part C. YOU MUST BE READY FOR A CHANGE OF STYLE. There is a considerable variation of style here. The dialogues are usually in fairly conversational English, though this tends to be less idiomatic than in Parts A and B. The talks are usually in formal, academic, spoken English, and if an announcement is included in this part, it is in the formal, impersonal, spoken English appropriate to providing information to the general public. In all cases, the content is important.

Section 2

Structure and Written Expression. YOU MUST BE READY FOR ANOTHER CHANGE OF STYLE *AND* A CHANGE IN CONTENT. There is a clear change of style from Section 1. Now you must deal with formal, *written* English. More important still, you must change *your attitude* towards the content. This content is factual, and deals with such matters as American history, science and technology, etc., with the subject matter changing abruptly from one item to the next. However, *you must not be distracted* by the subject matter, since the questions fundamentally deal with the *structures* involved.

Section 3

Vocabulary, Part A. The style and content of the vocabulary section remains similar to that in Section 2. Again, *do not be distracted* by the subject matter of the sentences. Focus your attention on the meaning of the underlined word or expression.

Reading Comprehension, Part B. BE READY TO CHANGE YOUR ATTITUDE AGAIN. The style and content again remain similar (generally formal and factual), but here the sentences clearly relate to one another within each passage. The biggest change must be in *your attitude* towards the content. Now it is the *content*, rather than the structure, which is supremely important. In the previous three parts, it was your *knowledge* of English structure and vocabulary that was tested. Now it is your *understanding* of written English that is being tested.

Tactics for Filling in the Answer Sheet

You will be given a separate answer sheet. Remember to mark it clearly and heavily in a dark (2B) pencil. Only blacken the circle that corresponds to the answer you want. Because the answer sheet will be graded by a machine, any extra markings may count as errors.

If you change your mind about an answer, be sure to erase completely so the machine will be able to read your answer accurately.

For each question you must only mark one answer. If you mark more than one, your answers will be counted wrong. Do answer every question, however—even if you only guess at some answers. It is a good idea to guess, because you will not be penalized for wrong answers. When guessing, you should first eliminate the answers that are clearly wrong, and then choose quickly between the remaining ones. Mark your guess on the answer sheet and put a very light dot beside the question so you can go back to it again later if you have time.

If you find that you have marked your answers in the wrong order, raise your hand for the examiner to help you. You should also raise your hand for the examiner if there is something wrong with your answer sheet or test booklet.

Remember to sit up straight when you take the test (you should do this for the practice tests as well). Use both hands: the one with your pencil should be used to keep your place on the answer sheet, the other to keep your place in the question booklet. Do not lift the booklet or answer sheet up; leave them on the desk in front of you.

Scoring the Practice Tests

Caution: These guidelines are very approximate ones. They are for information only and are certainly not guarantees of actual TOEFL scores.

If you take a whole test at the same time and follow the procedure and restrictions of the actual TOEFL as closely as possible, the following table offers a *very general* idea of what you *might* score on the TOEFL:

Percent correct on all three sections	Number correct on each section	Approximate TOEFL score
80%	40—32—48	550
70%	35—28—42	500
60%	30—24—36	450
45%	22/23—18—27	400

PRACTICE TEST I

Section 1: Listening Comprehension

Time: 40 minutes

You will need to play the tape for all the questions in Section 1. (The tapescripts are printed on pages 233-237. This material is designated by the symbol  .)

In this section of the test, you will have an opportunity to demonstrate your ability to understand spoken English. There are three parts to this section, with special directions for each part.

Part A

Directions: For each question in Part A, you will hear a short statement. The statements will be spoken just one time. They will not be written out for you, and you must listen carefully to understand what the speaker says.

After you hear a statement, read the four sentences in your test book, marked (A), (B), (C), and (D), and decide which *one* is closest in meaning to the statement you heard. Then, on your answer sheet, find the number of the question and blacken the space that corresponds to the letter of the answer you have chosen so that the letter inside the oval cannot be seen.

Example I

Sample Answer
(A) (B) (C) ●

You will hear:

You will read: (A) I've already had two classes with that teacher.

(B) I tried out for the teacher's role.

(C) I telephoned the teacher about class.

(D) I arrived after class had begun.

Sentence (D), "I arrived after class had begun," means most nearly the same as the statement "The teacher had already called the roll by the time I got to class." Therefore, you should choose answer (D).

Example II

Sample Answer
● (B) (C) (D)

You will hear:

You will read: (A) We have a new piece of copper furniture.

(B) The cobbler made our new table.

(C) There's a fresh pot of coffee on the copper table.

(D) We can't make out who that new policeman is.

Sentence (A), "We have a new piece of copper furniture," is closest in meaning to the sentence "Our new coffee table is made out of copper." Therefore, you should choose answer (A).

GO ON TO THE NEXT PAGE

1. (A) Students without tickets are not eligible.
   (B) Students may not own cars.
   (C) Report cards are available after fees are paid.
   (D) Students are penalized for not paying fees.

2. (A) Sue is still looking for an apartment.
   (B) Sue is out of work.
   (C) She hasn't collected our rent yet.
   (D) Sue won't share her apartment.

3. (A) May I borrow your number three vise?
   (B) Could you give me some advice?
   (C) Do you have any extra ice cubes?
   (D) Vice is not just a matter of inconvenience.

4. (A) The twins are now over thirteen.
   (B) The winners are already having tea.
   (C) The ten-year-olds haven't been seen for ages.
   (D) The twins seem older than their age.

5. (A) The reactor was no laughing matter.
   (B) I thought his response was ridiculous.
   (C) The comedians went on strike.
   (D) His actions always amuse me.

6. (A) She can be found in the spire.
   (B) She is sure about her co-workers.
   (C) The dents can be worked out.
   (D) Her fellow workers trust her.

7. (A) We wore our coolest dresses.
   (B) We thought it would be cooler.
   (C) The felt hat didn't match the dress.
   (D) I prefer pants over dresses.

8. (A) They continued working after the bell.
   (B) The students kept their compositions.
   (C) They began writing when the bell rang.
   (D) They turned in their essays when class ended.

9. (A) His story ends on the date of publication.
   (B) This book is not available any longer.
   (C) Current facts contradict this book's information.
   (D) You must not keep this book past the due date.

10. (A) They must be waiting in the Chicago airport.
    (B) They probably didn't make it to Chicago today.
    (C) They must be close to the air-cargo terminal.
    (D) They couldn't send their air cargo today.

11. (A) I enjoyed seeing that show.
    (B) I can picture myself in that show.
    (C) I got us two seats in row C.
    (D) I couldn't get tickets for that show.

12. (A) The building we own is fully insured.
    (B) This year's rent increase will be lower.
    (C) The owner reserved a place for us.
    (D) Our rent won't change this year.

13. (A) It wasn't easy for Jeff to find work.
    (B) Jeff's last job was harder than this one.
    (C) Jeff wanted an easier job.
    (D) Jeff's quite difficult to work with.

14. (A) Travelers must check in at number eight.
    (B) Traveler's checks are sold by another cashier.
    (C) The widow paid her restaurant bill by check.
    (D) Travelers can eat whatever they buy.

15. (A) I've never seen a mill that wonderful.
    (B) The steak was rare, but delicious.
    (C) That was one of the best meals I've ever had.
    (D) I have rarely had a good meal.

16. (A) They've written to their parents once.
    (B) They ride once in a while.
    (C) Their parents wrote from Leeds.
    (D) They should write more often.

17. (A) The state requires that all sports be registered.
    (B) Bidding must follow state guidelines.
    (C) Not all states allow gambling.
    (D) Some states do not permit competitive sports.

18. (A) They had two old pieces of luggage.
    (B) They got the man to help them.
    (C) They had the man over to discuss their case.
    (D) They bought a carrying case from the old man.

19. (A) That is not allowed.
    (B) I'm sure you're able.
    (C) I'm surprised you find it difficult.
    (D) You must undo what you've done.

20. (A) Why don't you call on us more often?
    (B) Can't you babysit for us anymore?
    (C) How are you going to visit us next time?
    (D) How did you use to get here?

Part B

Directions: In Part B you will hear short conversations between two speakers. At the end of each conversation, a third voice will ask a question about what was said. The question will be spoken just one time. After you hear a conversation and the question about it, read the four possible answers in your test book and decide which _one_ is the best answer to the question you heard. Then, on your answer sheet, find the number of the question and blacken the space that corresponds to the letter of the answer you have chosen.

Example

Sample Answer
Ⓐ Ⓑ ● Ⓓ

You will hear:

You will read: (A) He is very decisive.

(B) He needs shoes.

(C) He'd like some advice.

(D) His offer is unacceptable.

From the conversation you know that the man needs some help in making up his mind about the offer. The best answer, then, is (C), "He'd like some advice." Therefore, you should choose answer (C).

21. (A) Go out to dinner.
    (B) Go to the lab.
    (C) Write a report.
    (D) Join her friends later.

22. (A) There are no tickets for the early show.
    (B) Everyone has left.
    (C) The ticket line is on the left.
    (D) The last tickets have already been sold.

23. (A) Broken wagons.
    (B) A bad check.
    (C) Monitoring station breaks.
    (D) A problem with the woman's car.

24. (A) Skipping the meeting.
    (B) Going to the meeting by car.
    (C) Eating when the meeting ends.
    (D) Having dinner before eight.

25. (A) Take some clothing for a cold climate.
    (B) Not go to the places she used to.
    (C) Keep her worms in a can.
    (D) Take some aspirin and keep warm.

26. (A) She always wears the latest fashions.
    (B) She's often not on time for work.
    (C) She doesn't work late.
    (D) She's been doing a lot of new things recently.

27. (A) There aren't enough potatoes for everyone else.
    (B) The woman has to think about her request.
    (C) The woman has more potatoes than the man has.
    (D) The woman shouldn't eat any more potatoes.

28. (A) Lawyer.
    (B) Gardener.
    (C) Electrician.
    (D) Heart Surgeon.

29. (A) The woman should invite the policeman.
    (B) The policeman probably knows the route.
    (C) He doesn't want to go to the sports center.
    (D) The sports center is near the police station.

30. (A) Make a purchase.
    (B) Insist on a better price.
    (C) Try elsewhere.
    (D) Think about their budget.

31. (A) They disagree about it.
    (B) The woman hasn't tried it.
    (C) Neither likes it.
    (D) Both like it.

32. (A) Miss part of the performance.
    (B) Find their seats in the theater.
    (C) Enter the mission.
    (D) Look for a gas station.

33. (A) Arrange a place for him to stay.
    (B) Help him with some heavy work.
    (C) Go away for the weekend.
    (D) Give him her spare change.

34. (A) He confirms the directions for the trip.
    (B) He expresses his disappointment in the election results.
    (C) He hopes the woman will have a good vacation.
    (D) He wishes to congratulate the woman.

35. (A) At a birthday party.
    (B) At a convention for engineers.
    (C) At a graduation ceremony.
    (D) At a housewarming party.

Part C

<u>Directions:</u> In this part of the test, you will hear several short talks and conversations. After each talk or conversation, you will be asked some questions. The talks and questions will be spoken just one time. They will not be written out for you, so you will have to listen carefully to understand what the speaker says.

After you hear a question, read the four possible answers in your test book and decide which <u>one</u> is the best answer to the question you heard. Then, on your answer sheet, find the number of the question and blacken the space that corresponds to the letter of the answer you have chosen.

<u>Sample Answer</u>
Ⓐ ● Ⓒ Ⓓ

Listen to this sample talk.
You will hear:
Now look at the following example.
You will hear:
You will read: (A) Experienced secretaries.
(B) People with an interest but no training in business.
(C) People with bachelor's degrees in business administration.
(D) Office managers.

The best answer to the question "Who is the program designed for?" is (B), "People with an interest but no training in business." Therefore, you should choose (B).

<u>Sample Answer</u>
● Ⓑ Ⓒ Ⓓ

Now look at the next example.
You will hear:
You will read: (A) It depends on the course.
(B) A degree in office technology.
(C) Most bachelor's degree programs.
(D) Only towards completion of a two-year program.

The best answer to the question "What will the credits earned in this program count towards?" is (A), "It depends on the course." Therefore, you should choose answer (A).

36. (A) Seventeenth-century writers.
    (B) Thomas Tusser's importance to farmers.
    (C) Difficulties faced by early settlers.
    (D) Farming methods in the 1600's.

37. (A) The way farming knowledge was passed on.
    (B) The type of people who became farmers.
    (C) The number of farmers who could read and write.
    (D) The methods for preserving meat.

38. (A) Early settlers in England.
    (B) Seventeenth-century peasant farmers around the world.
    (C) The men who worked for Thomas Tusser.
    (D) Seventeenth-century farmers in North America.

39. (A) How to be a good husband.
    (B) How to be good parents or grandparents.
    (C) How to be a good farmer.
    (D) How to pass on traditional wisdom.

40. (A) Airline ground hostess.
    (B) Hotel receptionist.
    (C) Clerk in a store.
    (D) Tourist guide.

41. (A) A plane ticket.
    (B) New luggage.
    (C) A comb.
    (D) Requisition forms.

42. (A) Very far from the hotel.
    (B) In the hotel lobby.
    (C) Right beside the hotel.
    (D) A few blocks from the hotel.

43. (A) He usually buys toilet articles in hotels.
    (B) He was not expecting to stay at the hotel.
    (C) He always stays in the same hotel when in town.
    (D) He forgot some things when he packed his suitcase.

44. (A) She was helpful.
    (B) She was officious.
    (C) She was certain.
    (D) She was difficult.

45. (A) Natural disasters in urban areas.
    (B) The significance of Thanksgiving.
    (C) The nature of thunderstorms.
    (D) Dealing with lightning outside of cities.

46. (A) Floods.
    (B) Tornados.
    (C) Thunderstorms.
    (D) Hurricanes.

47. (A) 400
    (B) 300
    (C) 200
    (D) 100

48. (A) Young country-dwellers.
    (B) Sailors.
    (C) Weathermen.
    (D) City-dwellers.

49. (A) On an ocean liner at sea.
    (B) On a horse in a treeless field.
    (C) In a dense forest.
    (D) In a 25-story downtown office building.

50. (A) It is safe if you are in a boat.
    (B) Remain in a pond or lake until the storm passes.
    (C) Stay away from it.
    (D) If you are within a tenth of a mile of water, you will probably be a casualty.

Section 2: Structure and Written Expression

Time: 25 minutes

This section is designed to measure your ability to recognize language that is appropriate for standard written English. There are two types of questions in this section, with special directions for each type.

Part A

<u>Directions:</u> Questions 1-15 are incomplete sentences. Four words or phrases, marked (A), (B), (C), and (D), are given beneath each sentence. You are to choose the *one* word or phrase that best completes the sentence. Then, on your answer sheet, find the number of the question and blacken the space that corresponds to the letter of the answer you have chosen so that the letter inside the oval cannot be seen.

Example I

Sample Answer
(A) (B) (C) ●

_______ four major championships on the professional golf tour.

(A) They are
(B) The
(C) In all
(D) There are

In English, the sentence should read, "There are four major championships on the professional golf tour." Therefore, you should choose (D).

Example II

Sample Answer
● (B) (C) (D)

Sesame _______ a herbaceous plant native to the tropics.

(A) is
(B) which
(C) from
(D) it is

In English, the sentence should read, "Sesame is a herbaceous plant native to the tropics." Therefore, you should choose (A).

1. The algebra of sets ________ Boolean algebra.
   (A) is called
   (B) which is called
   (C) known as
   (D) called

2. ________ pitched his first major-league game, Joe Nuxhall was only fifteen years old.
   (A) Because of he
   (B) He
   (C) When he
   (D) Surprisingly he

3. The serval, a large African wildcat, hunts like a dog ________ like other members of the cat family.
   (A) so
   (B) rather than
   (C) instead
   (D) rather not

4. ________, William Shakespeare is the most widely known.
   (A) With all writers in English
   (B) All writers in English
   (C) All of the writers in English
   (D) Of all writers in English

5. The Cathedral of Seville enjoys the distinction ________ the largest medieval cathedral in the world.
   (A) of being
   (B) to be
   (C) being
   (D) it being

6. ________, the catfish is prized for its taste.
   (A) It is ugly-looking
   (B) Ugly-looking it is
   (C) With ugly-looking
   (D) Ugly-looking

7. ________ to develop immunity to rheumatic fever.
   (A) It not being possible
   (B) It is not possible
   (C) Not possible
   (D) Is not possible

8. The fuel used in nuclear-powered ships is usually uranium in either the metallic ________.
   (A) as well as the oxide form
   (B) but also the oxide form
   (C) or the oxide form
   (D) and the oxide form

9. ________ the coming of autumn, thousands of tourists follow the Blue Ridge Trail to observe the brilliant autumnal foliage.
   (A) As soon as
   (B) With
   (C) Arrived
   (D) When

10. In a rental contract the user ________ possession of, but not title to, the goods.
    (A) obtaining
    (B) with
    (C) without
    (D) obtains

11. If the United States had not entered the Second World War, probably the 1940 unemployment rate of 14% ________ still further.
    (A) would rise
    (B) would risen
    (C) would have risen
    (D) had risen

GO ON TO THE NEXT PAGE ▶

12. A pet can act as a barometer _______.
    (A) it measures anxiety in a family
    (B) by which anxiety in a family may be measured
    (C) it measures anxiety which in a family may be
    (D) that which measures anxiety in a family

13. _______ the formulation of explanatory laws, the first step in scientific research is the collection and description of facts.
    (A) Although science's ultimate aim is
    (B) Although science's ultimate aim it is
    (C) Although it is science's ultimate aim
    (D) Although being science's ultimate aim

14. The rhinoceros has a rather poor sense of smell, nor _______.
    (A) can it see well
    (B) it well can see
    (C) it can see well
    (D) well can it see

15. _______ is the cause of most small-business failures is virtually an economic truism.
    (A) Undercapitalization
    (B) Undercapitalization that
    (C) Where undercapitalization
    (D) That undercapitalization

Part B

<u>Directions:</u> In questions 16-40 each sentence has four words or phrases underlined. The four underlined parts of the sentence are marked (A), (B), (C), and (D). You are to identify the *one* underlined word or phrase that should be corrected or rewritten. Then, on your answer sheet, find the number of the question and blacken the space that corresponds to the letter of the answer you have chosen.

Example I

Sample Answer
● Ⓑ Ⓒ Ⓓ

<u>Many</u> of Gauguin's work <u>was</u> <u>lost</u> on the
 A   B   C
South Sea island where he lived <u>until</u> his
                             D
death.

Answer (A), the underlined word <u>many</u>, would not be accepted in carefully written English; the word <u>much</u> is used with the collective noun <u>work</u>. Therefore, the sentence should read, "Much of Gauguin's work was lost on the South Sea island where he lived until his death." To answer the question correctly, you would choose (A).

Example II

Sample Answer
Ⓐ ● Ⓒ Ⓓ

Students seeking to register at <u>some</u> Ameri-
                                 A
can colleges <u>can</u> to <u>do</u> so <u>by</u> mail.
                B   C   D
Answer (B), the underlined words <u>can to</u>, would not be accepted in carefully written English; the modal auxiliary <u>can</u> is not followed by <u>to</u>. Therefore, the sentence should read, "Students seeking to register at some American colleges can do so by mail." To answer the question correctly, you should choose (B).

16. The seventy-million-year old remains of a large mammal, somewhat as a modern rhi-
     A   B
noceros, have been found in Brazil.
            C   D
17. Both government and private industry make use of cryptoanalysis, that is, persons who
     A   B   C
make and break codes.
  D
18. A survey has shown that the states Californians most readily identify by their shapes
            A   B
are California itself, Alaska, Texas, Florida, as well as Michigan.
              C   D
19. It is the key car which, when turned in the ignition, prevents some car alarms from
              A   B   C
going off.
  D
20. It is claimed that as many as 1.5 billion people may have watched to the the opening
     A   B   C
game of the 1982 World Cup finals held in Spain.
                                    D
21. Although there are Spanish-speaking people in many parts of the United States, there
     A   B
is a particularly high concentration in South-west.
        C   D
22. The first postage stamps, issued in 1840, costed one penny, which was actually
                                              A   B   C
quite a lot of money.
     D
23. After eighteen seasons of playing for the Yankees, Mickey Mantle told that he intended
                        A   B   C
to retire.
  D
24. Aspirin was first commercially market just before the turn of the century.
                                A   B   C   D
25. Cartilage is total immune to invasion by cancer.
                  A   B   C   D
26. During the course of a day, the average man takes 17,300 breaths, whereas the average
     A   B   C
woman, with their smaller lungs, takes 28,800.
              D
27. Ninety-eight percent of all animal species in history had died out.
                                A   B   C   D
28. It is driving on the left what causes visitors to Britain the most trouble.
        A   B   C   D

29. People planning <u>to travel</u> <u>by car</u> to North Dakota <u>in the winter</u> are advised to equip
A   B   C
their cars with snow tires and <u>bringing</u> warm clothing.
D

30. Recent work on the theory of tectonic plates <u>it suggests</u> that the <u>western</u> edge of the
A   B
United States <u>may have</u> <u>once</u> been part of South America.
C   D

31. The doctrine <u>of</u> environmental determinism, <u>which enunciated</u> originally by Hip-
A   B
pocrates in the <u>fifth</u> century B.C., enjoyed a great following in the <u>mid-nineteenth</u> cen-
C   D
tury.

32. Computer software <u>consisting of</u> programs <u>in</u> languages <u>not spoken</u> by <u>any</u> human
A   B   C   D
race.

33. The female lunar moth exudes theramon, a scent a male <u>of the species</u> can <u>pick up</u> at a
A   B
distance of twenty miles, but which cannot <u>be sensed</u> by <u>any another</u> species.
C   D

34. The Federal Reserve Board, <u>created</u> <u>in</u> 1913, <u>is often called</u> the <u>more high</u> court of fi-
A   B   C   D
nance in the United States.

35. Basketball has become <u>increasingly</u> popular <u>from</u> 1891, when <u>it</u> <u>was invented</u> by James
A   B   C D
Naismith of the YMCA.

36. <u>In</u> the early 1960's the Civil Rights movement <u>made</u> great efforts <u>for registering</u> mem-
A   B   C
bers of minorities <u>to vote.</u>
D

37. By observing the <u>sun's</u> corona during eclipses, scientists have discovered many
A
<u>incredible and unbelievable</u> facts <u>about</u> <u>that body.</u>
B   C   D

38. Death Valley contains the place <u>in where</u> the American continent reaches <u>its</u> <u>greatest</u>
A   B   C
depth <u>below</u> sea level.
D

39. The Rose Bowl parade <u>takes place</u> every year <u>in</u> Pasadena <u>in</u> <u>New Year's Day.</u>
A   B   C   D

40. Scales both help <u>to protect</u> <u>fish</u> <u>against</u> disease and infection <u>or</u> serve as an external
A   B   C   D
skeleton preserving body shape.

Section 3: Reading Comprehension and Vocabulary

Time: 45 minutes

This section is designed to measure your ability to understand various kinds of reading materials, as well as your ability to understand the meaning and use of words. There are two types of questions in this section, with special directions for each type.

Part A

Directions: In questions 1-30 each sentence has a word or phrase underlined. Below each sentence are four other words or phrases marked (A), (B), (C), and (D). You are to choose the *one* word or phrase that *best keeps the meaning* of the original sentence if it is substituted for the underlined word or phrase. Then, on your answer sheet, find the number of the question and blacken the space that corresponds to the letter you have chosen so that the letter inside the oval cannot be seen.

Example

Sample Answer

Ⓐ Ⓑ ● Ⓓ

The American bald eagle is not really <u>bald</u> in the usual sense.

(A) mighty
(B) majestic
(C) hairless
(D) flightless

The best answer is (C) because "The American bald eagle is not really hairless in the usual sense" is closest in meaning to the original sentence, "The American bald eagle is not really bald in the usual sense." Therefore, you should choose answer (C).

As soon as you understand the directions, begin work on the questions.

1. <u>Eyeglasses</u> have been in use since about 1300.
   - (A) Spectacles
   - (B) Goblets
   - (C) Binoculars
   - (D) Telescopes

2. Hair is found <u>exclusively</u> in mammals.
   - (A) particularly
   - (B) commonly
   - (C) exceptionally
   - (D) only

3. While <u>endeavoring</u> to find a new route to India, Columbus discovered America by accident.
   - (A) sailing
   - (B) failing
   - (C) trying
   - (D) hoping

4. Many countries nowadays restrict the exportation of <u>genuine</u> archeological artifacts.
   - (A) particular
   - (B) rare
   - (C) authentic
   - (D) costly

5. The design of wildlife refuges is still a matter of considerable <u>controversy</u>.
   - (A) significance
   - (B) debate
   - (C) urgency
   - (D) concern

6. Patrick Henry <u>delivered</u> his speech asking for "liberty or death" at a church in Richmond, Virginia.
   - (A) made
   - (B) went over
   - (C) announced
   - (D) handed over

7. Cashiers must generally account for <u>discrepancies</u> between money taken in and the amount recorded on register tapes.
   - (A) deficits
   - (B) delays
   - (C) inconsistencies
   - (D) uncertainties

8. With the coming of the Christmas shopping season, downtown traffic is often <u>diverted</u>.
   - (A) entertained
   - (B) re-routed
   - (C) delayed
   - (D) deterred

9. The inland Caspian Sea is <u>saline</u>.
   - (A) salubrious
   - (B) extensive
   - (C) navigable
   - (D) salty

10. <u>Aside from</u> its reproduction on the one-dollar bill, the reverse of the Great Seal of the United States has hardly been used.
    - (A) Except for
    - (B) Since
    - (C) As a result of
    - (D) In addition to

11. <u>Carpets</u> from countries such as Persia and Afghanistan often fetch high prices in the United States.
    - (A) Artifacts
    - (B) Rugs
    - (C) Pottery
    - (D) Textiles

12. After the tremendous improvements of recent years, the <u>hugeness</u> of the first computers is almost shocking to us today.
    (A) slowness
    (B) primitive appearance
    (C) ugliness
    (D) vast size

13. After attempting to join a religious order in 1862, Auguste Rodin finally <u>yielded to</u> his inclination to pursue an artistic career.
    (A) resisted
    (B) understood
    (C) gave in to
    (D) returned to

14. The diver's task was complicated by the fact that, <u>besides</u> the gold, the wreck contained bombs and ammunition.
    (A) next to
    (B) away from
    (C) allied to
    (D) in addition to

15. The 1961 missile crisis brought the world to the <u>verge</u> of all-out war.
    (A) horror
    (B) brink
    (C) prospect
    (D) danger

16. Theodore Roosevelt was blessed with a <u>hearty</u> constitution.
    (A) robust
    (B) legal
    (C) weak
    (D) cardiac

17. <u>Given</u> current economic trends, liberal increases in the money supply appear unlikely in the extreme.
    (A) Following
    (B) Presenting
    (C) In view of
    (D) In lieu of

18. Engineers are still trying to come up with a commercially <u>viable</u> replacement for internal-combustion engines.
    (A) desirable
    (B) driveable
    (C) accessible
    (D) feasible

19. It takes <u>roughly</u> 4,000 pounds of petals to make a single pound of rose oil.
    (A) as much as
    (B) amazingly
    (C) more or less
    (D) relatively

20. Further arms limitations talks were <u>called off</u> when Congress failed to ratify the treaty.
    (A) cancelled
    (B) postponed
    (C) scheduled
    (D) interrupted

21. Professional gamblers will rarely back <u>a long shot</u>.
    (A) an unlikely winner
    (B) an inconsistent player
    (C) a distant target
    (D) an away game

22. <u>Enraged</u> by being taxed without being given representation, New Englanders tipped tea into Boston harbor.
    (A) Disappointed
    (B) Infuriated
    (C) Alienated
    (D) Endangered

23. Probably <u>due to</u> her failure to recognize the male of the species, the female praying mantis often devours him.
    (A) reflecting
    (B) aside from
    (C) causing
    (D) because of

24. In a period of economic stagnation, finding a job is <u>particularly</u> difficult for those in certain groups.
    (A) individually
    (B) fundamentally
    (C) especially
    (D) privately

25. The <u>degree</u> to which heat affects tennis players' performance depends in part on the level of humidity.
    (A) extent
    (B) temperature
    (C) height
    (D) strength

26. Some critics claim that links between academics and biotechnology companies are <u>a menace</u> to unfettered research.
    (A) an incentive
    (B) a nuisance
    (C) a threat
    (D) an invitation

27. The practical applications of the gyroscope received <u>added</u> impetus during the two world wars.
    (A) considerable
    (B) extra
    (C) summary
    (D) infinite

28. Even a century after the end of the Civil War, old grievances still <u>rankled</u>.
    (A) prevailed
    (B) threatened
    (C) appeared
    (D) irritated

29. John F. Kennedy was born into a <u>well-to-do</u> Massachusetts family in 1917.
    (A) privileged
    (B) prosperous
    (C) famous
    (D) respected

30. In 1981, the world recession and conservation measures combined to <u>curb</u> demand for oil.
    (A) restrict
    (B) involve
    (C) spread
    (D) affect

GO ON TO THE NEXT PAGE

Part B

Directions: The rest of this section is based on a variety of reading material (single sentences, paragraphs, and the like) followed by questions about the meaning of the material. For questions 31-60, you are to choose the _one_ best answer, (A), (B), (C), or (D), to each question. Then, on your answer sheet, find the number of the question and blacken the space that corresponds to the letter of the answer you have chosen.

Answer all questions following a passage on the basis of what is _stated_ or _implied_ in that passage.

Read the following passage.

Fitness entrepreneur, Jacki Sorenson, introduced the term "aerobic dancing" with a record of that name in 1980. Between that time and the end of 1982, the number of aerobic dancing records grew very quickly and their sales picked up the spirits of record company executives. "Dancercising" records have been put out by movie stars, exercise experts, athletes, and even Mickey Mouse. The people who buy them want the convenience and economy of getting in shape at home (a record is cheaper than joining an exercise class or a gym), and they want some upbeat music that allows them to forget that what they have really bought is a fairly rigorous exercise program.

Example I

Sample Answer

It can be inferred from the passage that

(A) Jacki Sorenson is a movie star.
(B) the end of 1982 saw a drop in aerobic dancing record sales.
(C) aerobic dance records have been good investments for record companies.
(D) "dancercising" is more complicated than aerobic dancing.

The passage says that sales of aerobic dancing records "picked up the spirits of record company executives." Therefore, you should choose answer (C).

Example II

Sample Answer

According to the passage, all of the following are true about people who buy aerobic dance records _except_

(A) they want to improve their physical condition.
(B) they prefer exercising at a gymnasium.
(C) they like working out to music.
(D) they are looking for an inexpensive exercise program.

The passage states that one of the reasons for buying an aerobic dance record is that it "is cheaper than joining an exercise class or a gym." Therefore, you should choose answer (B).

Questions 31-35

There are basically two kinds of printer worth considering these days for use with a small home or business computer, both of them of the impact variety, that is, those which strike through an inked ribbon in order to deposit the impression on the paper. The first, and by far the most popular, is the dot matrix variety, which is cheaper and faster than the second type, the formed character printer. This latter type, characterized by its use of a "daisywheel" arrangement, while suffering from the disadvantages mentioned, as well as from a lack of ability to reproduce graphics, is the only kind so far which can offer quick changes of type style or size and which gives professional quality printing.

31. What is an impact printer?
    (A) the only printers available for home computers
    (B) a printer which uses business computers
    (C) a printer which uses an inked ribbon
    (D) a printer which makes impression-able deposits

32. It may be inferred from the passage that
    (A) some computer printers are not impact printers.
    (B) all impact printers are cheap.
    (C) dot-matrix printers were the first impact printers.
    (D) impact printers can only be used with small computers.

33. Formed-character printers have the advantage over dot-matrix printers of
    (A) graphics production.
    (B) printing excellence.
    (C) cost.
    (D) speed.

34. With a "daisywheel" arrangement, the user can
    (A) use a dot-matrix printer.
    (B) do without a formed-character printer.
    (C) reproduce graphics.
    (D) vary his typeface.

35. What would be the most suitable title for this passage?
    (A) Small Computer Printers: Some Considerations
    (B) The Impact of Printers on Computer Sales
    (C) Small Home and Business Computers
    (D) Dot-matrix Printers Superior to Formed-character Printers

GO ON TO THE NEXT PAGE

Questions 36-39

Amber is created when the resins produced by certain trees in tropical or subtropical climates undergo a transformation process that usually takes millions of years, and which is still not fully understood. The Baltic Sea area, now a temperate zone, probably holds the best-known and most highly-prized supply of amber, which is used in jewelry. In addition, in earlier centuries, magical properties were attributed to amber because of the electricity it acquires when rubbed. The substance is also of great interest to scientists since it has been the means of preserving fossils, especially of insects, as much as 40 million years old. Amber varies greatly according to the place where it is formed, the amber in each location having its characteristic color, hardness, and even odor.

36. What can be inferred about the Baltic Sea area?
    (A) It produces more amber than any other.
    (B) It was once dryer than it is today.
    (C) It has won many prizes for its amber.
    (D) It was once hotter than it is today.

37. According to the passage, what can be said about the transformation process that results in amber?
    (A) It is a very lengthy one.
    (B) It is made into jewelry.
    (C) It is magical.
    (D) It has only recently been described completely.

38. Which of the following *cannot* be inferred from the passage?
    (A) Amber is of interest for a number of reasons.
    (B) The oldest fossils in amber found so far are about 40 million years old.
    (C) Not all amber has the same characteristics.
    (D) Only insect fossils are found in amber.

39. The characteristics of amber vary according to
    (A) how old it is.
    (B) how much it interests scientists.
    (C) where it is found.
    (D) how hard it is to find.

Questions 40-46

The Currier and Ives firm of lithographers was founded by Nathaniel Currier in 1834. James Ives joined the firm as a bookkeeper eighteen years later just after becoming Currier's brother-in-law, and was made a partner in 1857. The pair showed an uncanny ability to predict what the American public would rush to buy in the way of cheap art, and literally hundreds of thousands of prints from as many as 7,000 individual pictures were turned out and sold from the firm's shop in lower New York by street vendors and over shop counters throughout the country and even in Europe. Though in the course of time the firm employed some of America's finest artists, artistic excellence could certainly not be counted among the firm's real goals. Nevertheless, some time after it went out of business in 1907, the prints enjoyed new popularity as collectors' items, the rarer examples fetching thousands of dollars in the 1920's.

40. According to the passage, the firm of lithographers described was in existence for about
    (A) 85 years.
    (B) 75 years.
    (C) 50 years.
    (D) 17 years.

41. Which of the following correctly describes when Ives became a partner?
    (A) as soon as he married Currier's sister
    (B) when he could predict American taste in cheap art better than Currier
    (C) after eighteen years of service to the firm
    (D) when he had worked for the company for about five years

42. According to the passage, what was the particular factor that seemed to make the firm so successful?
    (A) its feeling for what the public would buy
    (B) its choice of shop site in lower New York
    (C) the fact that it published prints that became collectors' items
    (D) its ability to identify upcoming great American artists

43. Which of the following can be inferred from the passage?
    (A) During its whole history, it sold 7,000 prints.
    (B) The firm's prints were especially popular in Europe.
    (C) The average number of prints from each picture was fewer than 7,000.
    (D) Street vendors were the firm's most effective sales force.

44. Which of the following best describes Currier and Ives' distribution network?
    (A) European
    (B) Widespread
    (C) Nation-wide
    (D) Gallery-based

45. After the firm ceased producing prints, which of these became most valuable to collectors?
    (A) the ones by the best artists
    (B) the ones produced earliest
    (C) the ones of which fewest survived
    (D) the ones which were most popular originally

46. Which of the following *cannot* be inferred from the passage?
    (A) The issuing of a Currier and Ives print was of some interest to the American public.
    (B) Some of the best American artists of the day were employed by Currier and Ives.
    (C) The popularity of Currier and Ives prints did not end when the business closed.
    (D) Currier and Ives' primary goal was to be remembered as patrons of the arts.

GO ON TO THE NEXT PAGE

Questions 47-51

Recent research into whether people who are good at solving brain twisters are more intelligent than those who are not suggests that the "experts" make use of a special type of insight. However, not only do they appear to be good at this (choosing which elements to process, to combine, or to compare from the information given), but they are also clever at making use of "general" or prior knowledge and at monitoring their own progress with a particular problem. In addition, they appear capable of adopting an appropriate cognitive style consisting of a combination of impulse and reflection. Just what this combination is still mystifies the researchers, and so does the original question, to which their answer is a somewhat frustrating "possibly."

47. What is the best title for this passage?
    (A) The Nature of Intelligence
    (B) Are Brain Twisters Tests of Intelligence? Doubt Lingers
    (C) Brain Twisters: How Everyone Can Solve Them
    (D) The Cognitive Style of Brain-Twister Writers

48. Which of the following may *not* be inferred from the passage?
    (A) Experts at brain twisters use different talents from non-experts.
    (B) There are several factors affecting success with brain twisters.
    (C) Both impulsive and reflective thinking play a role in solving brain twisters.
    (D) The researchers were frustrated by brain twisters.

49. According to the passage, the experts' insight involves
    (A) a selection process.
    (B) making use of general knowledge.
    (C) monitoring their own progress.
    (D) a combination of impulse and reflection.

50. How does the author seem to feel about the research?
    (A) selectively interested
    (B) interested but in partial disagreement
    (C) interested but somewhat dissatisfied
    (D) interested but rather mystified

51. What was the researchers' main purpose?
    (A) to prove that brain-twister experts are unusually intelligent
    (B) to seek a correlation between solving brain twisters and intelligence
    (C) to identify the experts' monitoring process
    (D) to describe the process of solving brain twisters

Questions 52-58

As more women in the United States move up the professional ladder, more are finding it necessary to make business trips alone. Since this is new for many, some tips are certainly in order. If you are married, it is a good idea to encourage your husband and children to learn to cook a few simple meals while you are away. They will be much happier and probably they will enjoy the experience. If you will be eating alone a good deal, choose good restaurants. In the end, they will be much better for your digestion. You may also find it useful to call the restaurant in advance and state that you will be eating alone. You will probably get better service and almost certainly a better table. Finally, and most importantly, anticipate your travel needs as a businesswoman; this starts with lightweight luggage which you can easily manage even when fully packed. Take a folding case inside your suitcase; it will come in extremely handy for dirty clothes, as well as for business documents and papers you no longer need on the trip. And make sure you have a briefcase so that you can keep currently required papers separate. Obviously, experience helps, but you can make things easier on yourself from the first by careful planning, so that right from the start you really can have a good trip!

52. Who is the author's intended audience?
    (A) working women who have no time for cooking
    (B) husbands and children of working women
    (C) working women who must travel on their own
    (D) hotel personnel who must cater to working women

53. Which of the following can be inferred from the passage?
    (A) A greater percentage of women are advancing professionally in the U.S. than previously.
    (B) Professional men refuse to accompany their female colleagues on business trips.
    (C) Each year there are more female tourists in the United States.
    (D) Businesswomen become successful by showing a willingness to travel alone.

54. In this passage, what advice does the author have for married women?
    (A) Stay home and take care of your family.
    (B) Encourage your husband and kids to be happy and have fun while you are away.
    (C) Help your family learn to prepare food for themselves.
    (D) Have your whole family take gourmet cooking classes together.

55. Why are better restaurants especially preferable for frequent travelers?
    (A) The food is usually better for your health.
    (B) The tables are better.
    (C) You can call ahead for reservations.
    (D) You will not have to eat alone.

56. Why is lightweight luggage important for the traveling businesswoman?
    (A) It provides space for dirty clothes.
    (B) It allows for mobility.
    (C) It can double as a briefcase.
    (D) It is usually big enough to carry all business documents.

57. What is the main idea of this passage?
    (A) Business trips are more difficult for women than for men.
    (B) More women are finding the road to success in American business.
    (C) Good business trips result from careful organization before the trip.
    (D) Careful planning makes most business ventures successful.

58. Where would this passage most likely appear?
    (A) in a magazine specifically for women
    (B) in a restaurant and hotel guide
    (C) in a news magazine
    (D) in a journal for top-ranking businessmen and women

Questions 59-60. For each of these questions, choose the answer that is *closest in meaning* to the original sentence. Note that several of the choices may be factually correct, but you should choose the one that is the *closest restatement of the given sentence*.

59. It was not until the advent of the atomic bomb and the swift expansion of the air age that a widespread, popular interest in science fiction stories occurred.
    (A) The most popular science fiction stories have always been based on the development of the atomic bomb and aeronautics.
    (B) Only after the atomic bomb had been created and developments in air travel had taken off, did science fiction really become popular.
    (C) The birth of science fiction, the creation of the atomic bomb, and the growth of space exploration occurred at about the same time.
    (D) Science fiction literature was much more popular and widespread prior to the so-called atomic age.

60. Since scurvy is caused by a lack of dietary vitamin C which is abundant in raw fruit and vegetables, it is doubtful that primitive man, living close to nature, was subject to this deficiency.
    (A) Primitive man lacked the necessary dietary information to prevent the vitamin deficiency which leads to scurvy.
    (B) The first known cases of scurvy can be traced to primitive man who had very little to eat other than raw fruit and vegetables.
    (C) The natural conditions in which primitive humans lived subjected them to all sorts of diseases including scurvy.
    (D) The natural environment of primitive human beings probably provided them with enough vitamin C to prevent scurvy.

Answer Key
Practice Test I

Section 1: Listening Comprehension

Part A

1. D
2. A
3. C
4. A
5. B
6. D
7. B
8. A
9. C
10. B
11. D
12. D
13. A
14. B
15. C
16. D
17. C
18. B
19. C
20. A

Part B

21. C
22. A
23. D
24. C
25. A
26. B
27. D
28. B
29. B
30. C
31. A
32. A
33. B
34. D
35. C

Part C

36. B
37. A
38. D
39. C
40. B
41. C
42. D
43. B
44. A
45. D
46. C
47. A
48. A
49. B
50. C

Section 2: Structure and Written Expression

Part A

The explanations of why given answers are wrong have been kept as brief as possible. Indications of how particular incorrect answers might be made correct are provided as a stimulus to thinking about English sentence structure. The references marked FE are to the Focused Exercises which may be of help in further explaining why particular answers are correct or incorrect and in offering more practice.

1. A Correct
   B Creates dependent clause leaving incomplete main clause
   C Creates subject without predicate
   D See 1-C

2. A Noun not clause must follow preposition "in spite of"
   B Creates two unacceptably linked main clauses
   C Correct (FE-10)
   D See 2-B

3. A Unacceptable conjunction
   B Correct (FE-15)
   C Preposition must be followed by noun not clause
   D Does not create a comparison

4. A "with" wrong preposition
   B "William Shakespeare" is subject; this gives two subjects (FE-1)
   C See 2-B
   D Correct (FE-1)

5. A Correct
   B Incorrect complementation to previous phrase
   C See 2-B
   D Repeats subject "Cathedral of Seville" (FE-3)

6. A Creates two unacceptably linked main clauses
   B "it is" redundant
   C Meaningless
   D Correct (FE-12)

7. A Creates participial phrase without main clause
   B Correct (FE-4)
   C Needs anticipatory "it" and verb
   D Needs anticipatory "it" (FE-4)

8. A Wrong coordinate conjunction with "either"
   B See 8-A
   C Correct
   D See 8-A

9. A Needs to be followed by a clause (FE-10)
   B Correct
   C This type of absolute construction in English is impossible
   D See 9-A

10. A Creates dependent participial phrase with no main clause
    B Adjectival phrase, no main clause
    C See 10-B
    D Correct (FE-6)

11. A Wrong tense sequence (FE-29)
    B Impossible form
    C Correct (FE-29)
    D See 11-A

12. A Creates two unacceptably linked main clauses
    B Correct
    C See 12-A, plus misplaced prepositional phrase (FE-13)
    D "that which" combination unacceptable; correct without "that"

13. A Correct (FE-10)
    B "it" repeats subject of clause (FE-3)
    C Anticipatory "it" unacceptable, cre-
       ates subject repetition
    D No main verb in dependent clause
       (FE-10)

14. A Correct (FE-18)
    B, C, and D   Incorrect word order af-
    ter "nor"

15. A Verb repeated
    B Creates nonsense sentence
    C No subject for main clause
    D Correct (noun clause as subject,
       FE-2)

Part B

In every case the answer is given first. Where there is an FE reference, this indicates the number of the Focused Exercise which may offer useful further practice of the point in question. Where words in quotation marks follow the letter of the correct answer, these show what would be needed for the sentence to be correct. This usually occurs in cases where none of the Focused Exercises is applicable.

16. B ("somewhat like") (FE-25)
17. C (FE-39)
18. D ("and")
19. A (FE-34)
20. C (FE-28)
21. D (FE-37)
22. A (FE-30)
23. B (either "said" or "told" +
       indirect object)
24. B (FE-30)
25. A (FE-23)
26. D (FE-18)
27. C (FE-29)
28. C (FE-20)
29. D (FE-14,33)
30. A (FE-3,18)
31. B (FE-8,31)
32. A ("consist") (FE-6)
33. D ("any other")
34. D (FE-24)
35. B (FE-27)
36. C (FE-32)
37. B (FE-40)
38. A (FE-20)
39. C (FE-27)
40. D (FE-26)

Section 3: Reading Comprehension and Vocabulary

Part A

1. A
2. D
3. C
4. C
5. B
6. A
7. C
8. B
9. D
10. A
11. B
12. D
13. C
14. D
15. B
16. A
17. C
18. D
19. C
20. A
21. A

22. B	25. A	28. D
23. D	26. C	29. B
24. C	27. B	30. A

Part B

31. C	41. D	51. B
32. A	42. A	52. C
33. B	43. C	53. A
34. D	44. B	54. C
35. A	45. C	55. A
36. D	46. D	56. B
37. A	47. B	57. C
38. D	48. D	58. A
39. C	49. A	59. B
40. B	50. C	60. D

Strategies: A Reminder**

Section 1: Listening Comprehension

STRATEGY for Part A: look at all the answer choices before you hear the sentence.
STRATEGY for Part B: aim for a more general understanding than in Part A but more specific than Part C.
STRATEGY for Part C: aim for a general understanding of what you hear.

Section 2: Structure and Written Expression

GENERAL STRATEGY: work at a steady pace and read each possible answer very carefully.
STRATEGY for Part A: read carefully and choose the one correct sentence completion.
STRATEGY for Part B: choose the one incorrect part.

Section 3: Reading Comprehension and Vocabulary

GENERAL STRATEGY: do Part A quickly to allow yourself more time for Part B.
STRATEGY for Part A: work quickly; if you do not know the meaning, guess and continue on to the next item.
STRATEGY for Part B: think about the items and recheck them against the information given.

**See the Preview to the Practice Tests (pp. 42-45) for more specific strategies.

PRACTICE TEST II ————

Section 1: Listening Comprehension

Time: 40 minutes

You will need to play the tape for all the questions in Section 1. (The tapescripts are printed on pages 238-242. This material is designated by the symbol  .)

In this section of the test, you will have an opportunity to demonstrate your ability to understand spoken English. There are three parts to this section, with special directions for each part.

Part A

<u>Directions:</u> For each question in Part A, you will hear a short statement. The statements will be spoken just one time. They will not be written out for you, and you must listen carefully to understand what the speaker says.

After you hear a statement, read the four sentences in your test book, marked (A), (B), (C), and (D), and decide which <u>one</u> is closest in meaning to the statement you heard. Then, on your answer sheet, find the number of the question and blacken the space that corresponds to the letter of the answer you have chosen so that the letter inside the oval cannot be seen.

Example I

<u>Sample Answer</u>
(A) (B) (C) ●

You will hear:

You will read: (A) My cousin will make you a lamp.

(B) My relative has gotten rid of her old wood.

(C) Mike's making a wooden lamb.

(D) I have a cousin who makes lamps.

Sentence (D), "I have a cousin who makes lamps," means most nearly the same as the statement "My cousin makes lamps out of driftwood." Therefore, you should choose answer (D).

Example II

<u>Sample Answer</u>
(A) ● (C) (D)

You will hear:

You will read: (A) Turn in your paper this week.

(B) There are eight more days for handing in term papers.

(C) Two essays are required weekly.

(D) Return my newspaper next week.

Sentence (B), "There are eight more days for handing in term papers," is closest in meaning to the sentence "Term papers are due a week from tomorrow." Therefore, you should choose answer (B).

GO ON TO THE NEXT PAGE ➡

1. (A) He should have re-signed the contract.
   (B) I called the repairman an hour ago about this chair.
   (C) These antique chairs are signed by the craftsman.
   (D) I think he should've stepped down by now.

2. (A) Can I lend you my notes?
   (B) Did you make any notes on the reading?
   (C) I'd like to have a look at your notes.
   (D) I need to borrow against these notes.

3. (A) We should let them know we're glad they've returned.
   (B) Let's call and ask them to our party.
   (C) Why haven't they come home?
   (D) Let's find out about leasing a home phone.

4. (A) You never give me enough
   (B) No more for me, thanks.
   (C) I've had enough from you.
   (D) They can't take anymore.

5. (A) I expect you to pay the speaker.
   (B) Don't let your mind wander when I'm speaking.
   (C) I'll pay back that ten soon.
   (D) Stand at attention during the lecture.

6. (A) Kay opened a boarding house for retired people.
   (B) When tired, Kay suffers from tension.
   (C) Kay found it difficult to pay attention.
   (D) Kay didn't get a pension.

7. (A) We continued diving after you left.
   (B) It's not my custom to dry what's left.
   (C) I usually drive on the right.
   (D) I'm used to agreeing with the right side.

8. (A) Can you empty the garbage cans for us?
   (B) Can someone clean out the garage tomorrow?
   (C) We can't get rid of the garbage.
   (D) Surely we can clean out the garage before tomorrow.

9. (A) Would you hand me the phone?
   (B) Someone called before you got up.
   (C) Answer the phone before it stops ringing.
   (D) Phone me while you're up there.

10. (A) Chris doesn't type as well as Carolyn.
    (B) Carolyn is a better type of person than Chris.
    (C) Carolyn is more of a betting type than Chris.
    (D) Chris hasn't worked as a typist as long as Carolyn.

11. (A) Did you enjoy that movie?
    (B) You should have liked that movie.
    (C) I can't believe you liked that movie.
    (D) Wasn't that movie like real life?

12. (A) No one else knew about the course.
    (B) I didn't know about the course in time.
    (C) I was the only person registered for the course.
    (D) That's the only course I'm taking right now.

13. (A) Most graduate students are very reserved.
    (B) Library science is a graduate course.
    (C) This area is for graduate students only.
    (D) Books for graduate courses are in the reserve section.

14. (A) He didn't compete in the race.
    (B) He joined the race late.
    (C) He finished in last place.
    (D) He made a drawing of the last race.

15. (A) There are no good seats right now.
    (B) Someone will show you to a seat shortly.
    (C) The stewardess is sitting down, waiting for take-off.
    (D) The receptionist is waiting for you to sit down.

16. (A) The climate there is very wet.
    (B) The northern population is hearty.
    (C) More people are moving north.
    (D) Due to the weather, few people live there.

17. (A) This is Phil's last semester.
    (B) Phil graduated last term.
    (C) Phil is teaching the course.
    (D) Phil is repeating the course.

18. (A) Sam sold me his computer.
    (B) Sam is renting my apartment.
    (C) Sam is using my computer.
    (D) Sam stopped working at the mine.

19. (A) Whatever happens, Peter plans to remain in Alaska.
    (B) Peter is staying in Alaska in spite of the cold.
    (C) Peter tends to stay where the weather is good.
    (D) Because he has found gold, Peter will remain in Alaska.

20. (A) You show more skill than imagination.
    (B) I'm surprised at your skill.
    (C) I imagined you would be more skillful.
    (D) You need to show more skill and imagination.

Part B

Directions: In Part B you will hear short conversations between two speakers. At the end of each conversation, a third voice will ask a question about what was said. The question will be spoken just one time. After you hear a conversation and the question about it, read the four possible answers in your test book and decide which <u>one</u> is the best answer to the question you heard. Then, on your answer sheet, find the number of the question and blacken the space that corresponds to the letter of the answer you have chosen.

Example

<u>Sample Answer</u>
(A) ● (C) (D)

You will hear:

You will read: (A) Go to a restaurant.
           (B) Fix dinner in the back yard.
           (C) Build a bonfire.
           (D) Go out to see a show.

From the conversation you know that the people are discussing fixing dinner at home. The best answer, then, is (B), "Fix dinner in the back yard." Therefore, you should chose answer (B).

21. (A) At a university registrar's office.
    (B) At a weigh station.
    (C) At a student employment center.
    (D) On a loading platform.

22. (A) The woman can read the writing, but the man can't.
    (B) The signature has been erased.
    (C) The woman has seen this signet ring before.
    (D) Neither of the people can understand the signature.

23. (A) Many ancient pots have been found there.
    (B) It's famous for its lottery system.
    (C) It contains the essential ingredient for pottery making.
    (D) The first claim to the valley was the right one.

24. (A) He's a taxi driver.
    (B) He's a real estate salesman.
    (C) He's a meter reader.
    (D) He works at a fair.

25. (A) He's more efficient than he is punctual.
    (B) She thinks he should make up the time he has missed.
    (C) She would prefer him to be more efficient.
    (D) His punctuality makes up for his mistakes.

26. (A) She'd prefer to go to the park in the morning.
    (B) She's had enough exercise for today.
    (C) She can't leave until Jim gets back.
    (D) She doesn't want to change apartments.

27. (A) He doesn't know what the gift means.
    (B) He can't remember who gave him the gift.
    (C) He wants to know how much the gift cost.
    (D) He wants to express his thanks for the gift.

28. (A) He painted it by himself.
    (B) It needs to be printed.
    (C) It isn't beautifully painted.
    (D) He hired his brother to paint it.

29. (A) The party lasted all night.
    (B) She didn't go to Susan's.
    (C) She didn't like the party.
    (D) The party was someplace else.

30. (A) There's a westbound train every six minutes.
    (B) He doesn't know about the westbound trains.
    (C) She's on the wrong platform.
    (D) He can't keep track of the express trains.

31. (A) Charges on checking accounts.
    (B) A hotel regulation.
    (C) Banking hours.
    (D) Library fines.

32. (A) The apartment will probably be too expensive.
    (B) He hopes it can be arranged.
    (C) They don't need a new range.
    (D) The neighborhood is too far away.

33. (A) To the post office.
    (B) To a meeting.
    (C) To the club.
    (D) To Chris' house.

34. (A) He's very forgetful.
    (B) He likes to play tricks.
    (C) His tests are difficult.
    (D) It's very easy to pass his courses.

35. (A) Food they are eating.
    (B) Two species of fish.
    (C) A fire on the mountain.
    (D) A set of dishes.

1 1 1 1 1 1 1 1 1

Part C

Directions: In this part of the test, you will hear several short talks and conversations. After each talk or conversation, you will be asked some questions. The talks and questions will be spoken just one time. They will not be written out for you, so you will have to listen carefully to understand what the speaker says.

After you hear a question, read the four possible answers in your test book and decide which _one_ is the best answer to the question you heard. Then, on your answer sheet, find the number of the question and blacken the space that corresponds to the letter of the answer you have chosen.

Sample Answer
(A) (B) ● (D)

Listen to this sample talk.
You will hear:
Now look at the following example.
You will hear:
You will read: (A) Americans should import goldenrod.
(B) The goldenrod is an easily eliminated garden weed.
(C) The goldenrod has been underrated as a garden plant.
(D) Most people are either unable to find or to afford goldenrod.

The best answer to the question "Which of the following best expresses the speaker's opinion?" is (C), "The goldenrod has been underrated as a garden plant." Therefore, you should choose answer (C).

Sample Answer
● (B) (C) (D)

Now look at the next example.
You will hear:
You will read: (A) in an open field.
(B) in a plant shop.
(C) in a fancy garden.
(D) in a desert.

The best answer to the question "Where would you be most likely to find goldenrod?" is (A), "in an open field." Therefore, you should choose answer (A).

36. (A) She wasn't interested in the topic.
    (B) She had a date this afternoon.
    (C) She went to the race track instead.
    (D) She was not feeling well.

37. (A) American history.
    (B) Theology.
    (C) American geography.
    (D) Criminal law.

38. (A) As soon as she finishes her term paper.
    (B) After she has visited Salem, Massachusetts.
    (C) At the beginning of the next week.
    (D) Sometime this weekend.

39. (A) They feel guilty about the nineteen hangings.
    (B) They are surprised at the number of people convicted of being witches.
    (C) They are especially interested in present-day trials.
    (D) They are surprised to learn that these trials were conducted.

40. (A) write her term paper about witchcraft.
    (B) talk to Professor Jones about her ideas for a term paper.
    (C) rest and catch up with her school work.
    (D) do research on Salem, Massachusetts.

41. (A) in a cooking class.
    (B) in a retail fish market.
    (C) in an expensive restaurant.
    (D) on an airplane.

42. (A) in New York.
    (B) in most parts of America.
    (C) in Nova Scotia.
    (D) in unfamiliar locations.

43. (A) to sell bluefin tuna.
    (B) to explain how to judge bluefin tuna.
    (C) to interest investors in a fish restaurant.
    (D) to analyze the market for fish in New York City.

44. (A) He thinks it should be frozen before it is eaten.
    (B) He thinks it is delicious when eaten raw.
    (C) He thinks it should only be eaten in restaurants.
    (D) He thinks most Americans will not like it.

45. (A) blue.
    (B) the brightest red.
    (C) the color is unimportant.
    (D) it depends on individual taste.

46. (A) The audience will go to a retail fish market.
    (B) The speaker will show photographs of the bluefin tuna.
    (C) Everyone will taste raw fish from a restaurant.
    (D) The speaker will demonstrate how to fix bluefin tuna.

47. (A) It is surprising that coin collecting is so old.
    (B) It is unbelievable that stamp collecting did not start before it did.
    (C) There are obvious reasons why stamp collecting is newer than coin collecting.
    (D) Stamp collecting is older than coin collecting.

48. (A) since 1836.
    (B) since the middle of the 1850's.
    (C) for about 2,000 years.
    (D) possibly for 3,000 years.

49. (A) the invention of a new kind of stamp.
    (B) the introduction of a postal service.
    (C) a group of enthusiasts in the 1850's.
    (D) the familiarity of the stamps.

50. (A) It was a long time in coming.
    (B) It attracted followers quite quickly.
    (C) It started in Scotland.
    (D) It only showed potential.

STOP STOP STOP STOP STOP STOP STOP

Section 2: Structure and Written Expression

Time: 25 minutes

This section is designed to measure your ability to recognize language that is appropriate for standard written English. There are two types of questions in this section, with special directions for each type.

Part A

Directions: Questions 1-15 are incomplete sentences. Four words or phrases, marked (A), (B), (C), and (D), are given beneath each sentence. You are to choose the <u>one</u> word or phrase that best completes the sentence. Then, on your answer sheet, find the number of the question and blacken the space that corresponds to the letter of the answer you have chosen so that the letter inside the oval cannot be seen.

Example I

Sample Answer
Ⓐ ● Ⓒ Ⓓ

________ thirty-five African nations where the elephant still exists.

(A) Are
(B) There are
(C) They are
(D) Those

In English, the sentence should read, "There are thirty-five African nations where the elephant still exists." Therefore, you should choose (B).

Example II

Sample Answer
Ⓐ Ⓑ ● Ⓓ

Anthony Burgess is not only a successful novelist, ________ an expert linguist.

(A) and therefore
(B) however
(C) but also
(D) and also

In English, the sentence should read, "Anthony Burgess is not only a successful novelist, but also an expert linguist." Therefore, you should choose (C).

1. David Bushnell, of Yale, _______ a sub-marine in 1775.
   (A) has built
   (B) built
   (C) he built
   (D) was built

2. The bombardier beetle gets its name because _______ its prey with caustic liquid.
   (A) shooting
   (B) of it shoots
   (C) it shoots
   (D) to shoot

3. Today's typewriter keyboard is _______ Shole's 1867 keyboard.
   (A) as same as
   (B) the same as
   (C) the same than
   (D) a same one as

4. Electron storage rings _______ in investigations of the structure of materials.
   (A) they are used
   (B) that are used
   (C) used
   (D) are used

5. The All Pueblo Council is said _______ from 1598.
   (A) to date
   (B) it dates
   (C) dating
   (D) dated

6. The volume of Hawaii's Mauna Loa is fifty times _______ Mount Everest.
   (A) of
   (B) more of
   (C) that of
   (D) than of

7. _______ professional baseball is played, the more certain it becomes that Walter Johnson's shut-out record will never be beaten.
   (A) The longer than
   (B) How long
   (C) However long
   (D) The longer

8. _______ the bones of prehistoric man, scientists hope to determine what their owners ate.
   (A) By studying
   (B) In study of
   (C) To study
   (D) Studying

9. _______ the Christmas shopping season begins.
   (A) That is after Thanksgiving
   (B) After Thanksgiving it is
   (C) It is after Thanksgiving that
   (D) It is Thanksgiving that

10. Progressive farmers use several methods to prevent top soil _______ .
    (A) from running off
    (B) to run off
    (C) from to run off
    (D) to running off

11. *The Baltimore American* first tried to nominate Theodore Roosevelt for the Presidency _______ .
    (A) when he had only twenty-eight years
    (B) when he was only twenty-eight
    (C) when he was age twenty-eight years
    (D) at age twenty-eight years

12. ________, the Mauritius parakeet, and the Japanese crested ibis are among the most endangered of the world's birds.
    (A) Including the Marianas mallard
    (B) Being the Marianas mallard
    (C) There are the Marianas mallard
    (D) The Marianas mallard

13. Not until the mid-nineteenth century ________ achieve recognition.
    (A) had El Greco's work
    (B) did El Greco's work
    (C) El Greco's work
    (D) El Greco's work did

14. Abolitionist writer and former slave, Frederick Douglass, was impressed with Lincoln ________ he found him entirely free of prejudice.
    (A) because
    (B) who
    (C) therefore
    (D) because of

15. In elections held in 1982, an unusual number of well-known political figures campaigned on behalf of children ________ who were running for office.
    (A) theirs
    (B) of them
    (C) of theirs
    (D) their

Part B

Directions: In questions 16-40 each sentence has four words or phrases underlined. The four underlined parts of the sentence are marked (A), (B), (C), and (D). You are to identify the *one* underlined word or phrase that should be corrected or rewritten. Then, on your answer sheet, find the number of the question and blacken the space that corresponds to the letter of the answer you have chosen.

Example I

Sample Answer
● Ⓑ Ⓒ Ⓓ

A heat used to make popcorn changes the
  A   B
moisture in the kernels of corn into steam.
                          C   D

Answer (A), the underlined words *A heat*, would not be accepted in carefully written English; the words *The heat* should be used because the sentence describes a specific kind of heat. Therefore, the sentence should read, "The heat used to make popcorn changes the moisture in the kernels of corn into steam." To answer the question correctly, you should choose (A).

Example II

Sample Answer
Ⓐ Ⓑ Ⓒ ●

Because he was found to have taken part in
                           A   B
professional team sports when younger,
                           C
Jim Thorpe was allowed to keep neither his

Olympic medals or his titles.
          D

Answer (D), the underlined word *or*, would not be accepted in carefully written English; the word *nor* should be used after *neither*. Therefore, the sentence should read, "Because he was found to have taken part in professional team sports when younger, Jim Thorpe was allowed to keep neither his Olympic medals nor his titles." To answer the question correctly, you would choose (D).

16. In the <u>early</u> nineteenth century, <u>it</u> was both economic <u>or</u> mechanical developments
      A   B   C
   that <u>accounted for</u> the quick spread of railroads.
        D

17. A natural laser <u>formed</u> by part <u>of</u> the <u>outer</u> Martian atmosphere.
              A   B C   D

18. Alaska is twice <u>as</u> <u>larger</u> as the <u>next</u> <u>largest</u> state, Texas.
               A   B   C   D

19. An adhesive, by <u>making</u> contact with molecules of two surfaces, <u>holds</u> <u>they</u> together.
      A   B   C   D

20. As the nation's first president, George Washington still <u>enjoys</u> a <u>very</u> <u>unparalleled</u> place
    A   B   C
   in American history.
        D

21. So <u>many</u> people suffer from problems with <u>the back</u> that this has become <u>the leading</u>
       A   B   C
   cause of <u>lost</u> work days in the United States.
           D

22. Scott reached <u>the</u> South Pole <u>by the time</u> Amundsen did, but found that his rival
               A   B
   had <u>beaten him</u> by a matter of <u>a</u> few days.
          C   D

23. Marathon runners are <u>prone to</u> stress fractures and a <u>large</u> <u>number</u> of <u>feet</u> ailments.
                        A   B   C   D

24. Before <u>to enter</u> <u>first</u> grade, <u>most</u> American children <u>attend</u> kindergarten.
           A   B   C   D

25. Two <u>from</u> North America's <u>most important</u> shipping <u>routes</u> are linked <u>by</u> the Illinois
        A   B   C   D
   waterway.

26. It was <u>hardly</u> surprising that Barker felt <u>wonderfully</u> after <u>pitching</u> only the thirteenth
            A   B   C
   perfect game <u>in</u> major league history.
               D

27. The <u>kilogram</u> is the <u>only</u> base <u>unitary</u> still defined by <u>a</u> physical object.
         A   B   C   D

28. The youth movement in <u>women's</u> professional tennis has gone <u>so far</u> <u>that</u> a
                         A   B   C
   <u>twelve-years-old</u> girl recently participated in a professional tournament.
         D

29. R.L. Stevenson's grass hut <u>was built</u> in Samoa but is now in Hawaii and tourists can
        A   B
   visit <u>throughout</u> the <u>year</u>.
     C   D

30. Despite <u>their</u> length, <u>the</u> giraffe's neck has the same number of vertebrae <u>as</u>
          A   B   C
   a <u>human being's</u>.
         D

GO ON TO THE NEXT PAGE ➤

31. The winner of the first auto race <u>held</u> in the United States, in 1895, <u>drived</u> his car <u>at a</u>
      _A   _B   _C
    speed of 7.5 <u>miles per hour.</u>
                 _D

32. <u>By the end</u> of the examination, Bill, <u>the most intelligent</u> student <u>in</u> the class, had been
    _A   _B   _C
    finished <u>since</u> more than an hour.
              _D

33. <u>Among the things</u> which may <u>improve</u> the cardiovascular system are exercising, diet-
    _A   _B
    ing, <u>giving up</u> smoking, and <u>you should avoid</u> stress.
          _C   _D

34. A bone marrow test, <u>what involves</u> extracting fluid from the marrow, <u>may be</u> necessary
                         _A   _B   _C
    <u>for diagnosing</u> leukemia.
    _D

35. As <u>their</u> standard of living <u>has improved,</u> most American families have become accus-
       _A   _B
    tomed <u>to enjoy</u> creature comforts previous generations only <u>dreamed of.</u>
           _C   _D

36. The progress <u>done</u> in the <u>field</u> of urban planning <u>over</u> recent years has resulted in a
                 _A   _B   _C
    different view <u>being taken</u> of downtown areas.
                   _D

37. *The Canterbury Gospels,* <u>given to</u> St. Augustine by Pope Gregory I <u>in</u> 597, is among the
                              _A   _B
    most valuable <u>book</u> in the <u>world.</u>
    _C   _D

38. Six of <u>the first ten</u> U.S. presidents <u>they</u> were <u>born</u> in the State <u>of</u> Virginia.
           _A   _B   _C   _D

39. The attractions <u>between</u> opposite <u>poles</u> on <u>differents atoms</u> <u>are</u> called Van der Waals
                    _A   _B   _C   _D
    forces.

40. The Mausoleum of Halicarnassus <u>has been erected</u> in 353 B.C. <u>to commemorate</u> King
                                    _A   _B
    Mausolos of Caria and <u>is the source</u> of the modern word "mausoleum."
                           _C   _D

Section 3: Reading Comprehension and Vocabulary

Time: 45 minutes

This section is designed to measure your ability to understand various kinds of reading materials, as well as your ability to understand the meaning and use of words. There are two types of questions in this section, with special directions for each type.

Part A

Directions: In questions 1-30 each sentence has a word or phrase underlined. Below each sentence are four other words or phrases marked (A), (B), (C), and (D). You are to choose the *one* word or phrase that *best keeps the meaning* of the original sentence if it is substituted for the underlined word or phrase. Then, on your answer sheet, find the number of the question and blacken the space that corresponds to the letter you have chosen so that the letter inside the oval cannot be seen.

Example I

Sample Answer
● Ⓑ Ⓒ Ⓓ

When the museum <u>unveiled</u> its plans, it expected a violent reaction.

(A) revealed
(B) made
(C) changed
(D) implemented

The best answer is (A) because "When the museum revealed its plans, it expected a violent reaction" is closest in meaning to the original sentence, "When the museum unveiled its plans, it expected a violent reaction." Therefore, you should choose answer (A).

Example II

Sample Answer
Ⓐ ● Ⓒ Ⓓ

The same questions repeated over and over soon made them <u>weary</u>.

(A) suspicious
(B) tired
(C) disturbed
(D) cautious

The best answer is (B) because "The same questions repeated over and over soon made them tired" is closest in meaning to the original sentence, "The same questions repeated over and over soon made them weary." Therefore, you should choose answer (B).

As soon as you understand the directions, begin work on the questions.

1. Modern techniques have made <u>dentures</u> virtually unnoticeable.
   (A) false teeth
   (B) surgical implants
   (C) artificial hair
   (D) plastic surgery

2. Early log cabins were <u>crude</u> if sturdy structures.
   (A) unpainted
   (B) resilient
   (C) unseasoned
   (D) rough

3. The first American Thanksgiving was <u>held</u> in Plymouth, Massachusetts in 1621.
   (A) retained
   (B) declared
   (C) celebrated
   (D) arranged

4. Though many scientific breakthroughs have resulted from <u>mishaps</u>, it has taken brilliant thinkers to recognize their potential.
   (A) misunderstandings
   (B) accidents
   (C) misfortunes
   (D) incidentals

5. Considerable energy savings are made in parts of California by <u>harvesting</u> melons at night.
   (A) picking
   (B) planting
   (C) watering
   (D) packing

6. The library has announced that <u>henceforth</u>, fines on overdue books will be 25 cents per day.
   (A) for the time being
   (B) across the board
   (C) from now on
   (D) as a result

7. When the tombs of two Zhongshan rulers were excavated, two of the <u>vessels</u> found, which were more than 2,200 years old, still had wine in them.
   (A) chambers
   (B) containers
   (C) remains
   (D) coffins

8. The kiwi is <u>a peculiar</u> flightless creature with furry feathers and a long, curved beak.
   (A) a particular
   (B) a solemn
   (C) an awkward
   (D) an odd

9. American children <u>customarily</u> go trick-or-treating on Halloween.
   (A) gaily
   (B) traditionally
   (C) readily
   (D) inevitably

10. Our knowledge of at least two-thirds of the world's languages remains <u>scanty</u>.
    (A) theoretical
    (B) meager
    (C) indeterminate
    (D) implicit

11. Though it can <u>sense</u> the slightest touch anywhere on the body, the brain itself is insensitive to pain.
    (A) intellectualize
    (B) reveal
    (C) sensualize
    (D) feel

12. Congress has <u>earmarked</u> funds for research into alternative sources of energy.
    (A) set aside
    (B) increased
    (C) turned down
    (D) discussed

13. Some hotels in the United States have imposed a <u>ban</u> on cigarette smoking.
    (A) restriction
    (B) guarantee
    (C) fine
    (D) prohibition

14. The production of hot glass necessitates a <u>fusion</u> of art and technology.
    (A) an explosion
    (B) a nucleus
    (C) a blending
    (D) a combatting

15. In her book of 1857, *A Selection of Synonyms*, Elizabeth Jane Whately evidences a closer affinity to the modern approach to synonyms than had <u>hitherto</u> been the case.
    (A) usually
    (B) traditionally
    (C) characteristically
    (D) formerly

16. It is no <u>simple</u> matter for chimpanzees accustomed to living with human beings to return to the wild.
    (A) foolish
    (B) easy
    (C) common
    (D) unique

17. Prospects for an upturn in the economy remain <u>bleak</u>.
    (A) dismal
    (B) indifferent
    (C) encouraging
    (D) unknown

18. The Supreme Court only takes on cases it believes <u>warrant</u> its attention.
    (A) demand
    (B) respect
    (C) merit
    (D) guarantee

19. The sabertooth tiger had very long, <u>slender</u> upper canines.
    (A) sharp
    (B) curved
    (C) thin
    (D) ferocious

20. The 1908 Siberian meteorite explosion <u>brought about</u> considerable depletion of the northern hemisphere's ozone layer.
    (A) was caused by
    (B) resulted in
    (C) brought back
    (D) was initiated by

21. Killing frosts occur when moisture <u>within</u> plant cells freezes.
    (A) inside
    (B) involved with
    (C) surrounding
    (D) combined with

22. Aristotle believed that a thrown ball traveled in a straight line until the force impelling it was <u>exhausted</u>.
    (A) used up
    (B) debilitated
    (C) diverted
    (D) tired out

23. Studies of climatology <u>indicate</u> that volcanic dust in the atmosphere may contribute to the onset of ice ages.
    (A) explain
    (B) insinuate
    (C) suggest
    (D) prove

24. Taillevent's fame as a <u>chef</u> has endured since the 14th century.
    (A) cook
    (B) soldier
    (C) diplomat
    (D) leader

25. From the first, President Reagan's avowed intention was to change the <u>course</u> of the American economy.
    (A) nature
    (B) productivity
    (C) uncertainty
    (D) direction

26. The word "antonym" was <u>coined</u> in 1857.
    (A) invented
    (B) current
    (C) codified
    (D) valued

27. Alexander Hamilton remained <u>adamantly</u> opposed to the policies of John Adams throughout the latter's presidency.
    (A) admirably
    (B) strongly
    (C) inflexibly
    (D) manfully

28. The use of Navajo code-talkers resolved a situation of the utmost <u>gravity</u> in World War II.
    (A) delicacy
    (B) seriousness
    (C) levity
    (D) deadliness

29. Rote learning is now considered to be of <u>dubious</u> worth.
    (A) dual
    (B) questionable
    (C) spurious
    (D) salient

30. Even more powerful computers are needed to process all the <u>pertinent</u> information required for accurate weather-forecasting.
    (A) sophisticated
    (B) complex
    (C) different
    (D) relevant

Part B

<u>Directions:</u> The rest of this section is based on a variety of reading material (single sentences, paragraphs, and the like) followed by questions about the meaning of the material. For questions 31-60, you are to choose the *one* best answer, (A), (B), (C), or (D), to each question. Then, on your answer sheet, find the number of the question and blacken the space that corresponds to the letter of the answer you have chosen.

Answer all questions following a passage on the basis of what is <u>stated</u> or <u>implied</u> in that passage.

Read the following passage.

The eradication of malaria has proved to be a much more intractable problem than ridding the world of what used to be regarded as a much more terrible scourge: smallpox. Even after decades of campaigns against the former disease, some 200 million people are infected annually, whereas fortunately the latter has now virtually disappeared. One of the more interesting approaches now being investigated to combat malaria is development of what would be the first altruistic vaccine—that is, one not aimed at protecting those who are immunized, nor at curing the disease, but one which would prevent carriers of the disease from transmitting it to others.

Example I   Sample Answer
● Ⓑ Ⓒ Ⓓ

Which of the following can be inferred from the passage about malaria and smallpox?

(A) Smallpox is more dreaded but now easier to prevent than malaria.

(B) Malaria is now almost unknown in most parts of the world.

(C) Malaria was previously the most feared type of epidemic.

(D) There are at least twice as many victims of smallpox as of malaria each year.

The passage says that "The eradication of malaria has proved to be a much more intractable problem than ridding the world of what used to be regarded as a much more terrible scourge: smallpox." Therefore, you should choose (A) as the best answer.

Example II   Sample Answer
Ⓐ Ⓑ Ⓒ ●

According to the passage, an altruistic vaccine is one which

(A) halts the development of malaria and related diseases.

(B) protects people who have been immunized against a specific ailment.

(C) provides the remedy for several major diseases.

(D) stops the transmission of the disease from person to person.

The passage says that an altruistic vaccine is "one which would prevent carriers of the disease from transmitting it to others." Therefore, you should choose answer (D) as the best completion of the sentence.

Questions 31-35

The fact that some naturally left-handed children are forced into becoming right-handed may even result in levophobia, an irrational fear of the left. Sufferers from this rare condition find their hearts pound as if a heart atack were coming on as a result of their brains releasing adrenalin at the mere prospect of a left-oriented maneuver. They refuse to stand on the left side of an elevator, make left-hand turns when driving, sometimes even to look to the left. Psychologists believe levophobia will only disappear entirely when left-handed children—a minority in all known societies—are fully accepted.

31. What was the preceding paragraph probably about?
    (A) other problems caused by attitudes towards left-handed children
    (B) the advantages of being right-handed as a child
    (C) other causes of levophobia
    (D) a definition of levophobia

32. It may be inferred from the passage that
    (A) levophobia affects a minority in all known societies.
    (B) levophobia attacks may occur before a left-handed movement is required.
    (C) excess adrenalin is a contributory cause in levophobia.
    (D) levophobia causes heart attacks.

33. The passage suggests that levophobia sufferers
    (A) are afraid of right-handed people.
    (B) generally refuse to use elevators unless forced to.
    (C) never look to their left-hand side.
    (D) often have to seek roundabout routes when driving.

34. It is believed that levophobia will not be eradicated until
    (A) certain general attitudes change.
    (B) left-handers are in a majority.
    (C) sufferers' irrational fears are dealt with by psychologists.
    (D) sufferers change their uncooperative ways.

35. According to the passage, levophobia
    (A) affects only children.
    (B) is likely to disappear soon.
    (C) is a psychological problem.
    (D) is a heart ailment.

Questions 36-41

Several hundred grave sites have been found throughout Iceland dating from the time of the first settlements, some 1,100 years ago, to the time the Icelandic people embraced Christianity around the year 1000 A.D. The evidence they offer of that pagan era suggests some Viking influence as bodies were occasionally laid in boats, but the dead were more commonly provided with one or, exceptionally, two small Icelandic horses. This custom, of course, equally connotes a journey to the land of the dead, and it also provides evidence both that these horses have been the Icelanders' companions from the very first and that the breed has remained pure over the centuries right down to the present day.

36. Approximately how long did the "pagan era" in Iceland last?
   (A) one hundred years
   (B) several hundred years
   (C) one thousand years
   (D) one thousand one hundred years

37. Which of the following can be said of the grave sites found in Iceland?
   (A) They are all located in the very first settlements.
   (B) They were discovered about 1,100 years ago.
   (C) They are located in many different parts of the country.
   (D) They were usually built by travelers.

38. What can be inferred from the passage about the first settlers?
   (A) They were unquestionably Vikings.
   (B) They arrived on horseback.
   (C) They embraced Christianity.
   (D) They were not Christians.

39. Which of the following *cannot* be said of the contents of the pagan graves?
   (A) The bodies were rarely laid in boats.
   (B) They occasionally evidenced Viking influence.
   (C) The bodies were generally accompanied by two small horses.
   (D) They had not been given a Christian burial.

40. According to the passage, the idea of a journey after death was believed by
   (A) the Vikings only.
   (B) the Vikings and the pagan Icelanders.
   (C) the Christian Icelanders.
   (D) the pagan Icelanders only.

41. Which of the following can be inferred from the passage?
   (A) The small Icelandic breed of horses has remained unchanged for over a thousand years.
   (B) The first Vikings brought Christianity to Iceland.
   (C) Icelandic horses live to a great age.
   (D) Horses were first brought to Iceland by Christian missionaries.

Questions 42-44

Sprinkler-based irrigation systems are claimed to be more efficient than gravity systems since they use less water to irrigate the same amount of land. In addition, it is said that they can be efficiently utilized both on sandy soil, and on hilly or uneven ground, neither of which is true of gravity systems.

42. How many advantages of sprinkler-based systems are suggested?
    - (A) one
    - (B) three
    - (C) four
    - (D) five

43. Which of the following may NOT be inferred from the passage?
    - (A) Gravity systems are said to require more water than sprinkler systems.
    - (B) The author agrees with the claims made.
    - (C) Sprinkler systems may be used on either hilly or uneven terrain.
    - (D) Gravity systems cannot be efficiently used on sandy soil.

44. Which of the following is claimed as an advantage for sprinkler-based irrigation systems?
    - (A) They are more often utilized.
    - (B) They can be used in addition to gravity systems.
    - (C) They are less economical with water.
    - (D) They are more versatile.

GO ON TO THE NEXT PAGE

Questions 45-53

Between 1977 and 1981, three groups of American women, numbering 27 in all, between the ages of 35 and 65, were given month-long tests to determine how they would respond to conditions resembling those aboard the space shuttle.

Though carefully selected from among many applicants, the women were volunteers and pay was barely above the minimum wage. They were not allowed to smoke or drink alcohol during the tests, and they were expected to tolerate each others' company at close quarters for the entire period. Among other things, they had to stand pressure three times the force of gravity and carry out both physical and mental tasks while exhausted from strenuous physical exercise. At the end of ten days, they had to spend a further twenty days absolutely confined to bed, during which time they suffered backaches and other discomforts, and when they were finally allowed up, the more physically active women were especially subject to pains due to a slight calcium loss.

Results of the tests suggest that women will have significant advantages over men in space. They need less food and less oxygen and they stand up to radiation better. Men's advantages in terms of strength and stamina, meanwhile, are virtually wiped out by the zero-gravity condition in space.

45. For how long was each woman tested?
    (A) four days
    (B) twenty days
    (C) twenty-seven months
    (D) one month

46. What was the average number of women in each group tested?
    (A) 9
    (B) 27
    (C) 33
    (D) 50

47. Which of the following can be inferred from the passage?
    (A) The tests were not carried out aboard the space shuttle.
    (B) The women involved had had previous physical fitness training.
    (C) The women were tested once a year from 1977 to 1981.
    (D) The tests were carried out on women of all ages.

48. Which would be the most suitable title for the passage.
    (A) Older Women, Too, Can Travel in Space
    (B) Space Testing Causes Backaches in Women
    (C) Poor Wages for Women Space-test Volunteers
    (D) Tests Show Women Suited for Space Travel

49. What can be said about the women who applied?
    (A) There were 27 in all.
    (B) They were anxious to give up either smoking or drinking.
    (C) They had previously earned the minimum wage.
    (D) They chose to participate in the tests.

50. According to the passage, physical and mental tasks were carried out by the women
    (A) prior to strenous exercise.
    (B) following strenuous exercise.
    (C) before they were subjected to unusual pressure.
    (D) after they were subjected to unusual pressure.

51. The calcium loss particularly affected
    (A) all the women tested.
    (B) those who had been particularly active in the previous ten days.
    (C) those who were generally very active.
    (D) those who had suffered backaches.

52. Which of the following is suggested as being least useful in space?
    (A) high resistance to radiation
    (B) unusual strength
    (C) low food intake
    (D) low oxygen intake

53. The physical advantages men enjoy in normal conditions are counteracted by
    (A) conditioning.
    (B) virtue.
    (C) zero gravity.
    (D) food and oxygen.

GO ON TO THE NEXT PAGE

Questions 54-58

In place of submitting a traditional application for admission, prospective students may choose to apply for admission under the Test Score Application System. Under this system, the University accepts as applications the official score reports from either the American College Test (ACT) or the Scholastic Aptitude Test (SAT). High school juniors and seniors who take the ACT or the SAT should indicate this university as a score recipient of their ACT or SAT registration form. Upon receipt of the ACT Student Profile report or the SAT report, the Admissions Office will notify students of their eligibility for admission. Under this system, it is unnecessary to submit a high school transcript until after graduation unless the student wishes to apply for a scholarship.

54. According to the passage, the Test Score Application System is
    (A) optional
    (B) preferable
    (C) traditional
    (D) required

55. A student using the Test Score Application System
    (A) submits scores from two tests.
    (B) is accepted by the University.
    (C) must be in high school.
    (D) has to take one of two tests.

56. Which of the following applicants would need to include a high school transcript with his test score?
    (A) someone who hoped to graduate from the University
    (B) someone who had received his Student Profile report
    (C) someone who hoped to be awarded a scholarship
    (D) someone who had notified the Admissions Office of his eligibility

57. What is the purpose of this announcement?
    (A) to promote a new application system
    (B) to advertise the SAT and the ACT
    (C) to offer university scholarships
    (D) to describe an admissions procedure

58. When will prospective students be advised of their acceptance by the University under the Test Score Application System?
    (A) after the University receives their official ACT or SAT scores
    (B) after they graduate from high school
    (C) immediately after taking the ACT or the SAT
    (D) after the University awards all available scholarships

Questions 59-60. For each of these questions, choose the answer that is *closest in meaning* to the original sentence. Note that several of the choices may be factually correct, but you should choose the one that is the *closest restatement of the given sentence*.

59. The almost legendary ten-year population cycle of the snowshoe hare may be determined by weather patterns, cyclic wildfires, predation, or a combination of causes.
    (A) The legends about the snowshoe hare often revolve around its problems with the weather, fires, predators, and other problems in the wild.
    (B) The fact that most snowshoe hares live to be only ten years old is caused by several dangerous factors in their environment.
    (C) The size of the snowshoe hare population follows a very famous pattern which is regulated by a variety of causes in the animal's environment.
    (D) The snowshoe hare's reproductive patterns are determined by several legendary causes.

60. Although there was not even a single other black student at Iowa State College when he was accepted, George Washington Carver was so successful that, after receiving a Master of Science degree, he was appointed to the faculty of his alma mater.
    (A) Even though he was accepted at Iowa State College and was awarded a Master of Science degree, George Washington Carver was never accepted as a professor at that school.
    (B) After finishing a Master of Science degree, George Washington Carver became a member of the Iowa State College faculty, having once been its first black student.
    (C) After finishing his program at Iowa State College, George Washington Carver ended his life as a single man and also became a successful member of the ISC faculty.
    (D) George Washington Carver was the first American black to receive a Master of Science degree and to become a college professor.

Answer Key/ Practice Test II ——————

Section 1: Listening Comprehension

Part A	*Part B*	*Part C*
1. D	21. A	36. D
2. C	22. D	37. A
3. A	23. C	38. C
4. B	24. A	39. B
5. B	25. C	40. C
6. D	26. B	41. A
7. C	27. D	42. C
8. D	28. D	43. B
9. A	29. B	44. B
10. A	30. C	45. D
11. C	31. B	46. D
12. B	32. A	47. C
13. C	33. D	48. D
14. A	34. C	49. A
15. B	35. A	50. B
16. D		
17. D		
18. C		
19. A		
20. B		

Section 2: Structure and Written Expression

Part A

The explanations of why given answers are wrong have been kept as brief as possible. Indications of how particular incorrect answers might be made correct are provided as a stimulus to thinking about English sentence structure. The references marked FE are to the Focused Exercises which may be of help in further explaining why particular answers are correct or incorrect and in offering more practice.

1. A Inappropriate tense (FE-29)
   B Correct (FE-6)
   C Repetition of subject (FE-3)
   D Passive is impossible (FE-7)

2. A Dependent clause needs subject and verb (FE-10)
   B "because of" must be followed by a noun
   C Correct (FE-10)
   D Would create dependent phrase needing subsequent completion of "because" clause

3. A "same" always preceded by "the"
   B Correct
   C "same" is not a comparative form, "than" therefore inappropriate (FE-15, 24)
   D See 3-A

4. A Repeated subject (FE-3, 18)
   B Creates subject only of main clause with no predicate (FE-6)
   C Creates subject with dependent phrase (See 4-B)
   D Correct

5. A Correct
   B, C, and D all impossible complementations of "is said"

6. A "of" cannot follow "fifty times"
   B "more" requires "than," but this would still be inadequate with reference word to "volume"—parallelism (FE-14, 33)
   C Correct
   D "fifty times" is not a comparative form, needed before "than" (FE-24, 25)

7. A, B, and C wrong because they do not provide link to "the more certain it becomes"
   D Correct (FE-15)

8. A Correct
   B Non-existent phrase
   C Structurally possible but meaning impossible ("in order to")
   D Participle form of verb needs "by" if desired meaning is "by means of"

9. A Only possible with comma after "that is" (meaning "i.e.") and previous referent
   B Only possible with comma after "Thanksgiving" and "that" before "begins"
   C Correct (FE-4)
   D Structurally possible but the "season" does not begin "Thanksgiving"

10. A Correct (FE-32)
    B Wrong preposition after "prevent"
    C Incorrect verb form after preposition (FE-32)
    D See 10-B

11. A Wrong verb; can't use "have" with age
   B Correct
   C Would be correct with "aged" and without "years"
   D Dependent phrase would refer to "Baltimore American" and could not have "years"

12. A Would create dependent participial phrase to "... ibis", needing entire main clause to follow
   B Meaningless
   C Produces "there are" and "are" (FE-5)
   D Correct (FE-14 and FE-1)

13. A "had" would require "achieved"
   B Correct (FE-8)
   C "not until" requires subject-verb inversion and anyway "achieving" impossible
   D Inversion requires question form (auxiliary before subject)

14. A Correct (FE-10)
   B "who" would make "Lincoln" subject of following clause, which would be structurally correct (though semantically different) without "he" (FE-10)
   C Theoretically possible (but a non-sequitur) if some punctuation after "Lincoln"
   D "because of" cannot be followed by a clause

15. A, B, and D all contain incorrect pronoun forms since the only possible pronoun structure following the noun to indicate possesive is "of" + "possessive" (FE-19)

   C Correct

Part B

In every case the answer is given first. Where there is an FE reference, this indicates the number of the Focused Exercise which may offer useful further practice of the point in question. Where words in quotation marks follow the letter of the correct answer, these show what would be needed for the sentence to be correct. This usually occurs in cases where none of the Focused Exercises is applicable.

16. C (FE-26)
17. A (FE-7, 31)
18. B (FE-24)
19. D (FE-19)
20. C (FE-40)
21. B (FE-21)
22. B (FE-28)
23. D (FE-35)
24. A (FE-32)
25. A (FE-28)
26. B (FE-23)
27. C (FE-22)
28. D (FE-35)

29. C ("visit it")
30. A (FE-17)
31. B (FE-30)
32. D (FE-27)
33. D (FE-14, 33)
34. A (FE-20)
35. C (FE-32)
36. A (FE-38)
37. D (FE-36)
38. B (FE-3, 18)
39. C ("different")
40. A (FE-29)

Section 3: Reading Comprehension and Vocabulary

Part A

1. A	11. D	21. A
2. D	12. A	22. A
3. C	13. D	23. C
4. B	14. C	24. A
5. A	15. D	25. D
6. C	16. B	26. A
7. B	17. A	27. C
8. D	18. C	28. B
9. B	19. C	29. B
10. B	20. B	30. D

Part B

31. A	41. A	51. C
32. B	42. B	52. B
33. D	43. B	53. C
34. A	44. D	54. A
35. C	45. D	55. D
36. A	46. A	56. C
37. C	47. A	57. D
38. D	48. D	58. A
39. C	49. D	59. C
40. B	50. B	60. B

Strategies: A Reminder**

Section 1: Listening Comprehension

STRATEGY for Part A: look at all the answer choices before you hear the sentence.
STRATEGY for Part B: aim for a more general understanding than in Part A but more specific than Part C.
STRATEGY for Part C: aim for a general understanding of what you hear.

Section 2: Structure and Written Expression

GENERAL STRATEGY: work at a steady pace and read each possible answer very carefully.
STRATEGY for Part A: read carefully and choose the one correct sentence completion.
STRATEGY for Part B: choose the one incorrect part.

Section 3: Reading Comprehension and Vocabulary

GENERAL STRATEGY: do Part A quickly to allow yourself more time for Part B.
STRATEGY for Part A: work quickly; if you do not know the meaning, guess and continue on to the next item.
STRATEGY for Part B: think about the items and recheck them against the information given.

**See the Preview to the Practice Tests (pp. 42-45) for more specific strategies.

PRACTICE TEST III

Section 1: Listening Comprehension

Time: 40 minutes

You will need to play the tape for all the questions in Section 1. (The tapescripts are printed on pages 243-247. This material is designated by the symbol  .)

In this section of the test, you will have an opportunity to demonstrate your ability to understand spoken English. There are three parts to this section, with special directions for each part.

Part A

Directions: For each question in Part A, you will hear a short statement. The statements will be spoken just one time. They will not be written out for you, and you must listen carefully to understand what the speaker says.

After you hear a statement, read the four sentences in your test book, marked (A), (B), (C), and (D), and decide which <u>one</u> is closest in meaning to the statement you heard. Then, on your answer sheet, find the number of the question and blacken the space that corresponds to the letter of the answer you have chosen so that the letter inside the oval cannot be seen.

Example I

Sample Answer
● Ⓑ Ⓒ Ⓓ

You will hear:

You will read: (A) Her family wanted her to work on the land.

(B) The older generation was tied to the farm.

(C) They couldn't pay the rent on the tractor.

(D) Her parents encouraged her to marry a pharmacist.

Sentence (A), "Her family wanted her to work on the land," is closest in meaning to the sentence "Her parents tried to attract her to farming." Therefore, you should choose answer (A).

Example II

Sample Answer
Ⓐ Ⓑ ● Ⓓ

You will hear:

You will read: (A) The game eventually went into overtime.

(B) Their demands annulled their major gains.

(C) There is support for holding the game yearly.

(D) Major Lee hopes to see the annual game.

Sentence (C), "There is support for holding the game yearly," is closest in meaning to the sentence "The major leagues hope to make the old-timers' game an annual event." Therefore, you should choose answer (C).

GO ON TO THE NEXT PAGE

1. (A) I haven't met anyone in the company.
   (B) I didn't know about your visitors.
   (C) I was surprised that you own your own company.
   (D) Excuse me for dropping your timpani class.

2. (A) Ben fulfilled his part of the agreement.
   (B) Ben threw away the rest of the dill.
   (C) Ben carried out the garbage after dinner.
   (D) Ben finished dealing the cards.

3. (A) Is that the right road?
   (B) This is exactly what you ordered.
   (C) Did you want it like that?
   (D) That's the weight you requested.

4. (A) The assignment is overly difficult.
   (B) The study is through those two doors.
   (C) The study is hot off the press.
   (D) The weather makes it difficult to study inside.

5. (A) Bill wins at shooting contests.
   (B) Bill is always losing his shoes.
   (C) Bill uses his gun to shoo away animals.
   (D) Bill never stops chewing gum.

6. (A) Even though Dave is strong, the strain was too much.
   (B) Dave needed to find a job after finishing his studies.
   (C) Dave is looking for a job with the railroad company.
   (D) Dave helped finish the training track.

7. (A) More people cast ballots than anticipated.
   (B) The candidate's tactics were heavy-handed.
   (C) The weather made boating unusually difficult.
   (D) It was difficult to lift the boat out of the water.

8. (A) I can't return the money before tomorrow.
   (B) I don't think I'll have enough money tomorrow.
   (C) Borrowing money is a bad policy in my view.
   (D) The idea doesn't seem worth the money to me.

9. (A) He forgave them for having missed the answer.
   (B) He was sorry to have given them the incorrect answer.
   (C) He's never forgiven them.
   (D) He felt he should have given them the short solution.

10. (A) Tracy must wear a cast on her ankle for a month.
    (B) Tracy's contract expires this month.
    (C) Tracy's uncle expected to hear from her by now.
    (D) Her uncle's monthly contract posed a problem.

11. (A) Allen did not find Maria's proposal acceptable.
    (B) Allen thought Maria favored growing roses.
    (C) Maria thought Allen's pose unacceptable.
    (D) Allen did not propose to Maria.

12. (A) Don't allow the game to upset you.
    (B) Don't worry about the weight you gained.
    (C) Be sure to get to the game on time.
    (D) Did you happen to forget the gains we've made?

13. (A) I wish I had been a more serious student last term.
    (B) It's difficult for me to study alone.
    (C) I shouldn't have spent my last quarter.
    (D) If I had tried harder, I wouldn't have had to study so much.

14. (A) Can you give me a hand?
    (B) Why do you need my help?
    (C) What would you like me to do?
    (D) How are you doing?

15. (A) The peaches make the trip worthwhile.
    (B) Plain marble can be found along the coast.
    (C) Our plans go back to our last vacation.
    (D) We'll return there for the beaches.

16. (A) Tony just managed to catch his bus.
    (B) Tony barely caught a ride.
    (C) Tony was out of breath because of running for his bus.
    (D) Tony's boss got to work a little later than he did.

17. (A) Jean does exactly as she pleases.
    (B) Jean can sew like a professional seamstress.
    (C) You don't know Jean.
    (D) Jean's suit wasn't made for this occasion.

18. (A) This map won't be of any use.
    (B) I can't find the mop anywhere.
    (C) This map's too faded to read.
    (D) This mat isn't going to be very helpful.

19. (A) Bill won't like this evening's show.
    (B) Even if Bill thinks it's important, he won't show you.
    (C) No matter what, Bill won't approve.
    (D) Bill won't agree with importing it.

20. (A) How long were you at the coast this summer?
    (B) Your cost of living used to be lower in the summer.
    (C) How much do you usually spend on your vacation?
    (D) You don't go to the coast anymore.

GO ON TO THE NEXT PAGE

Part B

Directions: In Part B you will hear short conversations between two speakers. At the end of each conversation, a third voice will ask a question about what was said. The question will be spoken just one time. After you hear a conversation and the question about it, read the four possible answers in your test book and decide which _one_ is the best answer to the question you heard. Then, on your answer sheet, find the number of the question and blacken the space that corresponds to the letter of the answer you have chosen.

Example

Sample Answer
(A) (B) (C) ●

You will hear:
You will read: (A) He's expecting a letter.
(B) He can't type.
(C) He'll type the letter after the post office closes.
(D) Someone else will have to type the letter.

From the conversation you know that the man could type the letter if he had time. The best answer, then, is (D), "Someone else will have to type the letter." Therefore, you should choose answer (D).

21. (A) The long wait.
    (B) Her paycheck.
    (C) The computer.
    (D) The bank's excuses.

22. (A) Go to an Italian restaurant.
    (B) Buy some garlic for the sauce.
    (C) Change the recipe for the sauce.
    (D) Taste the sauce.

23. (A) It was strange that the Johnsons didn't come.
    (B) The Johnsons came as expected.
    (C) The Johnsons turned down the invitation.
    (D) The Johnsons came, but not alone.

24. (A) Someone else bought it for him.
    (B) He bought it on his birthday.
    (C) He exchanged it for something else.
    (D) He doesn't remember where he got it.

25. (A) Have her eyes examined.
    (B) Discuss the work with her fellow workers.
    (C) Consult with her boss.
    (D) Divide the work with him.

26. (A) The number of crashes.
    (B) The small size of the part.
    (C) The condition of the park.
    (D) The lack of parking space.

27. (A) Read the magazine.
    (B) Postpone writing the article.
    (C) Fetch the article later.
    (D) Break her promise.

28. (A) She would like the tray from the garden.
    (B) She wants flowers throughout the living room.
    (C) She wishes the man would work outside.
    (D) She doesn't want dirt in the house.

29. (A) An Irish relative.
    (B) International politics.
    (C) The man's problems with his mother.
    (D) Something cooking.

30. (A) The woman doesn't know who he's talking about.
    (B) His old roommate has moved and is a writer.
    (C) Keith won't be coming back to be his roommate.
    (D) The woman read about Keith in a short story.

31. (A) She is in a different kind of business.
    (B) She feels her salary is a private matter.
    (C) She isn't learning a lot in her business course.
    (D) She doesn't want to work with the man anymore.

32. (A) Pediatrician.
    (B) House painter.
    (C) TV repairman.
    (D) Receptionist.

33. (A) Go on a diet.
    (B) See a doctor.
    (C) Consult a reference book.
    (D) Avoid foods containing vitamin A.

34. (A) All textile mills are in the South.
    (B) Oregon is in the South.
    (C) Jane is from Oregon.
    (D) Textiles are produced in Oregon and in the South.

35. (A) In an apartment for rent.
    (B) In an appliance store.
    (C) In a library.
    (D) At a carpenter's shop.

1 1 1 1 1 1 1 1 1

Part C

Directions: In this part of the test, you will hear several short talks and conversations. After each talk or conversation, you will be asked some questions. The talks and questions will be spoken just one time. They will not be written out for you, so you will have to listen carefully to understand what the speaker says.

After you hear a question, read the four possible answers in your test book and decide which _one_ is the best answer to the question you heard. Then, on your answer sheet, find the number of the question and blacken the space that corresponds to the letter of the answer you have chosen.

<u>Sample Answer</u>
(A) (B) (C) ●

Listen to this sample talk.
You will hear:
Now look at the following example.
You will hear:
You will read: (A) The achievements of American and Canadian builders.
(B) The beginning of a harmonious relationship between two countries.
(C) The opening of the Detroit River to tourists.
(D) The well-established friendship between two countries.

The best answer to the question "What does the International Peace Movement commemorate?" is (D), "The well-established friendship between two countries." Therefore, you should choose answer (D).

<u>Sample Answer</u>
(A) (B) ● (D)

Now look at the next example.
You will hear:
You will read: (A) In Detroit.
(B) In Windsor.
(C) On an island in the Detroit River.
(D) On the banks of the Detroit River.

The best answer to the question "Where is the International Peace Monument located?" is (C), "On an island in the Detroit River." Therefore, you should choose answer (C).

36. (A) Graduate students.
(B) Former students.
(C) Business leaders.
(D) University employees.

GO ON TO THE NEXT PAGE ▶

37. (A) To keep alumni in contact with the university.
    (B) To raise money.
    (C) To change the university's reputation.
    (D) To attract quality students.

38. (A) Since 1970.
    (B) Since the university opened.
    (C) For more than half a century.
    (D) This is its first meeting.

39. (A) They visit the campus.
    (B) They contribute money.
    (C) They sponsor alumni clubs.
    (D) They buy communication equipment.

40. (A) Receiving an alumni publication.
    (B) Expanding business contacts.
    (C) Notification of campus events.
    (D) Free tickets to social events.

41. (A) Current fashions in footwear.
    (B) Aristocratic extravagances in renaissance Europe.
    (C) Dangerous effects of fashion.
    (D) The unpractical nature of a shoe style from the past.

42. (A) They are more frivolous.
    (B) They are less extravagant.
    (C) They are more variable from year to year.
    (D) They are less noble.

43. (A) Five hundred years.
    (B) Until the beginning of the twentieth century.
    (C) From the twelfth to the fourteenth century.
    (D) One century.

44. (A) Everyone but the clergy.
    (B) All types of leaders.
    (C) Members of the upper classes.
    (D) Very practical people.

45. (A) He is running a high fever.
    (B) He is doing research on allergies.
    (C) He wants to make an appointment for a relative.
    (D) He has been having problems with his eyes and nose.

46. (A) By a skin test.
    (B) By a hay fever indicator.
    (C) By examining the pollen under a microscope.
    (D) By a complete physical examination.

47. (A) He works on a farm.
    (B) He is a public accountant.
    (C) He works in a library.
    (D) He works in a bookstore.

48. (A) Farm work.
    (B) Pollen.
    (C) The weather.
    (D) A bad cold.

49. (A) People in other parts of the state.
    (B) People who work outdoors.
    (C) People who have relatives with similar allergies.
    (D) People who are very sensitive to environmental conditions.

50. (A) To a drugstore.
    (B) To visit his family.
    (C) To the hospital.
    (D) To the university for a test.

Section 2: Structure and Written Expression

Time: 25 minutes

This section is designed to measure your ability to recognize language that is appropriate for standard written English. There are two types of questions in this section, with special directions for each type.

Part A

Directions: Questions 1-15 are incomplete sentences. Four words or phrases, marked (A), (B), (C), and (D), are given beneath each sentence. You are to choose the *one* word or phrase that best completes the sentence. Then, on your answer sheet, find the number of the question and blacken the space that corresponds to the letter of the answer you have chosen so that the letter inside the oval cannot be seen.

Example I

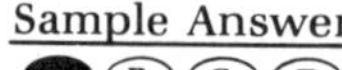
Sample Answer

________ techniques have been developed in recent years to diagnose genetic diseases in the developing fetus.

(A) Several
(B) There are several
(C) They are several
(D) Several of

In English, the sentence should read, "Several techniques have been developed in recent years to diagnose genetic diseases in the developing fetus." Therefore, you should choose (A).

Example II

Sample Answer

Trapeze artists usually rely on safety nets ________ through the air.

(A) flying
(B) they fly
(C) which fly
(D) when flying

In English, the sentence should read, "Trapeze artists usually rely on safety nets when flying through the air." Therefore, you should choose (D).

1. Pigs _______ certain characteristics with human beings.
   (A) which share
   (B) are sharing
   (C) while sharing
   (D) share

2. Albert Szent-Gyorgyi _______ the 1937 Nobel Prize for medicine for his synthesis of ascorbic acid.
   (A) was awarded
   (B) to award
   (C) awarded
   (D) awarding

3. _______ thirteen states in the original United States.
   (A) As there were
   (B) There were
   (C) Were
   (D) So were

4. Researchers have recently confirmed _______ Pygmies are missing an insulin-like growth factor.
   (A) and that
   (B) so that
   (C) because
   (D) that

5. The Order of Elks has been in existence _______ 1868.
   (A) starting in
   (B) since
   (C) after
   (D) founded

6. _______ to use pigeons for observation purposes on sea-rescue missions.
   (A) It is planned
   (B) There is planned
   (C) Has been planned
   (D) Is planned

7. Only under special circumstances _______ to test out of freshman composition and literature.
   (A) freshmen permitted
   (B) freshmen are permitted
   (C) are freshmen permitted
   (D) are permitted freshmen

8. _______ is so limited (64,000 transistors and 64,000 capacitors in about one-twentieth of a square inch), the manufacture of 64K random access memories requires highly sophisticated production technology.
   (A) Because space
   (B) As a result of space
   (C) Being space
   (D) Its space

9. Only one mammal, _______, is known to bear routinely four identical young.
   (A) it is the armadillo
   (B) being the armadillo
   (C) which the armadillo
   (D) the armadillo

10. One of the puzzles still mystifying biologists is _______ what to become in an embryo.
    (A) how do cells know
    (B) how know cells
    (C) how cells know
    (D) how cells knowing

11. Touch-typing was originally devised as an aid to _______.
    (A) the blinds
    (B) the blind
    (C) a blind one
    (D) blinds

GO ON TO THE NEXT PAGE

12. If a traveler had visited the San Diego Peninsula in the 1880's, _______ that coyotes and jackrabbits outnumbered the human population 10,000 to one.
(A) he had found
(B) he found
(C) had he found
(D) he would have found

13. The Appaloosa horse was brought to Mexico from Spain, was later introduced into the United States, and today _______.
(A) by American ranchers is prized
(B) is prized by American ranchers
(C) prized by American ranchers
(D) American ranchers prize it

14. _______ the news from war zones is inevitably censored.
(A) Although much of
(B) Assuming some of
(C) Much of
(D) Many of

15. There are now _______ methods for studying color vision in infants than there once were.
(A) more sophisticated than
(B) much more sophisticated
(C) much sophisticated
(D) sophisticated

GO ON TO THE NEXT PAGE

Part B

Directions: In questions 16-40 each sentence has four words or phrases underlined. The four underlined parts of the sentence are marked (A), (B), (C), and (D). You are to identify the *one* underlined word or phrase that should be corrected or rewritten. Then, on your answer sheet, find the number of the question and blacken the space that corresponds to the letter of the answer you have chosen.

Example I

<u>Sample Answer</u>
● Ⓑ Ⓒ Ⓓ

Most of the Menominee Indian men they
<u>A</u>
work at the tribe's sawmill on the Wolf River.
<u>B</u>   <u>C</u>   <u>D</u>
Answer (A), the underlined word *they*, would not be accepted in carefully written English; the subject has already been stated and the pronoun *they* is not necessary. Therefore, the sentence should read, "Most of the Menominee Indian men work at the tribe's sawmill on the Wolf River." To answer the question correctly, you should choose (A).

Example II

<u>Sample Answer</u>
Ⓐ Ⓑ Ⓒ ●

Well-stocked stores can usually offer foot-
<u>A</u>
wear not only in different shoe sizes but also
<u>B</u>
in a range of feet widths.
<u>C</u>   <u>D</u>
Answer (D), the underlined word *feet*, would not be accepted in carefully written English; the form *foot* should be used because the word is used as an adjective describing *widths*. Therefore, the sentence should read, "Well-stocked stores can usually offer footwear not only in different shoe sizes but also in a range of foot widths." To answer the question correctly, you should choose (D).

GO ON TO THE NEXT PAGE

16. Potatoes <u>grown</u> <u>in</u> vast <u>amounts</u> in <u>Southern</u> Idaho.
         A   B   C   D

17. Martin Heidegger <u>is generally regarded</u> <u>as</u> one of <u>the most influential</u> <u>founder</u> of exis-
                     A   B   C   D
tentialism.

18. <u>Because of</u> the divisive effect of the Vietnam War, Lyndon Johnson's supporters were
    A
unable <u>to persuade</u> him <u>running</u> for <u>the presidency</u> again in 1972.
         B   C   D

19. Night <u>falls</u> more <u>fast</u> in the tropics <u>than</u> in <u>other</u> latitudes.
       A   B   C   D

20. <u>It</u> <u>has been said</u> <u>that</u> the Pueblo Indians lived in America's <u>oldest and most ancient</u>
  A   B   C   D
apartment houses.

21. Sasswood is <u>the</u> <u>poisonous</u> bark of <u>an</u> <u>Africa</u> tree.
          A   B   C   D

22. The United States Patent Office was <u>set up</u> by <u>the</u> <u>three</u> <u>American</u> president, Thomas
                               A   B   C   D
Jefferson.

23. <u>Alike to</u> Mississippi and Georgia, Louisiana is <u>in</u> the deep South, but South Texas, fur-
    A   B
ther south than <u>any</u> of them is <u>thought of</u> as in the Southwest.
           C   D

24. <u>Top-grade</u> diamonds <u>had not</u> increased <u>so sharply</u> in value in <u>the late seventies</u> if one
    A   B   C   D
company had not controlled almost all of the world's supply.

25. The totally <u>deaf</u> <u>cannot</u> <u>listen</u> to even the loudest <u>of</u> noises.
        A   B   C   D

26. Saturn is the <u>most distance</u> of the planets <u>from</u> the earth that <u>can be seen</u>
               A   B   C
with the naked eye.
        D

27. Evariste Galois, <u>who</u> <u>was killed</u> in a duel <u>at the age of</u> twenty, <u>has been</u> responsible for
             A   B   C   D
the origins of group theory in mathematics.

28. Byron Nelson <u>once</u> performed the <u>feat extraordinary</u> of <u>winning</u> eleven golf tourna-
              A   B   C
<u>ments in a row</u>.
      D

GO ON TO THE NEXT PAGE

29. Based on <u>too</u> complex models stored in its memory, one computer is capable <u>of stating</u>
<u>A</u> <u>B</u>   C
the probability of finding particular minerals in <u>a given area</u>.
D

30. There are no known <u>society</u> in which <u>left-handed</u> people <u>predominate</u>.
<u>A</u>   <u>B</u>   C   D

31. Indians in pre-Colombian <u>times</u> developed <u>a wide range</u> of medicines <u>derived of</u> plants,
A   B   C
including digitalis, which they <u>utilized</u> in the treatment of heart disease.
D

32. The state of Washington, <u>which</u> entered the Union <u>in 1889</u>, <u>was named</u> <u>for honor of</u>
A   B   C   D
George Washington.

33. <u>Shortly</u> after John Lennon's death, more <u>than</u> thirty countries pledged contributions
A   B
<u>for to</u> refurbish a section of New York's Central Park <u>in his memory</u>.
C   D

34. The European bee eater <u>builds</u> <u>a</u> unlined nesting chamber <u>at</u> the end of a <u>yard-long</u>,
A   B   C   D
horizontal burrow.

35. The <u>real</u> year is six hours <u>longer than</u> <u>the</u> Julian year, <u>was introduced</u> by Julius Caesar.
A   B   C   D

36. The Earth's carbon dioxide <u>it</u> <u>contributes</u> fifty-five degrees Fahrenheit to <u>the</u> planet's
A   B   C
<u>average temperature</u>.
D

37. At sixty-nine, Ronald Reagan was <u>older than</u> <u>had</u> any President-elect among <u>his</u> thirty-
<u>A</u>   B   C   D
eight presidential predecessors.

38. Hell's Canyon, <u>with a depth</u> of 7,900 <u>feet</u>, is <u>deeper</u> <u>that</u> the Grand Canyon.
A   B   C   D

39. Legislative appropriations, <u>student</u> fees, and <u>receiving gifts</u> <u>constitute</u> the bases of the
A   B   C
financial support <u>enjoyed</u> by state universities.
D

40. La Paz, Bolivia is <u>the higher</u> capital city <u>in</u> the western hemisphere <u>and</u>
A   B   C
the <u>second-highest</u> in the world.
D

Section 3: Reading Comprehension and Vocabulary

Time: 45 minutes

This section is designed to measure your ability to understand various kinds of reading materials, as well as your ability to understand the meaning and use of words. There are two types of questions in this section, with special directions for each type.

Part A

<u>Directions:</u> In questions 1-30 each sentence has a word or phrase underlined. Below each sentence are four other words or phrases marked (A), (B), (C), and (D). You are to choose the *one* word or phrase that *best keeps the meaning* of the original sentence if it is substituted for the underlined word or phrase. Then, on your answer sheet, find the number of the question and blacken the space that corresponds to the letter you have chosen so that the letter inside the oval cannot be seen.

Example

<u>Sample Answer</u>
(A) (B) (C) ●

A series of <u>calamities</u> can severely affect underwriters' earnings.

(A) reports
(B) investments
(C) becalmings
(D) disasters

The best answer is (D) because "A series of disasters can severely affect underwriters' earnings" is closest in meaning to the original sentence, "A series of calamities can severely affect underwriters' earnings." Therefore, you should choose answer (D).

As soon as you understand the directions, begin work on the questions.

1. Diving is the <u>leading</u> cause of spinal-cord injuries.
   (A) primary
   (B) ultimate
   (C) conducive
   (D) utmost

2. The <u>choice</u> of a particular career is influenced by a number of factors.
   (A) usefulness
   (B) success
   (C) desirability
   (D) selection

3. Washington's army, consisting <u>mainly</u> of farmers and backwoodsmen, lacked military supplies.
   (A) exclusively
   (B) fortunately
   (C) principally
   (D) initially

4. United States presidents often <u>greet</u> foreign dignitaries on the White House lawn.
   (A) welcome
   (B) congratulate
   (C) address
   (D) accredit

5. Many <u>properties</u> of the atmosphere affect the amount of solar radiation that reaches the earth.
   (A) belongings
   (B) impurities
   (C) levels
   (D) characteristics

6. New chemical dyes for coating glasses have been developed which screen out <u>harmful</u> light rays.
   (A) invisible
   (B) damaging
   (C) dreadful
   (D) excessive

7. In ancient Egyptian paintings, royal figures were <u>differentiated</u> by making them several times larger than others.
   (A) distinguished
   (B) estranged
   (C) deferred
   (D) enlarged

8. The company possesses <u>unique</u> research capabilities.
   (A) single
   (B) only
   (C) unequalled
   (D) different

9. Chimpanzees are frequently used as <u>stand-ins</u> for human beings in experiments.
   (A) partners
   (B) role-models
   (C) stand-bys
   (D) substitutes

10. Viewers often find the paintings of the photo-Realist school <u>somewhat</u> disconcerting.
    (A) rather
    (B) thoroughly
    (C) very
    (D) instrinsically

11. Differences in positions adopted by oxygen and hydrogen atoms <u>account for</u> variations in the crystalline structure of different forms of ice.
    (A) are caused by
    (B) explain
    (C) derive from
    (D) constitute

GO ON TO THE NEXT PAGE

12. No other newspaper columnist has managed <u>as yet</u> to rival Ann Landers' popularity in terms of readership.
    (A) though
    (B) in spite of this
    (C) even
    (D) so far

13. Many politicians find that they can no longer afford the luxury of a personal <u>chauffeur</u>.
    (A) valet
    (B) driver
    (C) secretary
    (D) servant

14. The United States Food and Drug Administration has shown itself to be particularly <u>wary</u> with regard to alleged "miracle" drugs in recent times.
    (A) bellicose
    (B) exhausted
    (C) cautious
    (D) severe

15. The <u>plainer</u> a bower bird's plumage, the more brightly it decorates its nest to attract a mate.
    (A) more spectacular
    (B) duller
    (C) flatter
    (D) more melancholy

16. Attitudes on the two sides in the Revolutionary War <u>precluded</u> the possiblity of a peaceful solution.
    (A) presaged
    (B) prejudiced
    (C) anticipated
    (D) prevented

17. Cowrie shells were once in widespread use as <u>a token</u> of value.
    (A) a symbol
    (B) an amount
    (C) a thing
    (D) an investment

18. Because leeches' behavior patterns are simple, it is <u>relatively</u> easy to identify which neurons govern which behavior.
    (A) apparently
    (B) comparatively
    (C) obviously
    (D) consequently

19. <u>Adverse</u> reviews in the New York press may greatly change the prospects of a new Broadway production.
    (A) additonal
    (B) encouraging
    (C) unfavorable
    (D) subversive

20. Translating literally from one language to another <u>works</u> unsatisfactorily at best.
    (A) pays
    (B) functions
    (C) reads
    (D) labors

21. The army <u>permitted</u> Teddy Roosevelt's "Rough Riders" to carry six-shooters instead of regular army weapons.
    (A) allowed
    (B) forced
    (C) instructed
    (D) convinced

GO ON TO THE NEXT PAGE

22. The <u>quest</u> for supercomputers is intensi-
fying.
(A) investment
(B) challenge
(C) search
(D) demand

23. Some brush fires are set <u>on purpose</u>.
(A) deliberately
(B) at will
(C) spontaneously
(D) on impulse

24. A number of animals in Aesop's fables are
portrayed as being <u>crafty</u>.
(A) vain
(B) virtuous
(C) artistic
(D) cunning

25. The <u>founder</u> of the American Red Cross
was Clara Barton.
(A) leader
(B) backer
(C) discoverer
(D) originator

26. General acceptance of 3-D films may
prove hard to <u>come by</u>, as the experience
of three decades ago indicated.
(A) obtain
(B) explain
(C) understand
(D) discern

27. Perhaps more than anything else, it was
<u>onerous</u> taxes that led to the Peasants'
Revolt in England in 1381.
(A) multiple
(B) unjust
(C) burdensome
(D) infamous

28. Psychologists have recently mounted an
offensive against what they describe as
<u>nastiness</u> toward students by educators.
(A) arbitrariness
(B) unpleasantness
(C) severity
(D) aloofness

29. Recent research into aging suggests that
the body's defense mechanisms may lose
the ability to distinguish what is <u>alien</u>.
(A) insane
(B) infectious
(C) foreign
(D) poisonous

30. Jane Austen's *Persuasion* was not <u>pub-
lished</u> until 1818, after the author's death.
(A) edited
(B) issued
(C) publicized
(D) promoted

GO ON TO THE NEXT PAGE

Part B

Directions: The rest of this section is based on a variety of reading material (single sentences, paragraphs, and the like) followed by questions about the meaning of the material. For questions 31-60, you are to choose the _one_ best answer, (A), (B), (C), or (D), to each question. Then, on your answer sheet, find the number of the question and blacken the space that corresponds to the letter of the answer you have chosen.

Answer all questions following a passage on the basis of what is _stated_ or _implied_ in that passage.

Read the following passage.

Since an increasing amount of the information we take in today has been previously recorded and is then presented to us on radio, TV, or cassette, there are obvious advantages in speeding up recorded material. Up until now, the problem in doing this has been that simply increasing the speed of a recording makes the pitch of the voice unnaturally high. Now, a solution to this problem is offered by machines that lower the pitch and break down speech into tiny fragments. With the aid of a computer, certain unnecessary parts of the recording are eliminated and the speech is then put back together, the pitch returning to normal. This process allows TV programmers, for example, to reduce a thirty-minute broadcast by as much as 20% without leaving anything out.

Example I

Sample Answer

(A) ● (C) (D)

It can be inferred from the passage that the new machines referred to will

(A) require maintenance by computer experts.
(B) increase the amount of recorded information which can be contained in a given time period.
(C) eliminate the need for television programmers.
(D) reorder parts of a given recording and adjust the pitch at the same time.

The passage says that the process performed by these machines "allows TV programmers, for example, to reduce a thirty-minute broadcast by as much as 20% without leaving anything out." Therefore, you should choose (B) as the best completion of the sentence.

Example II

Sample Answer

(A) (B) ● (D)

According to the passage, simply speeding up recorded information results in a

(A) breakdown of sound.
(B) loss of certain information.
(C) distortion of the speaker's voice.
(D) need for specialized broadcasting equipment.

The passage says that "simply increasing the speed of a recording makes the pitch of the voice unnaturally high." Therefore, you should choose (C) as the best completion of the sentence.

128   Practice Test III

Questions 31-34

During the decade of the nineteen-fifties, Arizona, an inland state located in the Southwest and bordered by New Mexico, the country of Mexico, California, Nevada, Utah, and Colorado, had one of the fastest-growing populations in the nation, with a rate of growth surpassed by only three other states: Florida, Nevada, and Alaska. In the early part of the twentieth century, the population was predominantly rural but, by the time of the 1960 census, 74.5% was urban-dwelling, as compared with 55.5% at the decennial census ten years earlier.

31. Where did the state of Arizona rank in population growth rate in the 1950's?
    (A) fourth
    (B) third
    (C) tied for first
    (D) first

32. According to the passage, which of the following *cannot* be said of Arizona?
    (A) It shares its border with five other states of the Union.
    (B) It has no coastline.
    (C) Its population grew rapidly over the 1951-1960 period.
    (D) It was the fastest growing state in its area in the 1950's.

33. When was a majority of Arizona's population urban-dwelling for the first time?
    (A) in the early part of the twentieth century
    (B) during the course of the 1950's
    (C) sometime before 1950
    (D) in 1960

34. Which of the following can be inferred from the passage?
    (A) The population of Arizona increased by a greater number of people than that of all but three states in the 1950's.
    (B) A decennial census was taken in 1950.
    (C) There were more urban than rural dwellers in Arizona in 1940.
    (D) Alaska's population grew faster than that of Florida during the 1950's.

Questions 35-39

The Sphenisciformes order of birds is a particularly distinct, homogeneous one, comprising a single family, Spheniscidae, the penguins. The distribution of these birds is limited to the Southern Hemisphere. One species of the eighteen in this order, the Galapagos penguin, lives at the equator, and a few species inhabit temperate regions, but the majority breed on islands in subantarctic waters. Total populations of most species run into the millions and some are noticeably increasing, apparently due to sharp reductions in the numbers of Antarctic whales, which compete with penguins for the krill that form the basis of both animals' diets. Most species of penguins lay two eggs, though the emperor and king penguins lay only one, and incubation is performed by the male and female parent alternately, once the female has returned from some two weeks at sea, where she feeds and recovers from the effort of egg-laying. Here, too, the emperor penguin proves to be an exception to the rule, for the female usually has to walk from 50 to 100 miles to the sea and then walk the same distance back again, by which time incubation is complete.

35. The passage suggests that most orders of birds are
    (A) Spheniscidae.
    (B) homogeneous.
    (C) particular.
    (D) multi-family.

36. According to the passage, which of the following is not true?
    (A) All Spheniscidae are penguins.
    (B) All penguins are Spheniscidae.
    (C) All Spheniscidae belong to the order Sphenisciformes.
    (D) All Spheniscidae belong to the same species.

37. According to the passage, what is the probable reason for the recent increase in the numbers of some penguin species?
    (A) the drop in whale populations
    (B) the drop in krill availability
    (C) the fact that some species lay two eggs
    (D) the change in penguins' diet

38. It may be inferred from the passage that the species of penguins which have recently increased in number
    (A) live on the Galapagos Islands.
    (B) live in subantarctic regions.
    (C) live in temperate zones.
    (D) are not the emperor or king penguins.

39. It may be inferred from the passage that the male emperor penguin incubates the egg alone because the female
    (A) is too tired.
    (B) cannot lay another egg.
    (C) spends too long at sea recovering from egg-laying.
    (D) takes too long to return from the sea.

Questions 40-47

Chester Arthur, the twenty-first President of the United States, was an unlikely holder of the highest office in the land. Born in Vermont in 1830, he was the son of an Irish immigrant father and a New Hampshire mother. After becoming a lawyer in New York, he joined the Republican Party and eventually came to hold a number of state offices there, including a position as head of the New York Customs House. Though personally honest, Arthur's administration was marred by corrupt practices, and he was removed from office in 1878.

When James Garfield was elected as the Republican Party's presidential candidate in 1880, Arthur, who belonged to a faction that had supported the renomination of President Grant, was offered the Vice-presidency as a conciliatory gesture. Arthur accepted, and then, in 1881, was elevated to the Presidency following Garfield's assassination.

In view of his far-from-unblemished record and his lack of strong political support, even within his own party, Arthur's move to the White House was viewed with great concern by many Americans, but, to the astonishment of most, his administration proved to be a competent and honest one. However, he never was elected President in his own right, being defeated for the nomination at his party's convention in 1884, and dying in November two years later of Bright's disease during the presidency of a Democrat, Grover Cleveland.

40. How does the writer describe the fact that Arthur became President?
    (A) as disliked
    (B) as eventual
    (C) as improbable
    (D) as conciliatory

41. Chester Arthur was
    (A) of mixed Irish-American stock.
    (B) born of Irish parents.
    (C) born in New Hampshire.
    (D) born in New York.

42. Which of the following best describes Arthur's tenure as the head of the New York Customs House?
    (A) a thoroughly corrupt administration
    (B) one suffering from much corruption that Arthur, though not involved, failed to remedy
    (C) one which, in spite of the efforts of honest officials, was made corrupt by its leader
    (D) one in which corruption was not eradicated from Arthur's office until 1878

43. Why was Arthur invited to become Garfield's running-mate?
    (A) because his support for President Grant was half-hearted
    (B) because of his previous record in office
    (C) because Garfield wanted to hold the Republican Party together
    (D) because there was a danger of Garfield's being assassinated

44. During his years as President, Arthur was
    (A) a cause of great concern to the American people.
    (B) a pleasant surprise to most people.
    (C) far from unblemished in his conduct.
    (D) the focus of strong political support.

45. Who was the twentieth President of the United States?
    (A) Grover Cleveland
    (B) Ulysses S. Grant
    (C) Chester Arthur
    (D) James Garfield

46. In his bid for re-election, Arthur was defeated by
    (A) a fellow Republican.
    (B) Bright.
    (C) Grover Cleveland.
    (D) an unnamed Democrat.

47. How old was Chester Arthur when he died?
    (A) 48
    (B) 51
    (C) 54
    (D) 56

GO ON TO THE NEXT PAGE

Questions 48-53

Simply stated, computational linguistics is no more than the use of electronic digital computers in linguistic research. These machines are employed to scan texts and to produce, more rapidly and more reliably than is possible without their aid, such valuable tools for linguistic and stylistic research as word lists, frequency counts, and concordances. But more interesting and theoretically much more difficult than the compilation of lists, is the use of computers for automatic grammatical analysis and translation. A considerable amount of progress was made in the area of machine translation in the United States, Great Britain, the Soviet Union, and France between the mid-1950's and the mid-1960's, but much of the original impetus for this work has now disappeared, due in part to the realization that the problems involved are infinitely more complex than was at first envisaged. Thus, translation continues to remain as much an art as a science, if not more so.

48. According to the passage, computational linguistics involves
   (A) a reliance on computers.
   (B) a simplified computer language.
   (C) making electronic tools.
   (D) research into electronics.

49. In what way have the machines referred to proven to be helpful to researchers?
   (A) They can produce accurate lists of what a text contains.
   (B) They can translate texts more reliably than was possible in the past.
   (C) They can validate the theories of linguists and stylists.
   (D) They have been used to improve grammatical analysis.

50. How does the author describe the present state of machine translation?
   (A) It has been recognized as an art.
   (B) It has largely been abandoned.
   (C) It has received new impetus from a more artistic approach.
   (D) The complex problems previously envisaged have recently been solved.

51. According to the passage, which of the following problems is the most difficult to solve?
   (A) compilation of word lists and frequency counts
   (B) developing a theoretical approach to list compilation
   (C) grammatical analyses and translations
   (D) coming up with concordances which are useful for stylistic research

52. According to the passage, when approximately was significant progress made in translations by computers?
   (A) between 1950 and 1960
   (B) before 1950
   (C) after 1965
   (D) between 1955 and 1965

53. It can be inferred from the passage that translation
   (A) will never be done satisfactorily by machines.
   (B) is a science rather than an art.
   (C) is more complex than making lists.
   (D) is done particularly well in the United States, Great Britain, France, and the Soviet Union.

Questions 54-58

Blood is indeed in the news, for on the heels of that announcement comes a report of tests carried out in the United States and Japan on artificial blood. After an accident, time is crucial for a person suffering from extensive blood loss, and a transfusion of real blood must often be preceded by a time-consuming test for blood type. Plasma does not require such a test but, because it can carry little oxygen, it is not a wholly satisfactory substitute. Perfluorocarbons appear to offer an answer. They are utilized in combination with an emulsion called Fluosol-DA, which provides a number of additional advantages over real blood. These include the absence of a need for blood tests, the fact that it can be frozen for as long as two years, its elimination eventually as a gas through the lungs, and the impossiblity of its transmitting such problems as hepatitis.

54. What was the preceding paragraph probably about?
    (A) the benefits of a well-advertised foot product
    (B) the announcement of another blood-related development
    (C) an account of the nature of real blood
    (D) a description of other tests in the United States

55. Why, according to the passage, is a transfusion of real blood sometimes problematical?
    (A) because there is not enough time for a blood test
    (B) because oxygen must be injected into the plasma
    (C) because of the test necessitated by the use of plasma
    (D) because of tests being carried out with artificial blood

56. What can be inferred from the passage about perfluorocarbons?
    (A) They are utilized in a plasma emulsion.
    (B) They can carry considerable amounts of oxygen.
    (C) They are injected pure into the patient.
    (D) They require only a quick blood type test.

57. Which of the following is mentioned as being an advantage of Fluosol-DA over real blood?
    (A) It is a gas.
    (B) Blood tests are not required for two years.
    (C) It eliminates the risk of certain infections.
    (D) It is an emulsion.

58. What would be the most suitable title for this extract?
    (A) Too Many Accidents: Blood Loss Increases
    (B) Artificial Blood: A Vital Time Saver
    (C) Plasma a Problem in Blood Transfusions
    (D) More Blood Tests in the United States and Japan

Questions 59-60   For each of these questions, choose the answer that is *closest in mean-ing* to the original sentence. Note that several of the choices may be factually correct, but you should choose the one that is the *closest restatement of the given sentence.*

59. Had the economic climate been more favorable, there is little doubt that the monetary policy would have worked.
    (A) If the air-conditioning units had been cheaper, they would certainly have been worth buying.
    (B) It is certain that the money-supply policy functioned once economic conditions had improved.
    (C) The fact that the money policy did not work was due to unfavorable circumstances in the economy.
    (D) When the weather worsens, this usually heralds economic policy difficulties.

60. Grades of "incomplete" will be changed to failing grades if the unfinished work is not completed within two quarters of the end of the course.
    (A) For two terms before the end of any course, students who fail will have their work marked "incomplete."
    (B) Students have only two quarters in which to receive a passing grade for work they have failed to hand in by the end of their course.
    (C) A fifty-cent fine will be charged to all students who fail to complete assignments by the end of their courses.
    (D) Failing grades can be upgraded to "incomplete" during a two-quarter period following the end of a course.

Answer Key/
Practice Test III

Section 1: Listening Comprehension

Part A

1. B
2. A
3. C
4. D
5. D
6. B
7. A
8. C
9. B
10. C
11. D
12. A
13. A
14. C
15. D
16. D
17. B
18. A
19. C
20. D

Part B

21. A
22. C
23. D
24. A
25. B
26. C
27. B
28. D
29. D
30. B
31. B
32. C
33. C
34. D
35. A

Part C

36. B
37. A
38. C
39. B
40. D
41. D
42. B
43. A
44. C
45. D
46. A
47. C
48. B
49. C
50. A

Section 2: Structure and Written Expression

Part A

The explanations of why given answers are wrong have been kept as brief as possible. Indications of how particular incorrect answers might be made correct are provided as a stimulus to thinking about English sentence structure. The references marked FE are to the Focused Exercises which may be of help in further explaining why particular answers are correct or incorrect and in offering more practice.

1. A Creates dependent clause and leaves "pigs" without predicate (FE-6)
   B "share" in this sense is a stative verb and cannot be used with progressive form
   C See 1-A
   D Correct (FE-6)

2. A Correct
   B Would create a dependent phrase (with comma after "name") to "acid" and leave main clause without predicate (FE-6)
   C Needs passive (FE-7)
   D See 2-B

3. A Would create dependent clause without main clause (FE-10)
   B Correct (FE-5)
   C No subject (FE-1)
   D Meaningless

4. A "and" would have to link up with another verb
   B Would create adverbial clause which cannot function as object of "confirmed"
   C See 4-B
   D Correct (noun clause as object) (See FE-2 for noun clause as subject)

5. A "starting in" cannot be combined with present perfect here
   B Correct (FE-27)
   C See 5-A
   D Meaningless here

6. A Correct (FE-4)
   B Impossible (FE-5)
   C Needs anticipatory "it" (FE-4)
   D See 6-C

7. A Main verb needed (FE-6, 7, 31)
   B Need inversion after initial "only" (FE-8)
   C Correct (FE-8)
   D Question form inversion needed (FE-8)

8. A Correct (FE-10)
   B Would be correct if "being" instead of "is," creating prepositional phrase
   C Unacceptable introductory word to dependent clause (FE-10)
   D No introductory word; results in main clause unacceptably linked to following main clause (FE-10)

9. A Creates main clause unacceptably linked to following main clause
   B Possible if preceded by "this"
   C Needs verb (FE-10)
   D Correct (FE-9)

10. A Question word order incorrect here (FE-13, 34)
    B Subject-verb inverted
    C Correct (FE-13, 34)
    D "knowing" is not a finite verb form, required by the noun clause complement

11. A Adjective as noun always singular form (FE-35)
    B Correct (FE-35)
    C "one" has no referent
    D See 11-A

12. A Incorrect tense sequence (FE-29)
    B See 12-A
    C No inversion since no introductory word requiring it (FE-8)
    D Correct (FE-29)

13. A Incorrect word order (FE-13)
    B Correct (FE-14)
    C Needs "is" to parallel previous "was" (FE-14)
    D Not parallel (FE-14)

14. A "Although" creates dependent clause with no main clause (FE-10)
    B See 14-A
    C Correct (FE-1)
    D Subject-verb agreement; "news" is singular (FE-16)

15. A Superfluous "than"
    B Correct (FE-15, 24)
    C "much" does not provide the comparative form demanded by "than" (FE-25)
    D See 15-C

Part B

In every case the answer is given first. Where there is an FE reference, this indicates the number of the Focused Exercise which may offer useful further practice of the point in question. Where words in quotation marks follow the letter of the correct answer, these show what would be needed for the sentence to be correct. This usually occurs in cases where none of the Focused Exercises is applicable.

16. A (FE-7,31)
17. D (FE-36)
18. C (FE-32)
19. B (FE-24)
20. D (FE-40)
21. D ("African")
22. C ("third")
23. A (FE-15,25)
24. B (FE-29)
25. C (FE-38)
26. A (FE-22)
27. D (FE-29)
28. B (FE-34)

29. B (FE-25)
30. A (FE-16)
31. C (FE-28)
32. D ("in honor of")
33. C (FE-32)
34. B (FE-21)
35. D ("which was introduced") (FE-10)
36. A (FE-3,18)
37. C ("was")
38. D (FE-25)
39. B (FE-14,33)
40. A (FE-24)

Section 3: Reading Comprehension and Vocabulary

Part A

1. A	11. B	21. A
2. D	12. D	22. C
3. C	13. B	23. A
4. A	14. C	24. D
5. D	15. B	25. D
6. B	16. D	26. A
7. A	17. A	27. C
8. C	18. B	28. B
9. D	19. C	29. C
10. A	20. B	30. B

Part B

31. A	41. A	51. C
32. D	42. B	52. D
33. C	43. C	53. C
34. B	44. B	54. B
35. D	45. D	55. A
36. D	46. A	56. B
37. A	47. D	57. C
38. B	48. A	58. B
39. D	49. A	59. C
40. C	50. B	60. B

STRATEGIES: A REMINDER**

Section 1: Listening Comprehension

STRATEGY for Part A: look at all the answer choices before you hear the sentence.
STRATEGY for Part B: aim for a more general understanding than in Part A but more specific than Part C.
STRATEGY for Part C: aim for a general understanding of what you hear.

Section 2: Structure and Written Expression

GENERAL STRATEGY: work at a steady pace and read each possible answer very carefully.
STRATEGY for Part A: read carefully and choose the one correct sentence completion.
STRATEGY for Part B: choose the one incorrect part.

Section 3: Reading Comprehension and Vocabulary

GENERAL STRATEGY: do Part A quickly to allow yourself more time for Part B.
STRATEGY for Part A: work quickly; if you do not know the meaning, guess and continue on to the next item.
STRATEGY for Part B: think about the items and recheck them against the information given.

**See the Preview to the Practice Tests (pp. 42-45) for more specific strategies.

PRACTICE TEST IV

Section 1: Listening Comprehension

Time: 40 minutes

You will need to play the tape for all the questions in Section 1. (The tapescripts are printed on pages 248-252. This material is designated by the symbol .)

In this section of the test, you will have an opportunity to demonstrate your ability to understand spoken English. There are three parts to this section, with special directions for each part.

Part A

Directions: For each question in Part A, you will hear a short statement. The statements will be spoken just one time. They will not be written out for you, and you must listen carefully to understand what the speaker says.

After you hear a statement, read the four sentences in your test book, marked (A), (B), (C), and (D), and decide which <u>one</u> is closest in meaning to the statement you heard. Then, on your answer sheet, find the number of the question and blacken the space that corresponds to the letter of the answer you have chosen so that the letter inside the oval cannot be seen.

Example I

Sample Answer
● Ⓑ Ⓒ Ⓓ

You will hear:

You will read: (A) The students must speak French in class.
(B) Small groups visit the French class daily.
(C) The students are studying French verse.
(D) The group will visit France in the fall.

Sentence (A), "The students must speak French in class," is closest in meaning to the sentence "The French teacher usually has the students practice conversation in small groups." Therefore, you should choose answer (A).

Example II

Sample Answer
Ⓐ ● Ⓒ Ⓓ

You will hear:

You will read: (A) He wants an apartment with a courtyard.
(B) My lawyer must fix things with the court.
(C) It's my turn to tell a tale.
(D) Matt will bring everything we need to the court.

Sentence (B), "My lawyer must fix things with the court," means most nearly the same as the statement "My attorney needs to arrange the details with the court." Therefore, you should choose answer (B).

GO ON TO THE NEXT PAGE

Practice Test IV

141

1 1 1 1 1 1 1 1 1 1

1. (A) I finally recognized her.
   (B) I couldn't remember her name.
   (C) I never see her these days.
   (D) We won't see her again until the final reel.

2. (A) Can you get another car by this afternoon?
   (B) Do you get along with the others in your car pool?
   (C) You're positive you won't need your car later?
   (D) Can you take a long drive after lunch?

3. (A) The reporters took away their bread.
   (B) The information shocked them.
   (C) Newborns can't breathe right away.
   (D) The news came from a far away beach.

4. (A) Tryouts were held two months ago.
   (B) This is the theater's last month.
   (C) The latest production will be in the small auditorium.
   (D) Auditions will be held before the end of the month.

5. (A) I slipped on the exam.
   (B) I fell asleep after the roll call.
   (C) I wish you had called.
   (D) I made it to the examination.

6. (A) We didn't have pears for a month.
   (B) The hall is in need of repair.
   (C) The clothing department had a few fires last month.
   (D) The shopping center lost four weeks' sales.

7. (A) She was delighted with the tin can.
   (B) She was happy with the results of her sunbathing.
   (C) She came from a family of ten.
   (D) She got the best possible score.

8. (A) They thought they weren't behaving badly.
   (B) We bought the children a beehive.
   (C) Someone had taught them good manners.
   (D) I thought they were well now.

9. (A) He left the case with his boss.
   (B) He lost his briefcase.
   (C) He missed the bus.
   (D) The bus continued after a brief stop.

10. (A) Jane didn't get a haircut.
    (B) Jane has recently changed hairdressers.
    (C) Jane won't mind if you get your hair cut.
    (D) Jane is dissatisfied with her haircut.

11. (A) The mystery required them to adopt a new course.
    (B) At least chemistry students don't have to take math.
    (C) Majors must take courses in math too.
    (D) More than one math course is required for a chemistry degree.

12. (A) Cynthia and Paul are both almost right.
    (B) Paul is probably more intelligent than Cynthia.
    (C) Cynthia doesn't live near Paul.
    (D) Paul is less brilliant than Cynthia.

13. (A) The two of us had a good laugh.
    (B) We were on hand to see Richard off.
    (C) Richard was among the last wave of passengers.
    (D) Richard had to leave from the air-strip.

14. (A) The reporter was interviewing people at the track.
    (B) Everyone is talking about the new high-jump record.
    (C) The cost of food has risen lately in this area.
    (D) All changes in local food prices must be reported.

15. (A) Mr. Alexander wants you to deliver this message.
    (B) Have you thought of a message for Mr. Alexander?
    (C) Can you give this message to Mr. Alexander?
    (D) This message reminds me of Mr. Alexander.

16. (A) He should change his life style.
    (B) He was given a race car last night.
    (C) He would be better off with a smaller car.
    (D) He gave up his late-night job at the drive-in.

17. (A) The president makes all difficult decisions.
    (B) The president takes a long time making decisions.
    (C) The country has had several bad presidents.
    (D) The country needs better leadership.

18. (A) Think about what you are going to say.
    (B) Look at the concentric lines.
    (C) Try to remember those lies.
    (D) Concentrate your efforts on the best-selling lines.

19. (A) Mark is a fast-talking boat salesman.
    (B) Mark lent them his sailboat.
    (C) Mark was talked into sailing his boat.
    (D) They convinced Mark to get rid of his boat.

20. (A) You were in no mood to have your picture taken.
    (B) The weather wasn't very good for picture-taking.
    (C) I couldn't picture you with that doll.
    (D) I couldn't imagine taking you out in this weather

Part B

<u>Directions:</u> In Part B you will hear short conversations between two speakers. At the end of each conversation, a third voice will ask a question about what was said. The question will be spoken just one time. After you hear a conversation and the question about it, read the four possible answers in your test book and decide which <u>one</u> is the best answer to the question you heard. Then, on your answer sheet, find the number of the question and blacken the space that corresponds to the letter of the answer you have chosen.

Example

<u>Sample Answer</u>
● Ⓑ Ⓒ Ⓓ

You will hear:
You will read: (A) Miss at least one semester of school.
(B) Rely on her intui-
tion.
(C) Finish two more
semesters at school.
(D) Start her own finish-
ing school.

From the conversation you know that Amy doesn't have enough money to pay for school in the coming semester. The best answer, then, is (A), "Miss at least one se-mester of school." Therefore, you should choose answer (A).

21. (A) The high quality of the courses they are taking.
(B) The preparation needed for the lat-est bill in Congress.
(C) The excellence of their dinner.
(D) The size the mill should be.

22. (A) At a baseball game.
(B) In a card shop.
(C) In a history class.
(D) In a library.

23. (A) Bill will be back in just a second.
    (B) The man and woman will return before Bill.
    (C) The woman wants to wait for Bill.
    (D) Writing a message for Bill will take too much time.

24. (A) She would like a second opinion.
    (B) She is grateful for the accountant's help.
    (C) The accountant is responsible for the problem.
    (D) She has mistaken the man for the accountant.

25. (A) She didn't do as well as she expected.
    (B) It was the last race.
    (C) The first three laps didn't count.
    (D) She thinks she'll lose the other races.

26. (A) All of his money is in change.
    (B) He doesn't have fifty dollars.
    (C) He can't give the woman change.
    (D) He's tired of making changes.

27. (A) Not apologetic.
    (B) Not responsible.
    (C) Bewildered.
    (D) Broken-hearted.

28. (A) Watch the woman get the baby ready.
    (B) Take care of the child.
    (C) Help get everything else ready.
    (D) Postpone the trip until everything's ready.

29. (A) She should take it to the post office.
    (B) It is too big to send by mail.
    (C) She should return it to the sender.
    (D) It needs more stamps.

30. (A) French courses.
    (B) The man's trip.
    (C) How to get to New Orleans.
    (D) Contrasting opinions of New Orleans.

31. (A) Watch something on TV.
    (B) Go for a ride in the car.
    (C) Read the newspaper.
    (D) Leave for the airport.

32. (A) He hasn't looked anywhere for it.
    (B) His brother in the Navy borrowed it.
    (C) It's being dry cleaned.
    (D) He's too lazy to find it.

33. (A) The woman is sending a gift for Ann and the kids.
    (B) Ann shares a house with the woman and her children.
    (C) The conversation takes place late at night.
    (D) The man doesn't want to drive in the dark.

34. (A) He sells appliances.
    (B) He's an accountant.
    (C) He delivers mail.
    (D) He's a mechanic.

35. (A) Buy a new car.
    (B) Stay home and save their money.
    (C) Fly to Las Vegas.
    (D) Drive through Death Valley.

Part C

Directions: In this part of the test, you will hear several short talks and conversations. After each talk or conversation, you will be asked some questions. The talks and questions will be spoken just one time. They will not be written out for you, so you will have to listen carefully to understand what the speaker says.

After you hear a question, read the four possible answers in your test book and decide which _one_ is the best answer to the question you heard. Then, on your answer sheet, find the number of the question and blacken the space that corresponds to the letter of the answer you have chosen.

Sample Answer
Ⓐ ● Ⓒ Ⓓ

Listen to this sample talk.
You will hear:
Now look at the following example.
You will hear:
You will read: (A) Responsible first-year students.

(B) Someone to be in charge of four dormitories.

(C) On-campus housing for its staff and students.

(D) Residents for its freshman dorms.

The best answer to the question "What is Melford College looking for?" is (B), "Someone to be in charge of four dormitories." Therefore, you should choose answer (B).

Sample Answer
Ⓐ Ⓑ ● Ⓓ

Now look at the next example.
You will hear:
You will read: (A) Signing a five-year dormitory contract.

(B) Training other applicants for residence-hall work.

(C) Planning a social calendar for the freshman dorms.

(D) Sending out freshman application forms.

The best answer to the question "According to the announcement, which of the following will probably be a duty of the new director?" is (C), "Planning a social calendar for the freshman dorms." Therefore, you should choose answer (C).

GO ON TO THE NEXT PAGE ➡

36. (A) The island of Komodo.
    (B) Walter's recent trip.
    (C) A species of monitor lizard.
    (D) An extinct dragon.

37. (A) To study the Komodo dragon.
    (B) To spend his vacation.
    (C) To photograph rare animals.
    (D) To find a Komodo dragon for the San Diego Zoo.

38. (A) Human beings.
    (B) House cats.
    (C) Goats.
    (D) Lizards.

39. (A) Because they are unpredictable.
    (B) Because they are very large.
    (C) Because they are very curious.
    (D) Because they are ugly and ferocious looking.

40. (A) In Southern California.
    (B) Exclusively on the island of Komodo.
    (C) In Asian and African zoos.
    (D) On several South Pacific islands.

41. (A) In New York City.
    (B) On a lake.
    (C) In a small town.
    (D) In various places.

42. (A) To provide a summer vacation spot that combines educational and recreational activities.
    (B) To provide a different type of activity each week for summer vacationers.
    (C) To provide training for dramatists.
    (D) To provide a year-round center for the arts.

43. (A) For several hundred years.
    (B) More than a hundred years.
    (C) For fifty years.
    (D) A little more than a decade.

44. (A) They were in operation in the winter as well as in the summer.
    (B) They presented performances for only one week each summer.
    (C) They visited several locations each summer season.
    (D) Their participants traveled to the shows by car.

45. (A) It covers a wide range of topics and modes of presentation.
    (B) It is limited to concerts and lectures.
    (C) It focuses specifically on educational issues.
    (D) It includes the best radio and movie productions of the previous year.

46. (A) The superiority of the original Chautauqua Institute.
    (B) Competition from traveling Chautauquas.
    (C) Other types of popular entertainment.
    (D) Insufficient number of performers for their productions.

47. (A) A treatment for skin disease.
    (B) An advertising campaign.
    (C) The similarities between men and women's skin.
    (D) The psychology of the male consumer.

48. (A) It was too short.
    (B) It was offensive to women.
    (C) It was too original.
    (D) It was limited in appeal.

49. (A) They have become more interested in advertising.
    (B) They are less interested in being the boss.
    (C) They are concerned about women's rights.
    (D) They are taking better care of their skin.

50. (A) Work on her presentation.
    (B) Go to the movies.
    (C) Attend a meeting.
    (D) Call her boss.

STOP STOP STOP STOP STOP STOP STOP

Section 2: Structure and Written Expression

Time: 25 minutes

This section is designed to measure your ability to recognize language that is appropriate for standard written English. There are two types of questions in this section, with special directions for each type.

Part A

Directions: Questions 1-15 are incomplete sentences. Four words or phrases, marked (A), (B), (C), and (D), are given beneath each sentence. You are to choose the *one* word or phrase that best completes the sentence. Then, on your answer sheet, find the number of the question and blacken the space that corresponds to the letter of the answer you have chosen so that the letter inside the oval cannot be seen.

Example I

Sample Answer
(A) (B) (C) ●

John F. Kennedy was the first Catholic _______ elected President of the United States.

(A) having been
(B) who
(C) he was
(D) to be

In English, the sentence should read, "John F. Kennedy was the first Catholic to be elected President of the United States." Therefore, you should choose (D).

Example II

Sample Answer
(A) ● (C) (D)

One of the best indicators of past living standards that present-day investigators can point to _______.

(A) was being height
(B) is height
(C) being height
(D) was height

In English, the sentence should read, "One of the best indicators of past living standards that present-day investigators can point to is height." Therefore, you should choose (B).

2 2 2 2 2 2 2 2 2

1. Economics _______ the science of choice.
   - (A) are
   - (B) which is
   - (C) is
   - (D) and

2. _______ yak is taken below 11,000 feet, it is likely to become sick.
   - (A) A
   - (B) If a
   - (C) Frequently a
   - (D) Because of a

3. Juggling _______ at least 5,000 years to the early Egyptians.
   - (A) dating back
   - (B) is dating back
   - (C) which dates back
   - (D) dates back

4. _______, Hong Kong acts as a gateway into and out of the Republic of China.
   - (A) Strategically located
   - (B) It is located strategically
   - (C) Where strategically located
   - (D) Because located strategically

5. In 1964, Americans drank an average of 26 gallons of milk _______.
   - (A) each
   - (B) every one
   - (C) singly
   - (D) themselves

6. The summer ice pack appears _______ by about 150 miles since the 1930's.
   - (A) having shrunk
   - (B) to shrink
   - (C) to have shrunk
   - (D) to be shrinking

7. _______ undergraduate programs, American universities also offer graduate and professional courses.
   - (A) Except for
   - (B) Moreover
   - (C) Besides
   - (D) As

8. _______ are carcinogens now appears to be beyond dispute.
   - (A) If asbestos fibers
   - (B) Asbestos fibers
   - (C) While asbestos fibers
   - (D) That asbestos fibers

9. It is _______ Minnesota popular with outdoorsmen.
   - (A) lakes that make it
   - (B) its lakes that make
   - (C) that lakes make it
   - (D) lakes that it makes

10. _______ Thomas E. Selfridge was the first person to be killed in an airplane accident.
    - (A) One of an army team evaluating the Wright Brothers' plane,
    - (B) The Wright Brothers' plane was being examined by an army team,
    - (C) He was one of an army team evaluating the Wright Brothers' plane,
    - (D) Of an army team evaluating the Wright Brothers' plane, one

11. Satchel Paige pitched his last game in the major leagues when he _______.
    - (A) approximately sixty years old
    - (B) was nearly sixty
    - (C) about sixty was
    - (D) had almost sixty years

12. Both slate and marble chips can be melted and spun _______, and then made into a type of glass wool.
    (A) like to cotton candy
    (B) as like cotton candy
    (C) like cotton candy
    (D) cotton candy, alike

13. The traditional goal of science is to discover how things are, not how they ought _______.
    (A) are
    (B) be
    (C) can be
    (D) to be

14. Though the female has undisputed last word over the acceptability of a new nest, it is the male weaver bird who must build it entirely _______.
    (A) on his own
    (B) on himself
    (C) for themselves
    (D) by his own

15. Herbalists recommend the juice of barley plants as a means of slowing the aging process and also _______.
    (A) it to cancer patients recommend
    (B) to cancer patients recommend it
    (C) recommend it cancer patients
    (D) recommend it to cancer patients

GO ON TO THE NEXT PAGE

2 2 2 2 2 2 2 2 2

Part B

<u>Directions:</u> In questions 16-40 each sentence has four words or phrases underlined. The four underlined parts of the sentence are marked (A), (B), (C), and (D). You are to identify the *one* underlined word or phrase that should be corrected or rewritten. Then, on your answer sheet, find the number of the question and blacken the space that corresponds to the letter of the answer you have chosen.

Example I   Sample Answer

The winds on Venus <u>invariable</u> <u>blow</u> <u>in</u>
                   A   B   C
<u>a westerly direction.</u>
     D
Answer (A), the underlined word <u>invariable</u>, would not be accepted in carefully written English; the form <u>invariably</u> should be used because an adverb is needed to modify the verb <u>blow</u>. Therefore, the sentence should read, "The winds on Venus invariably blow in a westerly direction." To answer the problem correctly, you would choose (A).

Example II   Sample Answer

A reversible chemical reaction is <u>one</u> that is
                                       A
capable <u>to go</u> through <u>a series</u> of changes
          B   C
<u>in either direction.</u>
  D
Answer (B), the underlined words <u>to go</u>, would not be accepted in carefully written English; the form <u>of going</u> should be used after <u>capable</u>. Therefore, the sentence should read, "A reversible chemical reaction is one that is capable of going through a series of changes in either direction." To answer the problem correctly, you would choose (B).

As soon as you understand the directions, begin work on the problems.

16. A Battle of Yorktown was the last major battle of the Revolutionary War.
    A   B   C   D

17. Amniocentesis can reveal whether a fetus is suffering from any of a variety of
                  A   B   C
    chromosomal defect.
         D

18. The closer one comes to earth, the more denser the atmosphere becomes.
        A   B   C   D

19. Bluefin tuna can swim too fast that only mako sharks and killer whales are able
                         A   B
    to catch them.
       C   D

20. It is a phenomenon known as temperature inversion what causes the worst smog in
                       A   B   C
    places such as Los Angeles.
           D

21. How the huge Nazca figures were created remains a mysterious.
        A   B   C   D

22. Great Lakes, between the United States and Canada, contain enough water to cover the
        A   B   C
    whole continental United States to a depth of ten feet.
                                    D

23. Sarah Caldwell, one of the world's best-known female conductors, have performed in
                                                        A   B
    public since the age of five.
           C   D

24. At times during the longest twentieth-century eclipse of the moon, the earth's satellite
               A   B
    was appearing reddish.
        C   D

25. The rose is believed to have been the first flower cultivated by man, perhaps
        A   B   C
    because was the first to be doubled.
         D

26. Animals having not color are called albinos.
        A   B   C   D

27. Jimmie Davis was an amateur country music singer, a governor of Louisiana and
                    A   B   C
    wrote songs.
       D

28. Lasers are capable of measuring precisely how far are other planets from the earth.
                        A   B   C   D

29. The amount of sage in the stuffing for the Thanksgiving turkey varies considerably
                                                                  A   B
    according the preferences of the cook's family.
         C   D

30. The site of St. Louis <u>was occupied</u> <u>in</u> <u>prehistoric times</u>, but the present city
                            A   B   C
<u>had been founded</u> in 1764.
       D

31. Scientistis tried <u>to unlocking</u> the genetic code <u>for</u> many years <u>before</u> Watson and Crick
                  A   B   C
<u>finally</u> succeeded.
  D

32. There is <u>concluded</u> evidence that <u>it</u> was in central Mexico <u>that</u> human groups first
    A   B   C   D
selected wild grain and created corn.

33. Crude rubber is <u>an</u> elastic solid with a specific gravity of 0.911 and a refractive index of
              A
1.591, though <u>it</u> composition varies with different latexes <u>as well as</u> with the way it
         B   C
<u>is prepared</u> at the plantation.
      D

34. A recent study showed that <u>some</u> 88% of all working Americans felt it was personally
                            A
important to <u>them</u> to work hard and <u>doing their best</u> <u>on the job</u>.
         B   C   D

35. <u>Much</u> people <u>in</u> the United States <u>are concerned</u> that starch blockers <u>may have</u> unsus-
   A   B   C   D
pected side effects.

36. In state parks, notices <u>constantly</u> <u>remember</u> visitors <u>not to be</u> <u>careless</u> with fire.
                       A   B   C   D

37. Schist <u>is</u> a <u>finely</u> banded crystalline <u>rocky</u> <u>produced by</u> dynamic metamorphism.
       A   B   C   D

38. Children <u>are</u> often very <u>imaginary</u> in <u>their</u> use of color.
        A   B   C D

39. Video games in the early eighties <u>they</u> became one of the <u>most sensational</u>
                            A   B
<u>growth industries</u> <u>ever</u> in the United States.
      C   D

40. After the Coal Age, two types of trees, the sago palm and the gingko, <u>covered</u> the earth
                                                         A
<u>from</u> Greenland to Antarctica, <u>thanks to</u> <u>its</u> method of seed dispersal.
  B   C   D

Section 3: Reading Comprehension and Vocabulary

Time: 45 minutes

This section is designed to measure your ability to understand various kinds of reading materials, as well as your ability to understand the meaning and use of words. There are two types of questions in this section, with special directions for each type.

Part A

<u>Directions:</u> In questions 1-30 each sentence has a word or phrase underlined. Below each sentence are four other words or phrases, marked (A), (B), (C), or (D). You are to choose the *one* phrase that *best keeps the meaning* of the original sentence if it is substituted for the underlined word or phrase. Then, on your answer sheet, find the number of the question and blacken the space that corresponds to the letter you have chosen so that the letter inside the oval cannot be seen.

Example

Sample Answer

Ⓐ Ⓑ ● Ⓓ

The association came close to <u>foundering</u> early in the year.

(A) discovery
(B) recognition
(C) being wrecked
(D) being funded

The best answer is (C) because "The association came close to being wrecked early in the year" is closest in meaning to the original sentence, "The association came close to foundering early in the year." Therefore, you should choose answer (C).

As soon as you understand the directions, begin work on the questions.

1. President Eisenhower's confidence was <u>infectious</u>.
   (A) dangerous
   (B) contagious
   (C) subject to quarantine
   (D) prone to relapse

2. <u>Impending</u> changes in tax legislation should provide a boost to industry.
   (A) recommended
   (B) important
   (C) imminent
   (D) favorable

3. Certain diseases of the brain are suffered by human beings <u>alone</u>.
   (A) on their own.
   (B) singly
   (C) without help
   (D) only

4. Alexander Hamilton is generally <u>regarded</u> as the founder of the modern Republican party.
   (A) derided
   (B) reviled
   (C) concerned
   (D) viewed

5. Really bright comets, which <u>scare</u> some people, occur only a few times each century.
   (A) attract
   (B) frighten
   (C) affect
   (D) excite

6. Scientists have found surprising evidence of a <u>response</u> in plants to physical abuse.
   (A) reaction
   (B) warning signal
   (C) disposition
   (D) trigger mechanism

7. The <u>current</u> trend towards a lowering of interest rates is predicated on an upcoming loosening of the money supply.
   (A) electric
   (B) alternative
   (C) actual
   (D) present

8. Older brothers and sisters sometimes <u>unwittingly</u> reduce the confidence of younger siblings.
   (A) unfairly
   (B) seemingly
   (C) unintentionally
   (D) unpleasantly

9. Spain <u>gave up</u> its control of Guam in 1897.
   (A) relinquished
   (B) upgraded
   (C) strengthened
   (D) transferred

10. An odometer is <u>a device</u> for measuring distance traveled.
    (A) a hypothesis
    (B) an instrument
    (C) a figure
    (D) an engine

11. <u>Excavation</u> for the first atomic power plant at Shippingport, Pennsylvania, started officially in 1954.
    (A) planning
    (B) preparations
    (C) exploration
    (D) digging

12. A number of third-world nations have accumulated <u>staggering</u> foreign debts since the oil crisis of 1973-74.
    (A) overwhelming
    (B) intolerable
    (C) wobbling
    (D) surmountable

13. <u>In common with</u> his predecessors, the Japanese emperor bears a name never given to any other child.
    (A) in association with
    (B) in imitation of
    (C) like
    (D) ignoring

14. Although starfish are of great interest to scientists because of their extraordinary capacity for regenerating limbs, they are less so to skin divers, as they <u>exude</u> a paralyzing poison.
    (A) inflict
    (B) bring up
    (C) inject
    (D) give off

15. <u>Date books</u> make a popular Christmas gift.
    (A) appointment books
    (B) books of facts
    (C) cookbooks
    (D) calendars

16. Evidence exists that hearing problems may be <u>alleviated</u> by changes in diet and exercise habits.
    (A) initiated
    (B) lessened
    (C) cured
    (D) complicated

17. Martin Couney was <u>zealous</u> in his efforts to ensure the survival of premature babies.
    (A) creative
    (B) unusual
    (C) fervent
    (D) pioneering

18. Entertaining <u>on a lavish scale</u> sometimes pays off for businesses.
    (A) slavishly
    (B) extravagantly
    (C) exotically
    (D) snobbishly

19. In the history of the New York Stock Exchange, 1929 must be <u>rated</u> as the most shattering year.
    (A) condemned
    (B) quoted
    (C) ranked
    (D) impugned

20. <u>Mimicry</u> of other, unpalatable species enables many butterflies to protect themselves from potential predators.
    (A) imitation
    (B) camouflage
    (C) techniques
    (D) pursuit

21. Over the past ten years, more and more American men have begun to use <u>make-up</u> products.
    (A) artificial
    (B) diet
    (C) cosmetic
    (D) health

22. Mother Teresa's unceasing efforts <u>on be-half of</u> Calcutta's poor eventually brought her the Nobel Prize.
    (A) in the area of
    (B) directed at
    (C) at the behest of
    (D) for the benefit of

23. Scientists are expected to carry out thor-oughgoing studies to <u>back up</u> claims made concerning new drugs.
    (A) support
    (B) elevate
    (C) investigate
    (D) challenge

24. <u>Views</u> regarding private education appear to be changing.
    (A) intentions
    (B) foresights
    (C) opinions
    (D) projects

25. Nathan Hale <u>doggedly</u> refused to accept English rule of the colonies.
    (A) resolutely
    (B) animatedly
    (C) petulantly
    (D) faithfully

26. Many immigrants, when they first arrived in the United States, were forced to en-gage in <u>menial</u> jobs.
    (A) significant
    (B) lowly
    (C) rough
    (D) remedial

27. German meteorologists have correlated each of six weather phases with the <u>onset</u> of certain medical conditions, ranging from epilepsy to stomach pains.
    (A) worsening
    (B) pain
    (C) diagnosis
    (D) start

28. Only one of the world's ten highest peaks <u>lies</u> outside of the Himalayas.
    (A) rises up
    (B) is located
    (C) originates
    (D) is discernible

29. When new math was introduced into schools, many parents were <u>perplexed</u> by the approach it involved.
    (A) puzzled
    (B) shocked
    (C) frightened
    (D) annoyed

30. Throughout her career, Mary Baker Eddy <u>shrewdly</u> maintained tight control over the affairs of the Church of Christ-Scien-tist.
    (A) stubbornly
    (B) tactfully
    (C) astutely
    (D) ruefully

GO ON TO THE NEXT PAGE

Part B

Directions: The rest of this section is based on a variety of reading material (single sentences, paragraphs, and the like) followed by questions about the meaning of the material. For questions 31-60, you are to choose the *one* best answer, (A), (B), (C), or (D), to each question. Then, on your answer sheet, find the number of the question and blacken the space that corresponds to the letter of the answer you have chosen.

Answer all questions following a passage on the basis of what is *stated* or *implied* in that passage.

Read the following passage.

The university library's Self-Teaching Center was inaugurated at the beginning of this fall quarter. The center is a multi-media facility designed to individualize learning and allow students to work at their own pace. Students interested in self-instruction should visit the STC counter in the main wing of the library. A brochure is available there which describes the types of non-book instructional materials contained in the center as well as the subject matter they cover.

Example I

Sample Answer
(A) (B) ● (D)

What is the purpose of this announcement?

(A) To invite students to the inauguration of the STC.
(B) To encourage students to read books at the university library.
(C) To encourage students to investigate the opportunities available at the STC.
(D) To guide students away from traditional classroom instruction.

The passage explains what the STC is and how students can obtain information about the opportunities available there. Therefore, you should choose answer (C).

Example II

Sample Answer
● (B) (C) (D)

All of the following are true about the STC *except*

(A) It provides the student with many types of self-teaching books.
(B) It is less than a year old.
(B) It is located on the university campus.
(D) It allows different students to work at different speeds.

The passage says that the brochure "describes the types of non-book instructional materials contained in the center." Therefore, you should choose answer (A).

Questions 31-35

One of the most common large mammals in the western part of the United States is the mule deer, which occupies a variety of habitats, ranging from dense coastal forests to arid desert lowlands. Probably as a result of this variety, there have been differing reports as to some aspects of the mule deer's social behavior, some observers claiming that dominant males gather harems around them while others specifically refute this. Comparisons with the social behavior of other ungulates suggests that the formation of groups is more likely to occur where the habitat is fairly open, as with elk, and less likely in densely vegetated areas, as is the case with moose.

31. What is the main topic of this passage?
    (A) the frequency of large mammals in the western United States
    (B) differences in social behavior among mule deer, elk, and moose
    (C) the variations in the habitats of mule deer
    (D) the effect of habitat on the social behavior of mule deer

32. The author suggests that the observers referred to
    (A) produced reports that differed from what they actually saw.
    (B) claimed to be dominant males.
    (C) disagreed because the conditions they observed differed.
    (D) compared mule deer behavior with that of other ungulates.

33. Which of the following can be inferred from the passage?
    (A) Most mule deer live in arid deserts.
    (B) Mule deer are ungulates.
    (C) Mule deer are the largest mammals in the western United States.
    (D) Mule deer in desert habitats show inconsistent social behavior.

34. Some aspects of the social behavior of elks appear to resemble that of
    (A) mule deer in relatively treeless habitats.
    (B) mule deer in forest habitats.
    (C) dominant male mule deer.
    (D) moose in desert habitats.

35. The idea that some mule deer behavior varies according to where they live is put forward by the author as
    (A) a proven fact.
    (B) a theory he is skeptical about.
    (C) a discredited view.
    (D) a theory he supports.

Questions 36-43

The place which is now Annapolis, the capital of Maryland, was first settled by ten Puritan families from Virginia in 1649, and was given the name of the Town of Greenbury. It received its present name in 1695, having been made capital of the crown colony of Maryland a year previously, was chartered by Queen Anne in 1708, and incorporated as a city in 1796. For a period of a little less than nine months, from November 26, 1783, it was made the temporary capital of the nation and it was there, on January 14, 1784, that the peace treaty with England was signed, ending the Revolutionary War. The city, which retains its authentic colonial character, is probably best known today as the home of the United States Naval Academy. Much of its present layout dates from 1696, its radiating streets and interconnecting circles being notably similar to the plans by Sir Christopher Wren and John Evelyn for the rebuilding of London after the Great Fire of 1666.

36. The capital of Maryland has been located at its present site since
    (A) 1649
    (B) 1694
    (C) 1695
    (D) 1796

37. Which of the following can be inferred from the passage?
    (A) There were Puritan settlements in Virginia in the first half of the 17th century.
    (B) Annapolis was the largest city in Maryland in 1796.
    (C) Annapolis has formally been a city for about 330 years.
    (D) Annapolis was the nation's first capital in the eighteenth century.

38. When was the nation's capital moved from Annapolis?
    (A) in late 1783
    (B) on January 14, 1784
    (C) in the second half of 1784
    (D) in 1791

39. Where would this paragraph most probably appear?
    (A) in a tourist brochure
    (B) in a book about military academies
    (C) in a history of Puritanism
    (D) in an account of the Revolutionary War

40. Which of the following is noted as a similarity between Annapolis and the plans for rebuilding London?
    (A) Many of the streets in the two cities bear the same names.
    (B) Both cities were originally built in the 17th century.
    (C) The cities' basic street plans are similar.
    (D) The two cities were planned by Wren and Evelyn.

41. According to the passage, all of the following statements about Annapolis are false except
    - (A) It was the site of the final battle of the Revolutionary War.
    - (B) It was the tenth settlement established in Virginia.
    - (C) Queen Anne made an expedition there in 1708.
    - (D) It remained the capital of the nation after the Revolutionary War was formally ended.

42. Today, Annapolis is primarily known as
    - (A) a city with an authentic colonial character and good street planning.
    - (B) the location of one of America's national military academies.
    - (C) the previous capital of the nation.
    - (D) the old Town of Greenbury.

43. It may be inferred from the passage that
    - (A) the Town of Greenbury and Annapolis are the only names the site described has had since 1649.
    - (B) Annapolis was the capital of Maryland before Maryland became a state.
    - (C) Annapolis was destroyed by fire in 1696.
    - (D) Annapolis was the capital of the nation for most of the Revolutionary War period.

GO ON TO THE NEXT PAGE

Questions 44-48

One of the unknown factors with tax cuts is what consumers will do with the extra income thereby made available to them. Such cuts are usually made with the aim of stimulating a flagging economy, but the effects on growth tend to be negligible if consumers, instead of going on a spending spree buying durable goods such as home appliances, decide either to pay off their accumulated debts or hold on to the extra cash in the form of savings. And the fact is that usually when a tax cut is implemented, company investment tends to be running at a low ebb, and only the consumer has the wherewithal to provide a fresh impetus.

44. According to the passage, tax cuts automatically provide more money for
    (A) consumers.
    (B) companies.
    (C) banks and creditors.
    (D) home-appliance manufacturers.

45. According to the passage, the effects of a tax cut are
    (A) stimulating.
    (B) negligible.
    (C) unpredictable.
    (D) expensive.

46. It may be inferred from the passage that a government which reduces taxes usually wants consumers to
    (A) buy things like cars and refrigerators.
    (B) save their extra money.
    (C) pay off their debts.
    (D) invest their extra cash in things like gold.

47. According to the passage, under what circumstances are tax cuts generally introduced?
    (A) when consumers are on a spending spree
    (B) when company investment is providing a fresh impetus
    (C) when the economy needs a boost
    (D) when negligible growth is sought

48. The passage implies that
    (A) consumer spending may help the level of company investment.
    (B) when there is a tax cut, consumers do not know whether they will have extra income.
    (C) tax cuts are always resorted to if economic growth falls below a certain point.
    (D) if consumers are neglected they go on shopping sprees.

Questions 49-53

Desertification, the loss of the soil's biological productivity, occurs naturally to a limited extent. The pace at which the process has spread recently, however, is largely man's own doing. This fact was highlighted by the great Sahel drought of 1968-73. The worst effects of this drought were caused by nomadic peoples who had earlier been forced by national governments to adopt agricultural and grazing practices that were not in accord with their traditions. In common with those of other nomads around the world, such traditions involved never staying in one place so long as to exhaust the earth that provided them with sustenance. When these people were not allowed to follow this tradition, the process of desertification moved ahead quickly.

49. Which of the following can be said of desertification?
    (A) It is a wholly natural phenomenon.
    (B) The Sahel drought was the first example of it.
    (C) It does not occur naturally.
    (D) Man has worsened this natural process.

50. Where does the author appear to ultimately lay the blame for the effects of the Sahel drought?
    (A) on nomads around the world
    (B) on someone in authority over the Sahel nomads
    (C) on natural causes
    (D) on the traditions of the Sahel nomads

51. According to the passage, what can be said about the Sahel drought?
    (A) It lasted for a decade.
    (B) It emphasized the effects of changing nomadic traditions.
    (C) It spread to other parts of the world.
    (D) It forced the adoption of untraditional farming practices.

52. Which of the following may be inferred about the author of the passage?
    (A) He disapproves of the nomads' traditional attitude to the soil.
    (B) He approves of the recent pace of desertification.
    (C) He approves of the nomads' new grazing practices.
    (D) He approves of the nomads' traditional attitude to the soil.

53. Nomads in other parts of the world and the Sahel nomads
    (A) share similar customs.
    (B) share the same desert.
    (C) suffered particularly in the 1968-73 period.
    (D) adopted new grazing practices before 1968.

Questions 54-58

A long-range health study in Framingham, Massachusetts, which began in 1948 and continues to this day, involves checking the survivors among the same 5,200 men and women every two years and carefully determining the causes of any deaths occurring in the group. A rather surprising conclusion that emerged in 1980 was that the lightest men had the shortest life expectancy, while the only others for whom weight seemed to have a significant negative effect on life expectancy were those who weighed more than 25% above the national average. Much the same was true of women, with those in the lightest and heaviest groups dying earliest. These results certainly cast considerable doubts on the validity of the "Ideal Weights" tables in use since the forties which recommend weight to height ratios well below the national average. Indeed, they suggest that if any such ideal exists, it is slightly above the average, whatever fashion may dictate.

54. Which of the following would be the most suitable title for the passage?
    (A) The Framingham Health Study
    (B) 5,200 Men and Women Can't Be Wrong
    (C) Fashion Is Wrong about Weight
    (D) Weight and Life Expectancy: Unexpected Evidence

55. The Framingham study
    (A) still examines 5,200 men and women every two years.
    (B) was completed in 1980.
    (C) has been going for more than 30 years.
    (D) focused exclusively on life-expectancy of the heaviest and lightest groups.

56. Which of the following can be inferred from the passage?
    (A) The study and the use of "Ideal Weights" tables began in the same decade.
    (B) More deaths have occurred in recent two-year periods than before.
    (C) The study was designed to invalidate the "Ideal Weights" tables.
    (D) The same number of men and women in the study have died.

57. According to the study, men and women in the medium weight ranges
    (A) are in a majority.
    (B) have weight to height ratios below the national average.
    (C) have the best life expectancy.
    (D) have the shortest life expectancy.

58. Which of the following does the author of the passage suggest?
    (A) Most people should put on more weight.
    (B) The "Ideal Weights" tables may not be very accurate.
    (C) Most people should lose weight.
    (D) The Framingham study is of doubtful validity.

Questions 59-60. For each of these questions, choose the answer that is _closest in meaning_ to the original sentence. Note that several of the choices may be factually correct, but you should choose the one that is the _closest restatement of the given sentence_.

59. The most important contemporary problems in modern medicine are philosophical and ethical rather than scientific or technical.
    (A) Scientific problems are now being solved in all areas of medicine.
    (B) Philosophy and ethics account for greater problems in medicine now than do science and technology.
    (C) Contemporary problems in medicine are more of the scientific type than the philosophical.
    (D) The scientific and technical problems any doctor meets with today are less important than his philosophy or ethics.

60. To many, the environmental crisis goes far beyond the inconveniences and nuisances of modern life; it goes to the most fundamental levels of concern about the future of our species on this planet.
    (A) Many people are extremely worried about environmental problems, especially about the water levels on this planet.
    (B) Although there is a fundamental concern about future generations, today's environmental inconveniences and nuisances affect many in a much more direct way.
    (C) Planetary environmental concerns are very important today, not only because they are inconvenient and a nuisance.
    (D) Although people are worried about immediate environmental problems, even more important is what will happen to future generations.

Answer Key/
Practice Test IV

Section 1: Listening Comprehension

Part A

1. A
2. C
3. B
4. A
5. D
6. D
7. B
8. C
9. B
10. A
11. D
12. B
13. B
14. C
15. C
16. A
17. D
18. A
19. D
20. B

Part B

21. C
22. D
23. B
24. A
25. A
26. C
27. B
28. B
29. D
30. B
31. A
32. C
33. D
34. A
35. C

Part C

36. C
37. B
38. C
39. A
40. D
41. B
42. A
43. B
44. C
45. A
46. C
47. B
48. D
49. D
50. A

Section 2: Structure and Written Expression

Part A

The explanations of why given answers are wrong have been kept as brief as possible. Indications of how particular incorrect answers might be made correct are provided as a stimulus to thinking about English sentence structure. The references marked FE are to the Focused Exercises which may be of help in further explaining why particular answers are correct or incorrect and in offering more practice.

1. A Subject-verb agreement; "economics" is singular (FE-16)
   B Would create a dependent clause, leaving main clause without predicate (FE-10)
   C Correct (FE-6)
   D Creates a subject without predicate

2. A Creates two unacceptably linked main clauses
   B Correct (FE-10)
   C See 2-A
   D "Because of" must be followed by a noun, not a clause

3. A Would create a dependent participial phrase with comma after "juggling," with no main clause completion (FE-12)
   B Stative verb as used here cannot be used with progressive form
   C Would create dependent clause (FE-10); see 3-A
   D Correct (FE-6)

4. A Correct (FE-12)
   B Would create two main clauses, inappropriately linked
   C Structurally possible, but "Hong Kong" cannot be located in different places
   D "because" requires clause with subject + main verb (FE-10)

5. A Correct
   B "every" must precede noun
   C Meaningless
   D Emphatic "themselves" would require comparison with something else

6. A Impossible "-ing" form complementation after "appears"
   B Structurally possible after "appears," but not with "since"
   C Correct
   D See 6-B

7. A Would mean that "undergraduate" programs are graduate courses
   B "moreover" is an adverb; following noun requires preposition
   C Correct
   D See 7-A

8. A Creates dependent conditional clause, leaving following main clause without subject
   B Creates main clause; subsequent clause would have no subject
   C Dependent adverbial clause; see 8-A
   D Correct (FE-2)

9. A "it" repeats object "Minnesota" (FE-3)
   B Correct (FE-4)
   C See 9-A
   D "it" repeats initial anticipatory "it" (FE-3)

10. A Correct (FE-9)
    B Creates two inappropriately linked main clauses
    C See 10-B
    D Would need to be preceded by a noun

11. A Missing main verb (FE-6, 10)
    B Correct
    C Unnecessary inversion (FE-8)
    D Wrong verb ("have"); missing "old"

12. A "to" cannot follow "like" (FE-15, 25)
    B "as" and "like" as conjunctions of comparison cannot be used together
    C Correct
    D "alike" cannot be used in this way

13. A Incorrect complementation of "ought"
    B "ought" needs "to"
    C One modal cannot immediately complement another
    D Correct

14. A Correct
    B Structurally possible, but does not make sense
    C Reflexive should not be plural
    D Wrong preposition

15. A Verb in wrong position (FE-13)
    B Prepositional phrase in wrong position (FE-13)
    C "to" missing
    D Correct

Part B

In every case the answer is given first. Where there is an FE reference, this indicates the number of the Focused Exercise which may offer useful further practice on the point in question. Where words in quotation marks follow the letter of the correct answer, these show what would be needed for the sentence to be correct. This usually occurs in cases where none of the Focused Exercises is applicable.

16. A (FE-21)
17. D (FE-36)
18. C (FE-24)
19. A (FE-25)
20. B (FE-20)
21. D (FE-22)
22. A (FE-37)
23. B (FE-16)
24. C ("appeared")
25. D ("because it was") (FE-10)
26. B ("without")
27. D (FE-14, 33)
28. C (FE-13, 34)

29. C (FE-28)
30. D (FE-29)
31. A ("to unlock") (FE-32)
32. B (FE-39)
33. B (FE-19)
34. C (FE-14, 33)
35. A (FE-17)
36. B (FE-38)
37. C (FE-22)
38. B (FE-39)
39. A (FE-3, 18)
40. D (FE-17)

Section 3: Reading Comprehension and Vocabulary

Part A

1. B	11. D	21. C
2. C	12. A	22. D
3. D	13. C	23. A
4. D	14. D	24. C
5. B	15. A	25. A
6. A	16. B	26. B
7. D	17. C	27. D
8. C	18. B	28. B
9. A	19. C	29. A
10. B	20. A	30. C

Part B

31. D	41. D	51. B
32. C	42. B	52. D
33. B	43. B	53. A
34. A	44. A	54. D
35. D	45. C	55. C
36. B	46. A	56. A
37. A	47. C	57. C
38. C	48. A	58. B
39. A	49. D	59. B
40. C	50. B	60. D

Strategies: A Reminder**

Section 1: Listening Comprehension

STRATEGY for Part A: look at all the answer choices before you hear the sentence.
STRATEGY for Part B: aim for a more general understanding than in Part A but more specific than Part C.
STRATEGY for Part C: aim for a general understanding of what you hear.

Section 2: Structure and Written Expression

GENERAL STRATEGY: work at a steady pace and read each possible answer very carefully.
STRATEGY for Part A: read carefully and choose the one correct sentence completion.
STRATEGY for Part B: choose the one incorrect part.

Section 3: Reading Comprehension and Vocabulary

GENERAL STRATEGY: do Part A quickly to allow yourself more time for Part B.
STRATEGY for Part A: work quickly; if you do not know the meaning, guess and continue on to the next item.
STRATEGY for Part B: think about the items and recheck them against the information given.

**See the Preview to the Practice Tests (pp. 42-45) for more specific strategies.

PRACTICE TEST V

Section 1: Listening Comprehension

Time: 40 minutes

You will need to play the tape for all the questions in Section 1. (The tapescripts are printed on pages 253-258. This material is designated by the symbol  .)

In this section of the test, you will have an opportunity to demonstrate your ability to understand spoken English. There are three parts to this section, with special directions for each part.

Part A

<u>Directions:</u> For each question in Part A, you will hear a short statement. The statements will be spoken just one time. They will not be written out for you, and you must listen carefully to understand what the speaker says.

After you hear a statement, read the four sentences in your test book, marked (A), (B), (C), and (D), and decide which *one* is closest in meaning to the statement you heard. Then, on your answer sheet, find the number of the question and blacken the space that corresponds to the letter of the answer you have chosen so that the letter inside the oval cannot be seen.

Example I

Sample Answer
(A) (B) (C) ●

You will hear:

You will read: (A) They arrived at the station thirty minutes late.

(B) They were out of eggs so they had cereal instead.

(C) They passed the time by talking about destiny.

(D) They drove beyond the place they were headed for.

Sentence (D), "They drove beyond the place they were headed for," means most nearly the same as the statement "They missed the exit and ended up thirty miles past their destination." Therefore, you should choose answer (D).

Example II

Sample Answer
(A) (B) ● (D)

You will hear:

You will read: (A) They ask that no one smoke in their home.

(B) They watched the coverage of the fire on television.

(C) They were unhappy to see their home burn.

(D) They saw a depressing show about the dangers of cigarettes.

Sentence (C), "They were unhappy to see their home burn," is closest in meaning to the sentence "The family sadly watched as their home went up in smoke." Therefore, you should choose answer (C).

GO ON TO THE NEXT PAGE

1. (A) I couldn't make the early train.
   (B) I couldn't go riding because of the rain.
   (C) I got to the station on time.
   (D) I took the wrong road to the station.

2. (A) It's much easier to park near the university now.
   (B) The university final exams make sense now.
   (C) The university has recently built a fine new park.
   (D) Parking is difficult in the university area.

3. (A) Bill offered to locate the will.
   (B) They cannot find Bill's will.
   (C) Bill will not accept their offer.
   (D) Bill was made an officer unwillingly.

4. (A) Buy that tie with the money left over.
   (B) Most of the fans were overpriced.
   (C) Few people stayed for the end of the game.
   (D) The game went into overtime.

5. (A) This weather makes me nauseous.
   (B) I wish the weather would improve.
   (C) I've already had enough to eat.
   (D) I had dinner at the wedding.

6. (A) She shouldn't take so many courses.
   (B) Her grades have really dropped.
   (C) She really lies about every subject.
   (D) She ought to talk about something else.

7. (A) Jogging provides beneficial exercise.
   (B) The jockey agreed to ride.
   (C) Those jogging clothes fit perfectly.
   (D) The job is not within walking distance.

8. (A) Afterwards, he went to several stores.
   (B) The roof needed repairing after the bad weather.
   (C) The tree that was replaced would not take root.
   (D) We replaced our storm windows.

9. (A) Forecasts ought to be done yearly.
   (B) Industrial predictions are off this year.
   (C) Car sales will probably be low this year.
   (D) Economic conditions will make the trip difficult.

10. (A) They must get the boss this time.
    (B) We're wasting our time here.
    (C) They lost the cotton I gave them.
    (D) They probably can't find this place.

11. (A) Did you understand what I said, Fred?
    (B) Did you catch what Fred said?
    (C) Is this where you put it, Fred?
    (D) Is that Fred at the door?

12. (A) Start reviewing for your final exam immediately.
    (B) The final exam isn't until tomorrow evening.
    (C) There will be time to study after finals.
    (D) Exam grades will be posted after the term begins.

13. (A) Curries take a long time to cook.
    (B) Slow down, we have plenty of time.
    (C) Hurry, someone has taken your time card.
    (D) There's a huge rush to be on time.

14. (A) Cathy left that board.
    (B) I lived abroad for a year.
    (C) Neither of us is leaving.
    (D) I've never lived out of the country.

15. (A) Report your income to the tax department.
    (B) You would benefit from professional tax assistance.
    (C) Make your tax deductions as soon as possible.
    (D) You should help your relations with their taxes.

16. (A) The first line explains the rules of the contest.
    (B) There will be a test at the beginning of class.
    (C) The race will start when the competitors are in position.
    (D) The participants will contest the starting time.

17. (A) The election will be on Thursday.
    (B) The candidates will meet late Thursday.
    (C) We need glasses for Thursday's meeting.
    (D) He hurt his knees last Thursday.

18. (A) Bombs are scarce.
    (B) The physicians discussed his resume.
    (C) The discussion was interrupted by a bomb threat.
    (D) The physicists were designing a new bomb.

19. (A) I didn't enjoy going to the performance alone.
    (B) The soloist performed brilliantly.
    (C) One part of the orchestra audition was a solo performance.
    (D) The soloist made the concert unsatisfactory.

20. (A) You shouldn't have gone through the light.
    (B) Have the light in the waiting room changed.
    (C) You shouldn't gain any weight.
    (D) You'll have to wait to get change.

Part B

<u>Directions:</u> In Part B you will hear short conversations between two speakers. At the end of each conversation, a third voice will ask a question about what was said. The question will be spoken just one time. After you hear a conversation and the question about it, read the four possible answers in your test book and decide which *one* is the best answer to the question you heard. Then, on your answer sheet, find the number of the question and blacken the space that corresponds to the letter of the answer you have chosen.

Example

<u>Sample Answer</u>
Ⓐ ● Ⓒ Ⓓ

You will hear:
You will read: (A) A stereo system.
(B) An automobile.
(C) A traffic light.
(D) A medical problem.

From the conversation you know that the people are discussing problems that one has with an automobile. The best answer, then, is (B), "An automobile." Therefore, you should choose answer (B).

21. (A) Eight years.
    (B) Six years.
    (C) Four years.
    (D) Two years.

22. (A) Yes, because she wants to be help-ful.
    (B) Yes, because she has recently had her house redecorated.
    (C) No, because part of the house is be-ing fixed up.
    (D) No, because she's having another meeting there right now.

23. (A) It was thoughtfully prepared.
    (B) The course had covered all the test questions.
    (C) It was too long.
    (D) It was unfair.

24. (A) Some time next week.
    (B) At the movie.
    (C) When the woman gets home.
    (D) Later this evening.

25. (A) A telephone number.
    (B) Information about a specific work of art.
    (C) A company which paints homes.
    (D) The nearest telephone.

26. (A) She wants the man to take more basic courses.
    (B) She wants special permission to take the physics course.
    (C) She wants to be excused from taking the physics course.
    (D) She wants to convince the man to leave class early just one time.

27. (A) One of the actors has been delayed.
    (B) There is a robbery in progress.
    (C) Someone needs to go out for more jam.
    (D) One of the performers has been caught by the police.

28. (A) She's a nurse.
    (B) She's a caterer.
    (C) She's a high school teacher.
    (D) She's a bank teller.

29. (A) The accounts have to be up-to-date before Friday.
    (B) The company was closed for the last two weeks.
    (C) The woman will have half of Friday off.
    (D) The woman will miss her sister's wedding.

30. (A) Buying bicycles.
    (B) Trading in cars.
    (C) High cost of gasoline.
    (D) What service station to go to.

31. (A) Returning home from Texas.
    (B) Resting at home.
    (C) Visiting relatives in Texas.
    (D) Visiting relatives nearby.

32. (A) In a restaurant.
    (B) In an employment agency.
    (C) In a newspaper office.
    (D) In a police station.

33. (A) Angry.
    (B) Apologetic.
    (C) Speechless.
    (D) Sad.

34. (A) The long coastlines.
    (B) The inhospitable interior.
    (C) The sandy beaches.
    (D) The high standard of living in the interior.

35. (A) She's frightened of traveling.
    (B) She would like to import tea from the East.
    (C) She's a successful pottery designer.
    (D) She thinks she might be better at a different type of job.

Part C

Directions: In this part of the test, you will hear several short talks and conversations. After each talk or conversation, you will be asked some questions. The talks and questions will be spoken just one time. They will not be written out for you, so you will have to listen carefully to understand what the speaker says.

After you hear a question, read the four possible answers in your test book and decide which _one_ is the best answer to the question you heard. Then, on your answer sheet, find the number of the question and blacken the space that corresponds to the letter of the answer you have chosen.

Sample Answer
Ⓐ Ⓑ Ⓒ ●

Listen to this sample talk.
You will hear:
Now look at the following example.
You will hear:
You will read: (A) Historical Landmarks.
(B) John D. Spreckels.
(C) The Hotel del Coronado.
(D) The Glorietta Bay Inn.

The best answer to the question "What is this talk about?" is (D), "Glorietta Bay Inn." Therefore, you should choose answer (D).

Sample Answer
Ⓐ ● Ⓒ Ⓓ

Now look at the next example.
You will hear:
You will read: (A) Behind the meeting rooms.
(B) In the Mansion and the two additional wings.
(C) Only in the old Spreckels Mansion.
(D) Only in the wings.

The best answer to the question "Where are the guest rooms located in this hotel?" is (B), "In the Mansion and the two additional wings." Therefore, you should choose answer (B).

178 Practice Test V

36. (A) A letter of recommendation.
    (B) Information about jobs.
    (C) Permission to take two management courses.
    (D) Suggestions on how to improve her grades.

37. (A) He was evasive.
    (B) He was cooperative.
    (C) He was honest.
    (D) He was unfriendly.

38. (A) She was a natural leader.
    (B) She recognized her own limitations.
    (C) She looked for ways to practice what she'd learned in class.
    (D) She got very good grades on tests.

39. (A) By completing their degree in business administration.
    (B) By taking a minimum of two management courses.
    (C) By seeking outside experience offered through the department.
    (D) By observing their professors.

40. (A) Excellent grades in college.
    (B) Initiative in a group situation.
    (C) Proven leadership ability.
    (D) Acceptance of criticism.

41. (A) Try to be more cooperative when working with others.
    (B) Take another course from Professor Burnham.
    (C) Work in the Business Administration Department for another semester.
    (D) Try to persuade Professor Burnham to reconsider her request.

42. (A) The armadillo's survival tactics.
    (B) Contrasting friends and enemies of the armadillo.
    (C) The armadillo as the farmer's friend.
    (D) Correcting popular assumptions about the armadillo.

43. (A) It cannot be bitten through by carnivores.
    (B) It is not sought after by collectors of animal skins.
    (C) It protects the animal from thorny, rough plants.
    (D) The animal can hide its head and limbs inside the armor.

44. (A) 55 million years.
    (B) Between 50 and 55 thousand years.
    (C) 55 centuries.
    (D) Up to 55 years.

45. (A) It preys on wild dogs.
    (B) Its meat is edible and delicious.
    (C) It protects certain insects.
    (D) Its food is thorny bushes.

46. (A) The public through contributions.
    (B) A local school of architecture.
    (C) The radio station which broadcast it.
    (D) A group of professional architects.

47. (A) A professional test for architects.
    (B) A professional organization for architects.
    (C) Application procedures for schools of architecture.
    (D) Qualifications needed to receive an architect's license.

1 1 1 1 1 1 1 1 1

48. (A) Anyone not registering before the deadline.
    (B) Members of the Kansas State Board of Examiners.
    (C) Students who have received their M.A. in architecture.
    (D) Applicants not having a professional degree in architecture.

49. (A) Within the next ten days.
    (B) Any time before April 10.
    (C) With an extension, up until May 24.
    (D) Immediately after finishing the qualifying test.

50. (A) By calling the telephone number given.
    (B) By visiting the Kansas State Board of Education.
    (C) By asking at an accredited school of architecture.
    (D) By taking the qualifying test.

2 2 2 2 2 2 2 2 2

Section 2: Structure and Written Expression

Time: 25 minutes

This section is designed to measure your ability to recognize language that is appropriate for standard written English. There are two types of questions in this section, with special directions for each type.

Part A

Directions: Questions 1-15 are incomplete sentences. Four words or phrases, marked (A), (B), (C), and (D), are given beneath each sentence. You are to choose the *one* word or phrase that best completes the sentence. Then, on your answer sheet, find the number of the question and blacken the space that corresponds to the letter of the answer you have chosen so that the letter inside the oval cannot be seen.

Example I   Sample Answer
                                      (A) (B) (C) ●

_______ Rhode Island is much smaller than Texas, it has the same number of senators.

(A) If
(B) Because
(C) Unless
(D) Although

In English, the sentence should read, "Although Rhode Island is much smaller than Texas, it has the same number of senators." Therefore, you should choose (D).

Example II   Sample Answer
                                      ● (B) (C) (D)

The dominant male in a group of Alaskan Dall's sheep uses up far more energy _______ other males in the group.

(A) than do any
(B) any than do
(C) than any do
(D) do than any

In English, the sentence should read, "The dominant male in a group of Alaskan Dall's sheep uses up far more energy than do any other males in the group." Therefore, you should choose (A).

As soon as you understand the directions, begin work on the problems.

2　2　2　2　2　2　2　2　2

1. The planet Pluto _______ only this century.
   - (A) was discovered
   - (B) discovered
   - (C) has discovered
   - (D) it was discovered

2. _______ the windchill factor which gives the best idea of how a person will feel outside on a cold day.
   - (A) Is
   - (B) It is
   - (C) There is
   - (D) Because

3. John Glenn was not the first United States astronaut to orbit the earth _______ certainly became the most famous.
   - (A) and
   - (B) however
   - (C) and he
   - (D) but he

4. _______, Renaldo Nehemiah decided to take up professional football in 1982.
   - (A) Nevertheless he was unbeatable as a hurdler
   - (B) As a hurdler he was virtually unbeatable
   - (C) Virtually unbeatable as a hurdler
   - (D) He was virtually unbeatable as a hurdler

5. Snowflakes _______ an infinite variety of shapes.
   - (A) that exhibit
   - (B) in exhibiting
   - (C) exhibiting
   - (D) exhibit

6. Only one modern bird, _______, has claws on its wings as did prehistoric birds.
   - (A) the South American hoatzin it is
   - (B) which the South American hoatzin
   - (C) the South American hoatzin
   - (D) it is the South American hoatzin

7. _______ other fruits, cranberries are judged for quality by their bounce.
   - (A) Unlike the most
   - (B) Unlike most
   - (C) They are unlike most
   - (D) The most unlikely

8. Hawaii's state capitol building in Honolulu is unique in _______ no cupola.
   - (A) having
   - (B) it has
   - (C) not having
   - (D) that having

9. _______ former radio-broadcaster and actor, Ronald Reagan is an excellent speaker.
   - (A) Like
   - (B) As
   - (C) As a
   - (D) That a

10. Precautions are taken _______ a hurricane threatens to strike the coast of the United States.
    - (A) whenever
    - (B) however
    - (C) always
    - (D) whether

GO ON TO THE NEXT PAGE ▶

11. Modern design features have enabled the area of the "sweet spot" on tennis racquets ________ almost 300 percent.
    (A) increasing
    (B) increased
    (C) to increase
    (D) to be increased

12. ________ charcoal and sulphur, potassium nitrate forms an explosive mixture.
    (A) The combination of
    (B) Combining
    (C) To combine
    (D) When combined with

13. On no account ________ be removed from the library.
    (A) reference books may
    (B) may reference books
    (C) reference books cannot
    (D) reference books

14. ________ of decorating houses in eastern Kentucky in the 1930's, that of papering interior walls with catalogues and magazines was probably the most popular.
    (A) All the means
    (B) Of all the means
    (C) Means of all
    (D) The means

15. Bifocal glasses are among the inventions ________ Benjamin Franklin.
    (A) have been attributed to
    (B) which attributed to
    (C) attributed to
    (D) were attributed to

2 2 2 2 2 2 2 2 2

Part B

Directions: In questions 16-40 each sentence has four words or phrases underlined. The four underlined parts of the sentence are marked (A), (B), (C), and (D). You are to identify the _one_ underlined word or phrase that should be corrected or rewritten. Then, on your answer sheet, find the number of the question and blacken the space that corresponds to the letter of the answer you have chosen.

Example I

Sample Answer
Ⓐ ● Ⓒ Ⓓ

Stress, one of the characteristic features of (A) modern urban living, cause emotional (B) problems that were much less common (C) in earlier times. (D)

Answer (B), the underlined word cause, would not be accepted in carefully written English; the form causes should be used because stress is singular. Therefore, the sentence should read, "Stress, one of the characteristic features of modern urban living, causes emotional problems that were much less familiar in earlier times." To answer the problem correctly, you should choose (B).

Example II

Sample Answer
Ⓐ Ⓑ ● Ⓓ

With specialization having come to take on (A) supreme importance, it is highly improbably (B) (C) that any inventor today will manage to emulate the versatility of Benjamin Frank- (D) lin or Thomas Edison.

Answer (C), the underlined word improbably, would not be accepted in carefully written English; the form improbable should be used because an adjective is needed after a linking verb. Therefore, the sentence should read, "With specialization having come to take on supreme importance, it is highly improbable that any inventor today will manage to emulate the versatility of Benjamin Franklin or Thomas Edison." To answer the problem correctly, you should choose (C).

As soon as you understand the directions, begin work on the problems.

16. <u>Much</u> more dates <u>are grown</u> in the Californian desert, <u>not far from</u> Palm Springs, than
   A   B   C
most people <u>would believe</u>.
          D

17. Tristan da Cunha, in <u>the South Atlantic</u>, <u>is renowned</u> <u>as</u> one of the loneliest <u>island</u> in
                A   B   C   D
the world.

18. The <u>historic</u> Cathedral of Saint Louis, <u>which</u> <u>it</u> is located on the banks of the Missis-
     A   B   C
sippi in New Orleans, is the <u>oldest</u> in the United States.
                        D

19. The First World War, <u>which</u> <u>broke out</u> <u>on 1914</u>, was the first European war <u>for</u> sixty
                A   B   C   D
years.

20. Businessmen will remain hesitant to <u>lend</u> money from banks for investing <u>in</u> <u>their</u> com-
                                   A   B   C
panies while interest rates <u>stay</u> at high levels.
                            D

21. The incidence <u>of</u> poliomyelitis <u>has greatly reduced</u> <u>by</u> the introduction of <u>the</u> Salk vac-
             A   B   C   D
cine.

22. A <u>mighty</u> and <u>powerful</u> presidency characterizes American political life, but Congress
                      A
also <u>plays</u> <u>a</u> vital <u>role</u>.
  B   C   D

23. One of the key <u>factors</u> in <u>improving</u> golf scores <u>are</u> <u>concentration</u>.
               A   B   C   D

24. The "Sun-Belt" appears to <u>be growing</u> away <u>from</u> the Eastern states socially,
                           A   B
<u>economically</u>, attitudinally, and <u>in politics</u>.
    C   D

25. Today <u>it</u> is almost impossible <u>imagining</u> the world <u>as</u> it was before the invention of
       A   B   C
<u>the automobile</u>.
      D

26. East Liverpool, Ohio <u>is located</u> <u>on the banks</u> of the <u>Ohio River</u> in the foothills of
                    A   B   C
<u>Appalachian Mountains</u>.
         D

27. The imposition nationwide of the <u>fifty-five-miles an hour</u> speed limit <u>has reduced</u> the
    A   B   C   D
number of accidents.

28. It has been <u>announced</u> that the Joint Chiefs of Staff <u>will meet</u> <u>the next week</u>.

<u>A</u>   B   C   D

29. Babe Ruth, probably <u>the greater</u> power hitter <u>of all time</u>, revolutionized <u>the whole</u> game

      A   B   C

of baseball <u>in the twenties</u>.

     D

30. Of all the <u>world cities</u>, Auckland, New Zealand <u>has the highest</u> Polynesian population.

    A B   C   D

31. The eruption of Mount St. Helens, in the <u>western</u> United States, <u>constituted</u> a great

                  A   B

natural <u>disastrous</u> for the <u>inhabitants</u> of the area.

    C   D

32. The sequoia is the <u>largest</u> <u>living</u> organism <u>in</u> earth.

 <u>A</u>   B   C   D

33. Some doctors <u>nowadays</u> claim that <u>born-newly</u> babies can <u>be</u> very <u>expressive</u> of their

     A   B   C   D

feelings.

34. It <u>was until</u> almost thirty years after his death <u>that</u> a plaque <u>in</u> memory of Dylan

   A   B   C

Thomas <u>was placed</u> in Westminster Abbey.

    D

35. The great majority of <u>Americans</u> today see <u>theirselves</u> as <u>middle-class</u>.

 <u>A</u>   B   C D

36. <u>By</u> the <u>four</u> year of an American president's administration <u>the</u> public has usually

 <u>A</u> <u>B</u>   C

changed <u>its</u> perception of the man in the Oval Office.

   D

37. Apart from <u>showing</u> technical proficiency, airline pilots <u>must score</u> <u>good</u> on psycholog-

    A   B   C   D

ical tests.

38. Quantum <u>physics</u> <u>lies</u> at <u>a</u> heart of <u>the</u> physical sciences.

    A   B C   D

39. <u>Everest</u> is almost three times as high <u>than</u> the Matterhorn, <u>the highest</u> mountain <u>in</u>

 <u>A</u>   B   C   D

Europe.

40. Guam, now <u>a</u> United States territory, <u>discovered</u> by Magellan <u>in</u> 1521.

    <u>A</u>   B   C   D

Section 3: Reading Comprehension and Vocabulary

Time: 45 minutes

This section is designed to measure your ability to understand various kinds of reading materials, as well as your ability to understand the meaning and use of words. There are two types of questions in this section, with special directions for each type.

Part A

Directions: In questions 1-30 each sentence has a word or phrase underlined. Below each sentence are four other words or phrases, marked (A), (B), (C), and (D). You are to choose the *one* word or phrase that *best keeps the meaning* of the original sentence if it is substituted for the underlined word or phrase. Then, on your answer sheet, find the number of the question and blacken the space that corresponds to the letter you have chosen so that the letter inside the oval cannot be seen.

Example

Sample Answer

(A) ● (C) (D)

The forty-niners of the California gold rush had to <u>endure</u> extraordinary hardships.

(A) meet with
(B) suffer through
(C) encounter
(D) survive

The best answer is (B) because "The forty-niners of the California gold rush had to suffer through extraordinary hardships" is closest in meaning to the original sentence, "The forty-niners of the California gold rush had to endure extraordinary hardships." Therefore, you should choose answer (B).

As soon as you understand the directions, begin work on the questions.

GO ON TO THE NEXT PAGE

1. Certain nerve gases are extremely <u>toxic</u>.
   (A) dangerous
   (B) volatile
   (C) poisonous
   (D) ephemeral

2. Cattle raising began in Texas <u>well</u> before the Civil War.
   (A) just
   (B) properly
   (C) shortly
   (D) long

3. The <u>introduction</u> of Ford's ideas revolutionized the auto-making industry.
   (A) implementation
   (B) publication
   (C) production
   (D) presentation

4. From the <u>outset</u> it was clear that the Mediterranean fruit fly constituted a threat to agricultural production.
   (A) information
   (B) beginning
   (C) explanation
   (D) consequences

5. All efforts to persuade at least one of the residents of the Mount St. Helens area to leave were <u>to no avail</u>.
   (A) indecisive
   (B) imprudent
   (C) mistaken
   (D) unsuccessful

6. George Ravencroft's invention of lead crystal in the late seventeenth century was <u>crucial to</u> the development of optical lenses.
   (A) essential to
   (B) prior to
   (C) dependent on
   (D) instructive for

7. It was a <u>widespread</u> belief in the nineteenth century that railroads were the ultimate mode of transport.
   (A) contagious
   (B) expansive
   (C) common
   (D) broad

8. Tests by psychologists have shown that people conceive of intelligence as having three <u>facets</u>.
   (A) bases
   (B) aspects
   (C) definitions
   (D) levels

9. Government health campaigns have <u>fostered</u> an awareness of the dangers in certain social habits.
   (A) engendered
   (B) perfected
   (C) discovered
   (D) encouraged

10. Painters such as Thomas Eakins and Winslow Homer adapted themselves to the photographic image, but tried to <u>transcend</u> it.
    (A) go beyond
    (B) reach into
    (C) transmit
    (D) modify

11. The monetarist <u>case</u> has been vividly expressed by Milton Friedman.
    (A) issue
    (B) argument
    (C) example
    (D) strongbox

12. Registering a patent <u>entails</u> a number of expenses.
    (A) includes
    (B) saves
    (C) involves
    (D) precludes

13. There is no known cure for dyslexia, but neurologists are developing ways to help sufferers <u>cope with</u> it.
    (A) retard·
    (B) dispense with
    (C) deal with
    (D) eradicate

14. Detroit, founded a hundred years before Chicago, enjoys <u>a favorable</u> geographical location.
    (A) a preferential
    (B) a pleasing
    (C) an exceptional
    (D) an advantageous

15. Maps of the brain at work are becoming increasingly <u>accurate</u>.
    (A) complex
    (B) precise
    (C) disparate
    (D) confusing

16. In his book, William James did not hesitate to devote several pages to arguments he felt deserved careful <u>scrutiny</u>.
    (A) examination
    (B) exposition
    (C) detailing
    (D) recounting

17. The safety features make it almost impossible to open the door <u>inadvertently</u>.
    (A) dangerously
    (B) hastily
    (C) accidentally
    (D) incautiously

18. Electronics firms continue to <u>seek</u> ways of cramming more bits of information onto tiny silicon chips.
    (A) find
    (B) look for
    (C) stake out
    (D) reveal

19. Before he became president, Truman was given no <u>hint</u> regarding the atomic bomb project.
    (A) details
    (B) authority
    (C) explanation
    (D) indication

20. The series of breathing and clicking sounds that constitute the Kung language have so far <u>defied</u> transcription.
    (A) resisted
    (B) avoided
    (C) challenged
    (D) scorned

21. The first ice-boxes were quite <u>fancy</u> pieces of dining-room furniture.
    (A) whimsical
    (B) delightful
    (C) elaborate
    (D) delicate

22. The <u>bulk</u> of the wheat exported from the United States comes from the mid-west.
    (A) majority
    (B) surplus
    (C) best
    (D) profitability

23. Benjamin Lee Whorf has pointed out that the Hopi language <u>practically</u> forces its users to observe vibratory phenomena.
    (A) virtually
    (B) usefully
    (C) relatively
    (D) repeatedly

24. Coffee consumption by American coffee drinkers <u>diminished</u> to 2.06 cups per day by 1979.
    (A) amounted
    (B) improved
    (C) dropped
    (D) fluctuated

25. Many animals have evolved <u>complicated</u> ways of transferring environmentally learned information to other members of their species.
    (A) combined
    (B) complimentary
    (C) complicit
    (D) complex

26. Though often <u>quoted</u>, the "Hawthorne Effect" is viewed as defective by most psychologists.
    (A) valued
    (B) cited
    (C) touted
    (D) defended

27. In the late seventies, the price of gold rose sharply <u>on account of</u> a worldwide sense of insecurity.
    (A) on behalf of
    (B) in payment of
    (C) together with
    (D) because of

28. The word "you," originally a plural only, was first used in addressing one person as <u>a term</u> of respect.
    (A) a means
    (B) a show
    (C) an expression
    (D) an example

29. The <u>demise</u> of the dinosaurs still mystifies scientists.
    (A) bone-structure
    (B) extinction
    (C) behavior
    (D) origins

30. In the eighteenth century, William Harvey was <u>reviled</u> by many of his colleagues for claiming that blood circulated through the body.
    (A) attacked
    (B) vindicated
    (C) revered
    (D) exposed

Part B

Directions: The rest of this section is based on a variety of reading material (single sentences, paragraphs, and the like) followed by questions about the meaning of the material. For questions 31-60, you are to choose the *one* best answer, (A), (B), (C), or (D), to each question. Then, on your answer sheet, find the number of the question and blacken the space that corresponds to the letter of the answer you have chosen.

Answer all questions following a passage on the basis of what is *stated* or *implied* in that passage.

Read the following passage.

The squid begins its three-year life cycle at the bottom of the ocean, but soon after hatching makes its way to the surface. As it grows, the squid becomes a voracious predator, searching for food from the ocean floor to the surface. Aided by its ability to outswim most other ocean creatures, the squid frequently consumes crustaceans, sardines, herrings, mackerel, and anchovies. In addition, up to 25% of the young squid's diet may be made up of fellow squid.

Example I

Sample Answer
(A) (B) (C) ●

Squid spend most of their lives

(A) close to the water's surface.
(B) on the ocean floor.
(C) hiding from predators.
(D) moving throughout the ocean.

The passage says that squid search for food from the ocean floor to the surface. Therefore, you should choose answer (D) as the best completion of the sentence.

Example II

Sample Answer
● (B) (C) (D)

According to the passage, what is true about young squid?

(A) They are cannibalistic.
(B) They are not expert swimmers.
(C) They survive mainly on plant life.
(D) They have a 25% chance of living for at least one decade.

The passage says that "up to 25% of the young squid's diet may be made up of fellow squid." Therefore, you should choose (A).

As soon as you understand the directions, begin work on the questions.

Questions 31-37

Malinowski makes the highly relevant point that folklore cannot simply be viewed in terms of its content. Instead, he contends that, as anthropologists rather than literary critics or students of ancient documents, we must distinguish the social context and function of any given narrative. To this end we must consider how those affected by folklore view it. For instance, he refers to the Trobriand Islanders who differentiate between what he defines as fairy tales, legends, and myths. The first are frankly fictional tales, which are dramatically told at a specific season, and are vaguely believed by the islanders to have a beneficial effect on their recently-planted crops. The second, or legends, are seen as being true and as containing important factual information, but not as being in any sense magical in their effect. The last group, or myths, are considered not only true, but venerable and sacred, to be told in association with specific rituals or when the effectiveness of such rituals is called into question.

31. This passage was written by
    (A) a student of ancient manuscripts.
    (B) an unnamed anthropologist.
    (C) Malinowski.
    (D) an unnamed literary critic.

32. Malinowski suggests that the usual, non-anthropological way of looking at a narrative is in terms of its
    (A) relevance.
    (B) social context.
    (C) social function.
    (D) content.

33. It may be inferred from the passage that
    (A) literary critics are generally not much concerned with the social function of a narrative.
    (B) the Trobriand Islanders are a legendary people.
    (C) the author disagrees with Malinowski's main point.
    (D) the author is a student of Trobriand Island mythology.

34. When do Trobriand Islanders tell fairy tales?
    (A) during crop planting
    (B) just before crop planting
    (C) just after crop planting
    (D) just before harvesting crops

35. According to the passage, which of the following is NOT true of the Trobriand Islanders?
    (A) They see legends as being true and informative.
    (B) They see fairy tales as untrue but somehow beneficial.
    (C) They see myths and legends as functionally different.
    (D) They see myths as untrue but sacred.

36. It may be inferred from the passage that Malinowski
    (A) was only concerned with the folklore of the Trobrianders.
    (B) was only interested in tales the Trobrianders believed were true.
    (C) talked to the Trobrianders about the purposes of their folklore.
    (D) encouraged the Trobrianders to become involved in their folklore.

37. Which of the following would be the best title for the passage?
    (A) Fairy Tales, Legends, and Myths
    (B) An Anthropological Approach to Folklore
    (C) Crop-planting in the Trobriand Islands
    (D) Malinowski: Folklorist of the Trobrianders

Questions 38-40

Los Angeles, host of the 1932 and 1984 Olympics, was founded in 1781, though the oldest house still standing in the city goes back to only 1818. Unlike San Francisco, it was mainly settled by people who traversed the United States by land.

38. According to the passage, Los Angeles
    (A) is more than 200 years old.
    (B) goes back to 1818.
    (C) was founded by people who traversed the United States by land.
    (D) was founded in the seventeenth century.

39. It may be inferred from the passage that
    (A) the early settlers of San Francisco reached it by land.
    (B) no houses were built in Los Angeles between 1781 and 1818.
    (C) a few buildings in Los Angeles are more than 200 years old.
    (D) there are no eighteenth-century buildings in Los Angeles.

40. The first time the Olympic games were held there, Los Angeles was
    (A) 52 years old.
    (B) 114 years old.
    (C) over 150 years old.
    (D) over 200 years old.

Questions 41-44

Among the problems that must be solved if even more powerful but smaller computers are to become viable propositions is the heat computer circuits generate. The present market leader, with 300,000 chips in 100 cubic feet, requires a powerful refrigeration system; the kind of super-computers now being discussed might cram half a million chips into a space the size of a shoe box, and would probably need a bath of liquid nitrogen to keep them from melting.

41. Today's leading large computer
    (A) is cooled by a system based on liquid nitrogen.
    (B) generates considerable heat in its circuits.
    (C) is smaller in size than the super-computers referred to.
    (D) has half a million chips.

42. It may be inferred from the passage that
    (A) if chips are packed closer together, a computer needs stronger refrigeration.
    (B) a computer the size of a shoe-box generates more heat than a larger one.
    (C) more powerful computers tend to be smaller.
    (D) the leading large computer is now cooled by liquid nitrogen.

43. According to the passage, the super-computers referred to
    (A) are already viable propositions.
    (B) might melt in a bath of liquid nitrogen.
    (C) would pack 300,000 chips into about 100 cubic feet.
    (D) would be more compact than today's models.

44. The passage deals mainly with
    (A) the number of chips modern computers use.
    (B) the problem of cooling tomorrow's super-computers.
    (C) the optimum size for computers.
    (D) the cooling properties of liquid nitrogen.

GO ON TO THE NEXT PAGE

Questions 45-54

Cerro Prieto, twenty miles south of the Unted States border, is a large geothermal energy field likely to produce 1,000 megawatts of electricity annually by the early 1990's. This will be well above its initial 1973 capacity of 75 megawatts, which was doubled in 1979, with a further 30 megawatts added two years later to bring it up to its present capacity. However, in addition to the primary purpose of producing electricity, scientists at Cerro Prieto have developed several other uses for the geothermal heat and fluid, including some in aquaculture and hydroponics. In relation to the former, crayfish are raised in water kept at about 85°F. They feed on the minute crustaceans and algae occurring naturally in the geothermal fluid while special strains of bacteria have been introduced to clean the water along with small local crayfish that absorb salts harmful to the commercial variety. This variety's metabolism is speeded up by the controlled environment, which reduces growing time. The salt-rich geothermal fluid also produces striking results through the use of hydroponics, with yields of crops such as tomatoes and cucumbers as much as 300 per cent higher than in normal soil. Meanwhile, a ten-meter-long enclosed shed produces half a ton of barley grass per day, the grass reaching a height of five inches in only seven days from seed.

45. Cerro Prieto is
    (A) in the South of the United States.
    (B) not very large.
    (C) in a field.
    (D) not in the United States.

46. What was the generating capacity of the Cerro Prieto field in 1980?
    (A) 75 megawatts
    (B) 105 megawatts
    (C) 150 megawatts
    (D) 180 megawatts

47. By how much was the field's capacity expected to expand between the time of writing and the early 1990's?
    (A) 820 megawatts
    (B) 700 megawatts
    (C) 250 megawatts
    (D) 100 megawatts

48. The passage implies that
    (A) the field's generating capacity doubles every six years.
    (B) the field originally began producing in 1973.
    (C) engineers had to look further afield to find another 30 megawatts.
    (D) the latest addition to capacity was two years behind schedule.

49. According to the passage, which of the following is true?
    (A) The scientists have designed special food for the crayfish.
    (B) Scientists at Cerro Prieto are more interested in hydroponics than in generating electricity.
    (C) Commercial crayfish react badly to salts in the geothermal fluid.
    (D) Crayfish feed on special types of bacteria.

50. It can be inferred from the passage that
    (A) the local crayfish and the "commercial" crayfish live in different natural environments.
    (B) "commercial" crayfish have reduced growth in a controlled environment.
    (C) "commercial" crayfish raise the water temperature to 85°F.
    (D) the bacteria alluded to occur naturally in the geothermal fluid.

51. Scientists control the commercial crayfish's environment in order to
    (A) produce special bacteria.
    (B) reduce their growth.
    (C) shorten their growth time.
    (D) produce smaller, local crayfish.

52. The passage says that, compared with what is normal, the use of hydroponics at Cerro Prieto produces
    (A) more tomatoes and cucumbers.
    (B) higher tomatoes and cucumbers.
    (C) larger tomatoes and cucumbers.
    (D) comparable tomatoes and cucumbers.

53. The barley grass mentioned in the passage
    (A) grows up to ten meters high.
    (B) has half a ton of barley mixed with it.
    (C) grows about 3/4 inch per day.
    (D) is grown in a fenced-off field.

54. What is the best title for the passage?
    (A) Cerro Prieto: Increased Generating Capacity for the Nineties
    (B) Geothermal Energy's Surprising Bonuses
    (C) The Hydroponics Revolution
    (D) Geothermal Energy: Electricity from the Earth

GO ON TO THE NEXT PAGE

Questions 55-57

Undergraduate students may choose to take one course each quarter under the Pass-Fail Option, so long as the total number of hours of course credit taken as pass/fail does not exceed fifteen. Courses in the student's major, honors courses, and English courses required of all students may not be taken as pass/fail courses. Credits earned in pass/fail courses are not used in computing grade-point averages. Students considering the pass/fail option should note that some graduate schools do not recognize courses taken on this basis.

55. A student may take on a pass/fail basis
    (A) no fewer than one course.
    (B) only one honors course.
    (C) up to fifteen courses in all.
    (D) as many as fifteen credit hours.

56. In relation to pass/fail courses, the passage implies that
    (A) students should take the maximum number allowed.
    (B) honor students are accorded preference.
    (C) prospective graduate students might be ill-advised to take them.
    (D) they are not available for two categories of courses.

57. In what way do pass/fail courses affect the undergraduate student's final standing?
    (A) They count towards graduation, but not towards the student's final average.
    (B) They do not count as credit towards graduation.
    (C) They make it impossible for the student to be accepted in graduate school.
    (D) They prevent a student from graduating with honors.

Questions 58-60. For each of these questions, choose the answer that is *closest in meaning* to the original sentence. Note that several of the choices may be factually correct, but you should choose the one that is the *closest restatement of the given sentence*.

58. The tremendous influence of television on educational issues was underestimated by the majority of programmers and viewers alike in its early days.

    A. Most programmers and viewers influenced early educational issues on television.
    B. The impact of television on educational concerns was not appreciated by most people when television was new.
    C. Early programmers and viewers recognized the potential influence of television on educational problems.
    D. The use of television in the classroom has often been underestimated by both programmers and viewers.

59. Contrary to popular opinion, the severity of many handicaps such as deafness can be lessened by a prescribed program of diet and exercise.

    A. Many handicaps as severe as deafness are reduced by public attitudes towards prescribed dieting and exercise programs.
    B. A prescribed diet and exercise regimen must be lessened by the severity of a number of disabilities such as deafness, though this is not generally believed.
    C. Public opinion contradicts handicaps like deafness, though these are improved if diet and exercise programs are followed.
    D. Despite widely-held doubts, a number of physical disabilities may be alleviated by better eating and exercise habits.

60. Established in 1964, the Roosevelt Campobello International Park in Canada is administered jointly by the United States and Canada and is a symbol of friendship between the two nations.

    A. Though located entirely in Canada, the Roosevelt Campobello Park, which was opened in the mid-sixties, represents the friendly ties between the two countries—the United States and Canada—which together are responsible for running the park.

    B. Though established in 1964 and run jointly by the United States and Canada, the Roosevelt Campobello International Park in Canada is symbolic of the ties between the two countries.

    C. The Roosevelt Campobello Park has symbolized the joint administering of two friendly nations—the United States and Canada—since it was established in Canada in 1964.

    D. The Roosevelt Campobello Park in Canada symbolizes the friendship between this country and the United States established in 1964 and is run as a combination of the two countries.

Answer Key/
Practice Test V

Section 1: Listening Comprehension

Part A	Part B	Part C
1. A	21. A	36. A
2. D	22. C	37. C
3. C	23. D	38. D
4. C	24. D	39. C
5. B	25. B	40. B
6. D	26. B	41. A
7. A	27. A	42. D
8. B	28. B	43. C
9. C	29. C	44. A
10. D	30. C	45. B
11. A	31. D	46. C
12. A	32. C	47. A
13. B	33. A	48. D
14. D	34. B	49. B
15. B	35. D	50. A
16. C		
17. B		
18. C		
19. D		
20. A		

Section 2: Structure and Written Expression

Part A

The explanations of why given answers are wrong have been kept as brief as possible. Indications of how particular incorrect answers might be made correct are provided as a stimulus to thinking about English sentence structure. The references marked FE are to the Focused Exercises which may be of help in further explaining why particular answers are correct or incorrect and in offering more practice.

1. A Correct (FE-7)
   B Needs passive
   C See 1-B
   D Repeats subject (FE-3, 18)

2. A Needs anticipatory subject (FE-4)
   B Correct (FE-4)
   C No expletive "there" before defining clause (FE-5)
   D Introduces dependent clause; no main clause (FE-10)

3. A Contrasting conjunction needed
   B Would need semi-colon or period after "earth" and subject for new clause
   C See 3-A
   D Correct

4. A Would work if "nevertheless" were a subordinating conjunction
   B Makes two inappropriately linked main clauses (FE-12)
   C Correct (FE-12)
   D See 4-B (FE-12)

5. A Creates subject of whole sentence; no verb (FE-6)
   B See 5-A
   C See 5-A
   D Correct (FE-6)

6. A Irrelevant inversion
   B Would be correct if "is" follows "which" (FE-10)
   C Correct (FE-9)
   D Main clause, inappropriately linked to existing main clause; see 6-A

7. A "most" not a noun ("the majority of" would be correct)
   B Correct (FE-15)
   C Main clause; see 6-D
   D Creates noun subject; would be structurally correct if comma after "cranberries" (FE-9)

8. A Correct (FE-32)
   B Clause after preposition needs initial "that"
   C Creates double negative
   D Creates dependent participial phrase which would require a following main clause

9. A Needs "a" with profession and would imply "Ronald Reagan" was not himself a former actor
   B Needs "a" with profession
   C Correct
   D Would create a noun clause subject with comma after "Reagan" (FE-2)

10. A Correct
    B Meaningless since hurricanes do not threaten to strike in different ways
    C Needs "when" and "always when" = "whenever"
    D "whether" needs subsequent "or not"

11. A Passive form required by sense and "to" after "enable" (FE-7)
    B See 11-A
    C See 11-A
    D Correct

12. A Would be correct if "and" followed
"sulphur" instead of preceding it
B Sense makes this impossible: "potassium nitrate" obviously does not
combine "charcoal" and "sulphur"
C Does not offer the participial phrase
required
D Correct (FE-12)

13. A Subject-verb inversion required after
initial "on no account" (FE-8)
B Correct (FE-8)
C See 13-A (would also create double
negative)
D Auxiliary finite verb missing to make
"be removed" possible

14. A Fails to provide relationship with
main clause (FE-3)
B Correct (FE-3)
C Meaningless
D Provides subject of main clause "The
. . . 1930's" which would need following verb

15. A Needs initial "which" (FE-10)
B Needs "be" form for passive (FE-31)
C Correct (FE-1)
D See 15-A

Part B

In every case the answer is given first. Where there is an FE reference,
this indicates the number of the Focused Exercise which may offer useful
further practice of the point in question. Where words in quotation marks
follow the letter of the correct answer, these show what would be needed for
the sentence to be correct. This usually occurs in cases where none of the
Focused Exercises is applicable.

16. A (FE-17)
17. D (FE-36)
18. C (FE-3, 18)
19. C (FE-27)
20. A (FE-38)
21. B (FE-7, 31)
22. A (FE-40)
23. C (FE-16)
24. D (FE-14, 33)
25. B (FE-4)
26. D (FE-37)
27. C (FE-35)
28. D ("next week")

29. A (FE-24)
30. A ("world's")
31. C (FE-22)
32. D (FE-28)
33. B (FE-34)
34. A ("not until")
35. C (FE-19)
36. B ("fourth")
37. D (FE-23)
38. C (FE-21)
39. B (FE-25)
40. B (FE-7, 31)

Section 3: Reading Comprehension and Vocabulary

Part A

1. C	11. B	21. C
2. D	12. C	22. A
3. A	13. C	23. A
4. B	14. D	24. C
5. D	15. B	25. D
6. A	16. A	26. B
7. C	17. C	27. D
8. B	18. B	28. C
9. D	19. D	29. B
10. A	20. A	30. A

Part B

31. B	41. B	51. C
32. D	42. A	52. A
33. A	43. D	53. C
34. C	44. B	54. B
35. D	45. D	55. D
36. C	46. C	56. C
37. B	47. A	57. A
38. A	48. B	58. B
39. D	49. C	59. D
40. C	50. A	60. A

STRATEGIES: A REMINDER**

Section 1: Listening Comprehension

STRATEGY for Part A: look at all the answer choices before you hear the sentence.
STRATEGY for Part B: aim for a more general understanding than in Part A but more specific than Part C.
STRATEGY for Part C: aim for a general understanding of what you hear.

Section 2: Structure and Written Expression

GENERAL STRATEGY: work at a steady pace and read each possible answer very carefully.
STRATEGY for Part A: read carefully and choose the one correct sentence completion.
STRATEGY for Part B: choose the one incorrect part.

Section 3: Reading Comprehension and Vocabulary

GENERAL STRATEGY: do Part A quickly to allow yourself more time for Part B.
STRATEGY for Part A: work quickly; if you do not know the meaning, guess and continue on to the next item.
STRATEGY for Part B: think about the items and recheck them against the information given.

** See the Preview to the Practice Tests (pp. 42-45) for more specific strategies.

PRACTICE TEST VI

Section 1: Listening Comprehension

Time: 40 minutes

You will need to play the tape for all the questions in Section 1. (The tapescripts are printed on pages 259-263. This material is designated by the symbol  .)

In this section of the test, you will have an opportunity to demonstrate your ability to understand spoken English. There are three parts to this section, with special directions for each part.

Part A

Directions: For each question in Part A, you will hear a short statement. The statements will be spoken just one time. They will not be written out for you, and you must listen carefully to understand what the speaker says.

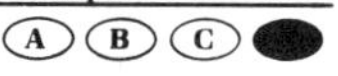

After you hear a statement, read the four sentences in your test book, marked (A), (B), (C), and (D), and decide which *one* is closest in meaning to the statement you heard. Then, on your answer sheet, find the number of the question and blacken the space that corresponds to the letter of the answer you have chosen so that the letter inside the oval cannot be seen.

Example I

Sample Answer
(A) (B) (C) ●

You will hear:
You will read: (A) He couldn't believe the changes on the reservation.
(B) He couldn't change the water in the reservoirs.
(C) He was hesitant to make any changes.
(D) He assumed he could change the reservations.

Sentence (D), "He assumed he could change the reservations," is closest in meaning to the sentence "When Tom made the reservations, he didn't know that they couldn't be changed." Therefore, you should choose answer (D).

Example II

Sample Answer
(A) (B) ● (D)

You will hear:
You will read: (A) Keith and his wife are not good bowlers.
(B) Keith won't vote for his wife.
(C) Keith's wife is the better bowler.
(D) Keith and his wife haven't been to a bowl game.

Sentence (C), "Keith's wife is the better bowler," means most nearly the same as the statement "Keith has never been as good at bowling as his wife is." Therefore, you should choose answer (C).

1. (A) What are Craig's favorite activities?
   (B) Can you describe Craig as a person?
   (C) What does Craig look like?
   (D) Can you compare Craig with anyone else?

2. (A) He went to four doctors before having surgery.
   (B) Three other members of his family are doctors.
   (C) The second sturgeon was caught by four doctors.
   (D) His relatives have never needed surgery.

3. (A) They were forced to count the resin.
   (B) The discovery was not pursued with force.
   (C) The accountant had to quit because of the missing funds.
   (D) Few causes of deafness have been accounted for.

4. (A) I didn't have enough money for the bar.
   (B) I couldn't carry the trash upstairs.
   (C) I couldn't afford to buy what I wanted.
   (D) The gun was too expensive for me.

5. (A) The police are timing the winter traffic.
   (B) You can't be kind in this traffic.
   (C) Don't leave your watch out in the rain.
   (D) Be careful of the cars and trucks in the rain.

6. (A) The restaurant went out of business in about a month.
   (B) The restaurant specialized in barley dishes.
   (C) They preferred to work in the old restaurant.
   (D) They rarely eat in a restaurant.

7. (A) The plant's underside shows that formation.
   (B) Those brochures are under a plant in my house.
   (C) Some new facts about house plants have been discovered.
   (D) Look at the pages devoted to house plants.

8. (A) Ken wanted to meet someplace else.
   (B) Ken didn't want dinner while studying.
   (C) Ken had to study at the meeting.
   (D) Ken was unclear about the objective.

9. (A) Can you count on Victor?
   (B) What system do you use for counting the fig trees?
   (C) To what do you attribute your success?
   (D) Was your accountant responsible for your triumph?

10. (A) The price of camp tents is rising.
    (B) Rents are usually high around the university.
    (C) You must be off campus by ten to two.
    (D) Campers must pay to stay on university grounds.

11. (A) We made it to a gas station in the nick of time.
    (B) We located the station just as the train pulled out.
    (C) We soon found that justice would be served.
    (D) We went to the memorial service right after class.

12. (A) I'd prefer a private journey.
    (B) I'm writing a diary.
    (C) I can't afford that prescription.
    (D) I wish I had the money for that subscription.

13. (A) Barbara can't see the doctor next week.
    (B) Barbara can see the doctor next Friday or Saturday.
    (C) The doctor can't be found.
    (D) The doctor is waiting to see Barbara.

14. (A) His unhealthy habits led to a heart attack.
    (B) Their hard attack made him tense.
    (C) His death was caused by ten attackers.
    (D) He was overwrought when he died.

15. (A) Sally spent her money shopping.
    (B) Sally can't go shopping until tomorrow.
    (C) Sally will cash your check soon.
    (D) Sally doesn't have any cash now.

16. (A) You must carry everything inside your suitcase.
    (B) Passengers must keep luggage under their feet.
    (C) Only bags of a certain size are permitted on board.
    (D) Do not carry on about your seat assignment.

17. (A) You would benefit from getting your tickets early.
    (B) The only tickets left are for the outer seats.
    (C) You will get a better fit if you go early.
    (D) There are no longer any tickets available.

18. (A) Late papers will not be accepted.
    (B) We don't have time to collect the rest of the exams.
    (C) Some of the exams will not be graded this evening.
    (D) All of the tests must be marked before tonight's deadline.

19. (A) I can't believe he's already a teenager.
    (B) He's very self-conscious about his age.
    (C) He's not old enough to think for himself.
    (D) It took him thirteen years to think of that.

20. (A) Check how much it's worth.
    (B) Use a dictionary.
    (C) It's at the top of the list.
    (D) Look at it carefully.

GO ON TO THE NEXT PAGE

1 1 1 1 1 1 1 1 1

Part B

Directions: In Part B you will hear short conversations between two speakers. At the end of each conversation, a third voice will ask a question about what was said. The question will be spoken just one time. After you hear a conversation and the question about it, read the four possible answers in your test book and decide which _one_ is the best answer to the question you heard. Then, on your answer sheet, find the number of the question and blacken the space that corresponds to the letter of the answer you have chosen.

Example

<u>Sample Answer</u>
● (B) (C) (D)

You will hear:

You will read: (A) She is not optimistic about the situation.
(B) She would prefer things to improve.
(C) She doesn't like the situation.
(D) She feels things will get better.

From the conversation you know that the woman does not expect things to improve. The best answer, then, is (A), "She is not optimistic about the situation." Therefore, you should choose answer (A).

21. (A) A beauty salon.
(B) An electrical company.
(C) A clothing store.
(D) A theater.

GO ON TO THE NEXT PAGE →

22. (A) He'll hook up the speakers.
    (B) He has the same problem with his stereo.
    (C) That model of stereo is difficult to fix.
    (D) He'll show the woman his stereo.

23. (A) An argument with David.
    (B) Bus transportation.
    (C) David's driving.
    (D) David's uncooperativeness.

24. (A) He's now doing better in medical school.
    (B) He's become a doctor in a very short time.
    (C) He's having a hard time at school now.
    (D) He's not planning to become a doctor.

25. (A) Give his salesmen a raise.
    (B) Take a vacation.
    (C) Hire a new employee.
    (D) Change his plans.

26. (A) She doesn't pay any attention to her schedule.
    (B) Everyone in her office is always telling jokes.
    (C) She doesn't work eight hours a day any more.
    (D) She likes her job so the hours aren't a problem.

27. (A) The quality of the shirt.
    (B) The service in the store.
    (C) Waiting in line.
    (D) The weight of the fabric.

28. (A) Apologizing.
    (B) Making excuses.
    (C) Procrastinating.
    (D) Disagreeing.

29. (A) She went to bed instead of watching the movie.
    (B) There was no movie on channel eight last night.
    (C) She had to turn in her assignment early.
    (D) She turned on her TV after the movie had ended.

30. (A) He's afraid of something.
    (B) He disagrees with the woman.
    (C) He feels ill.
    (D) He can't breathe.

31. (A) The religious affiliation of the college.
    (B) The location of the chapel.
    (C) The man's beliefs.
    (D) The most likely side to win.

32. (A) He's a student.
    (B) He's a bank teller.
    (C) He's a pilot.
    (D) He's a taxi driver.

33. (A) He'll deliver the lamp by car.
    (B) He won't take the lamp with him.
    (C) He doesn't need any help with the lamp.
    (D) He's changed his mind about the lamp.

34. (A) Jack's promotion.
    (B) A production problem.
    (C) A couple they met recently.
    (D) The end of a relationship.

35. (A) Because he was bored.
    (B) Because of a surprise meeting.
    (C) Because the meeting was so long.
    (D) Because he got up at four.

Part C

Directions: In this part of the test, you will hear several short talks and conversations. After each talk or conversation, you will be asked some questions. The talks and questions will be spoken just one time. They will not be written out for you, so you will have to listen carefully to understand what the speaker says.

After you hear a question, read the four possible answers in your test book and decide which _one_ is the best answer to the question you heard. Then, on your answer sheet, find the number of the question and blacken the space that corresponds to the letter of the answer you have chosen.

Sample Answer
● Ⓑ Ⓒ Ⓓ

Listen to this sample talk.
You will hear:
Now look at the following example.
You will hear:
You will read: (A) Various places in Morocco.
   (B) University courses in anthropology.
   (C) Modern Moroccan cities.
   (D) Mr. Talbott's last trip to Marrakech.

The best answer to the question "What is the film about?" is (A), "Various places in Morocco." Therefore, you should choose answer (A).

Sample Answer
Ⓐ Ⓑ ● Ⓓ

Now look at the next example.
You will hear:
You will read: (A) Librarian.
   (B) Film-maker.
   (C) Teacher.
   (D) Tour guide.

The best answer to the question "What is Paul Talbott's profession?" is (C), "Teacher." Therefore, you should choose answer (C).

36. (A) Provides instructors for computer classes.
   (B) Offers counseling for full-time students.
   (C) Helps students and faculty with research.
   (D) Supplies information about free community activities.

37. (A) By computer time required.
   (B) By the length of the project.
   (C) By the complexity of the project.
   (D) By the university status of the user.

GO ON TO THE NEXT PAGE

38. (A) To help students and faculty in computer and information sciences.
    (B) To help students, faculty, and employees of the university.
    (C) To help members of the computer club.
    (D) To help computer services staff members.

39. (A) To advertise the services of the Office of Computer Services.
    (B) To help people complete their projects.
    (C) To write summaries of projects.
    (D) To maintain the computer equipment.

40. (A) It encourages careful planning.
    (B) It is open for discussion.
    (C) It is very extensive.
    (D) It is an entirely written procedure.

41. (A) Ready to move back home.
    (B) Unable to afford new furniture.
    (C) Opposed to the woman's plan.
    (D) Unhappy with his old memories.

42. (A) Buy new furniture.
    (B) Move to a different apartment.
    (C) Open a secondhand furniture store.
    (D) Get a better job.

43. (A) They have redecorated their home.
    (B) They have gotten rid of most of their furniture.
    (C) They have changed apartments twice.
    (D) They have become more successful.

44. (A) It is old, but very comfortable.
    (B) It represents happy memories.
    (C) He wants to write a story about it.
    (D) It should be thrown out.

45. (A) Adventurous Americans.
    (B) Advances in crop dusting.
    (C) Restrictions on small aircraft.
    (D) A new way to fly.

46. (A) A simplified hang glider.
    (B) An airborne police car.
    (C) An adventure in speed.
    (D) A personal flying machine.

47. (A) The inventor of the ultralight.
    (B) The major producer of ultralights.
    (C) The man who placed the restrictions on ultralight use.
    (D) The man in charge of military uses of ultralights in Milwaukee.

48. (A) Limited restrictions on its use.
    (B) Its practical uses.
    (C) The chance to try something like pure flight.
    (D) The career opportunities surrounding it.

49. (A) Carrying less than five gallons of fuel.
    (B) Traveling without headlights.
    (C) Flying at night.
    (D) Using unrestricted airspace.

50. (A) Dusting crops.
    (B) Transporting fuel.
    (C) Police work.
    (D) Military surveillance.

Section 2: Structure and Written Expression

Time: 25 minutes

This section is designed to measure your ability to recognize language that is appropriate for standard written English. There are two types of questions in this section, with special directions for each type.

Part A

Directions: Questions 1-15 are incomplete sentences. Four words or phrases, marked (A), (B), (C), and (D), are given beneath each sentence. You are to choose the *one* word or phrase that best completes the sentence. Then, on your answer sheet, find the number of the question and blacken the space that corresponds to the letter of the answer you have chosen so that the letter inside the oval cannot be seen.

Example I

<u>Sample Answer</u>
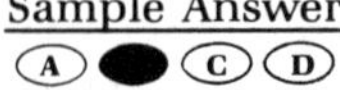

Philip Morrison, a professor at MIT, ________ as one of America's greatest teachers of science.

(A) has acknowledgement
(B) is acknowledged
(C) acknowledges
(D) acknowledged

In English, the sentence should read, "Philip Morrison, a professor at MIT, is acknowledged as one of America's greatest teachers of science." Therefore, you should choose (B).

Example II

<u>Sample Answer</u>
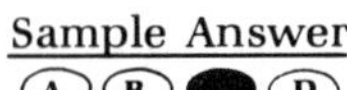

In the 16th century, people ________ insane were sometimes branded on the head as a form of treatment.

(A) considered being
(B) to consider
(C) considered to be
(D) in consideration

In English, the sentence should read, "In the 16th century, people considered to be insane were sometimes branded on the head as a form of treatment." Therefore, you should choose (C).

1. Moscow, Idaho _______ the home of the American Festival Ballet.
   - (A) which is
   - (B) formerly
   - (C) as
   - (D) is

2. _______ humans, the armadillo is the only mammal known to contract leprosy.
   - (A) Alongside
   - (B) As well as
   - (C) Like
   - (D) In conjunction with

3. There is evidence that Betelgeuse, a star in the constellation Orion, may _______ in size in the last 2,000 years.
   - (A) to have doubled
   - (B) have doubled
   - (C) double
   - (D) have doubling

4. _______ accurate, Audubon's work may be considered as falling within the mainstream of American realism.
   - (A) That scientifically
   - (B) Scientifically it was
   - (C) Scientifically
   - (D) It was scientifically

5. So involved with their computers _______ that leaders at summer computer camps often have to force them to break for sports and games.
   - (A) the children become
   - (B) become the children
   - (C) the children do become
   - (D) do the children become

6. Whatever _______ , members of Polar Bear clubs go for an outdoor swim on New Year's Day.
   - (A) cold
   - (B) weather
   - (C) it may be cold
   - (D) the temperature

7. _______ brilliant, Aaron Burr was unreliable.
   - (A) Though
   - (B) He was
   - (C) Though he
   - (D) Being

8. _______ adults, young children find little difficulty in imitating sounds in foreign languages.
   - (A) Not like
   - (B) Unlike
   - (C) Being not
   - (D) Not as

9. Paul Revere _______ political cartoonist.
   - (A) being a
   - (B) was a
   - (C) a
   - (D) was

10. _______ its olfactory functions, the nose warms the air passing into the lungs.
    - (A) In addition
    - (B) To add
    - (C) Additionally
    - (D) In addition to

GO ON TO THE NEXT PAGE ➤

11. The saiga, which _______ as the Russian antelope, is famous for the medicinal properties attributed to its horns.
    (A) is also known
    (B) also it is known
    (C) known also
    (D) it is also known

12. Darts are triangular folds of material _______ .
    (A) they are what give shape to a garment
    (B) give shape to a garment
    (C) which give shape to a garment
    (D) which giving shape to a garment

13. _______ Adam Smith's *The Wealth of Nations* that David Ricardo became fascinated by economic theory.
    (A) After reading
    (B) It was after reading
    (C) By reading
    (D) When he read

14. Before becoming President in 1928, Herbert Hoover _______ as Secretary of Commerce.
    (A) has served
    (B) was served
    (C) had served
    (D) serving

15. Electrical resistance is a common property of all materials, _______ .
    (A) differs only in degree
    (B) it only differs in degree
    (C) only in degree it differs
    (D) differing only in degree

GO ON TO THE NEXT PAGE

Part B

Directions: In questions 16-40 each sentence has four words or phrases underlined. The four underlined parts of the sentence are marked (A), (B), (C), and (D). You are to identify the *one* underlined word or phrase that should be corrected or rewritten. Then, on your answer sheet, find the number of the question and blacken the space that corresponds to the letter of the answer you have chosen.

Example I

Sample Answer

(A) (B) (C) ●

In the name of science, the eighteenth cen-
 A   B
tury explorer, Alexander Von Humboldt,
defied death by deliberately risking electro-
                      C
cuting him with an electric eel.
          D
Answer (D), the underlined word *him*, would not be accepted in carefully written English; the reflexive pronoun *himself* should be used after the verb form *electrocuting* in this sentence. Therefore, the sentence should read, "In the name of science, the eighteenth century explorer, Alexander Von Humboldt, defied death by deliberately risking electrocuting himself with an electric eel." To answer the problem correctly, you should choose (D).

Example II

Sample Answer

(A) ● (C) (D)

Modern banking, both private and govern-
                              A
mental, were among the most highly devel-
         B   C
oped capitalistic institutions in China in
the 1930's.
    D
Answer (B), the underlined word *were*, would not be accepted in carefully written English; the form *was* should be used with the singular subject *Modern banking*. Therefore, the sentence should read, "Modern banking, both private and governmental, was among the most highly developed capitalistic institutions in China in the 1930's." To answer the problem correctly, you should choose (B).

As soon as you understand the directions, begin work on the problems.

16. Merino sheep, its origins going back some three thousand years, are still the primary
                   A   B   C
    producers of the world's fine wool.
                    D

17. Sugar mill operators <u>use</u> saccharimeters in order <u>to measuring</u> <u>the amount of</u> sucrose
      A   B   C   D
in sugar cane.

18. Janet Guthrie, the first woman driver in the Indianapolis 500, <u>took part</u> in the race <u>each</u>
                        A   B
year <u>from</u> 1977 to 1979, her <u>better</u> finish being ninth in 1978.
    C   D

19. American children <u>are taught</u> <u>to treat</u> <u>their</u> pets <u>friendly</u>.
                  A   B   C   D

20. Cincinnati is <u>located</u> <u>cross</u> the <u>Ohio River</u> <u>from</u> Covington, Kentucky.
             A   B   C   D

21. Louis XIV of France saw <u>hisself</u> <u>as</u> <u>a</u> ruler <u>by</u> Divine Right.
                   A   B C   D

22. Only one <u>of</u> all the states <u>in</u> the United States <u>are</u> <u>larger</u> than Texas.
        A   B   C   D

23. <u>Contrary to</u> the ancient <u>believing</u> that <u>they</u> live in fire, salamanders <u>actually</u> delight in
       A   B   C   D
cool, moist places.

24. Many <u>industrial workers</u> in the <u>post-war years</u> won <u>improved</u> job security, excellent
               A   B   C
fringe benefits, and <u>earned more</u>.
                   D

25. <u>Since</u> Drew Barrymore is a member of one of America's most famous acting <u>families</u>,
    A   B
<u>many</u> people may have expected <u>she</u> to be an actress, but probably not by the age of
 C   D
seven.

26. Sabicu wood is <u>sometime</u> used <u>in</u> the construction of ships because of <u>its</u> durability
                 A   B   C
and <u>resistance to decay</u>.
           D

27. The Romans built <u>what</u> is known <u>as</u> Hadrian's Wall <u>to protect</u> their English possessions
                 A   B   C
from the Picts <u>in north</u>.
               D

28. Nutritionists urge that food <u>should be</u> <u>chewed and masticated</u> <u>thoroughly</u> before
                           A   B   C
<u>being swallowed</u>.
     D

29. In the 1880's it was <u>too</u> difficult <u>to distinguish</u> between Republican and Democratic
                A   B
party policies that electors voted according to <u>their</u> perceptions of the <u>candidate's</u>
                                           C   D
characters.

30. If <u>both</u> the President and Vice-president should be <u>simultaneously</u> incapacitated, <u>it is</u>
    A   B   C
the Speaker of the House of Representatives <u>which</u> is next in line.
                                              D

31. Robber crabs <u>are</u> a dangerous, <u>tree-climbing</u> <u>type</u> of crustaceans found <u>on</u> Pacific is-
              A   B   C   D
lands.

32. <u>High blood pressure</u> in a <u>pregnant woman</u> may <u>eventual</u> lead <u>to</u> heart disease in the
          A   B   C   D
unborn child.

33. Though <u>of</u> <u>extremely average</u> height <u>for</u> a professional football player, Don Nottingham
        A   B   C
was <u>effective as</u> a running back.
        D

34. Now smaller <u>as</u> several other buildings in North America, the Empire State Building
            A
<u>remains</u> the United States' <u>top</u> tall <u>tourist attraction.</u>
  B   C   D

35. Litmus paper <u>is used</u> <u>to test</u> <u>whether</u> a solution is alkaline or <u>an acid.</u>
             A   B   C   D

36. <u>It</u> was on his election <u>to</u> the Georgia Senate in 1962 <u>that</u> James Carter first became a
 A   B   C
full-time <u>politic.</u>
       D

37. The road runner can run <u>as fast</u> that it was <u>formerly</u> famous <u>for outrunning</u>
                     A   B   C
<u>horse-drawn</u> vehicles.
    D

38. After a <u>much-publicized</u> journey <u>through</u> Africa, Stanley <u>knew</u> Dr. Livingstone
          A   B   C
<u>for the first time</u> in the middle of the jungle.
       D

39. The first American bicycle <u>were manufactured</u> only fifteen years <u>before</u> Henry Ford
 A   B   C
built <u>his</u> first automobile.
   D

40. Because of <u>its</u> <u>cost and expense,</u> <u>above all,</u> the Medicaid program has come <u>under fire</u>
           A   B   C   D
recently.

Section 3: Reading Comprehension and Vocabulary

Time: 45 minutes

This section is designed to measure your ability to understand various kinds of reading materials, as well as your ability to understand the meaning and use of words. There are two types of questions in this section, with special directions for each type.

Part A

Directions: In questions 1-30 each sentence has a word or phrase underlined. Below each sentence are four other words or phrases, marked (A), (B), (C), and (D). You are to choose the _one_ word or phrase that _best keeps the meaning_ of the original sentence if it is substituted for the underlined word or phrase. Then, on your answer sheet, find the number of the question and blacken the space that corresponds to the letter you have chosen so that the letter inside the oval cannot be seen.

Example

Sample Answer
● Ⓑ Ⓒ Ⓓ

Porfirio Diaz is remembered in Mexican history for his long and <u>despotic</u> rule.

(A) dictatorial
(B) compassionate
(C) quixotic
(D) zealous

The best answer is (A) because "Porfirio Diaz is remembered in Mexican history for his long and dictatorial rule" is closest in meaning to the original sentence, "Porfirio Diaz is remembered in Mexican history for his long and despotic rule." Therefore, you should choose answer (A).

As soon as you understand the directions, begin work on the questions.

1. The energy crisis encouraged Americans to make more <u>sparing</u> use of scarce resources.
   (A) efficient
   (B) frugal
   (C) imaginative
   (D) discreet

2. The easternmost <u>point</u> in the United States is West Quoddy Head, Maine.
   (A) indication
   (B) direction
   (C) location
   (D) station

3. Crystallization is the most frequently <u>employed</u> technique for the purification of solid substances.
   (A) used
   (B) enjoined
   (C) belabored
   (D) added

4. New Year's Eve celebrations tend to be <u>livelier</u> than those marking Christmas Eve.
   (A) more animated
   (B) healthier
   (C) longer
   (D) more spiritual

5. <u>Notwithstanding</u> the fact that it is only one of Saturn's many moons, Titan is larger than the planet Mercury.
   (A) Considering
   (B) With regard to
   (C) In spite of
   (D) Ignoring

6. The Secretary of State's illness meant that his visit had to be <u>curtailed</u>.
   (A) postponed
   (B) shortened
   (C) cancelled
   (D) re-arranged

7. The <u>phonograph</u> brightened the lives of many people in the 1920's.
   (A) record player
   (B) electric light
   (C) radio
   (D) cinema

8. Cereal prototypes among <u>wild</u> grasses have not been identified.
   (A) uncultivated
   (B) savage
   (C) hybrid
   (D) intemperate

9. The old tea clippers were <u>largely</u> replaced by steamships during the nineteenth century.
   (A) gradually
   (B) imperceptibly
   (C) finally
   (D) mostly

10. The Arabic term from which the word "coffee" derives originally referred to the bitter quality of the <u>beverage</u> itself.
    (A) plant
    (B) substance
    (C) drink
    (D) infusion

11. Peat represents the first <u>stage</u> in the development of coal from vegetable matter.
    (A) era
    (B) phase
    (C) product
    (D) process

12. Cinnabar is the <u>sole</u> ore of mercury.
    (A) soldered
    (B) basic
    (C) essential
    (D) only

13. The United States armed forces maintain <u>cemeteries</u> in a number of foreign countries.
    (A) graveyards
    (B) foundations
    (C) bases
    (D) camps

14. Not until they were able to <u>discern</u> the Statue of Liberty did many European immigrants to the United States really believe they would reach their destination.
    (A) pass by
    (B) make out
    (C) embrace
    (D) visit

15. <u>Towards</u> the end of his life, W.C. Handy became totally blind.
    (A) By
    (B) Before
    (C) Near
    (D) Until

16. There were a number of limiting factors on the <u>output</u> of consumer durables in 1973-74.
    (A) outflow
    (B) production
    (C) income
    (D) reduction

17. The gila monster is a poisonous lizard with a <u>stout</u> body found in the southwestern deserts of the United States.
    (A) lengthy
    (B) powerful
    (C) muscular
    (D) thickset

18. New York is quite <u>muggy</u> in the summer.
    (A) hot and humid
    (B) dangerous
    (C) colorful and boisterous
    (D) abandoned

19. <u>Derided</u> by modern scientists, the view was once common among alchemists that an agent existed capable of turning base metals into gold.
    (A) Disproved
    (B) Scorned
    (C) Excluded
    (D) Disputed

20. The pioneer wagon trains were usually <u>escorted</u> by experienced frontiersmen.
    (A) organized
    (B) financed
    (C) accompanied
    (D) tracked

21. Chick-peas are now <u>extensively</u> grown in California.
    (A) widely
    (B) hardly
    (C) permanently
    (D) increasingly

22. Industrial <u>strife</u> seems to become more rampant in some countries in times of prosperity.
    (A) competition
    (B) demand
    (C) proliferation
    (D) conflict

23. Franklin D. Roosevelt was not <u>discouraged</u> even by the illness that <u>crippled</u> him.
    (A) disturbed
    (B) impoverished
    (C) disheartened
    (D) alienated

24. <u>Breeding</u> laboratory animals is a multi-million-dollar industry.
    (A) Investigating
    (B) Selling
    (C) Researching
    (D) Raising

25. Only very low-grade graphite is needed for lead pencils, <u>whereas</u> that used as a moderator in atomic piles must be thoroughly, and expensively, purified.
    (A) while
    (B) in addition
    (C) consequently
    (D) because

26. Since they thought that gold <u>resembled</u> the sun, the ancients represented this chemical element with a solar symbol.
    (A) derived from
    (B) looked like
    (C) reflected
    (D) symbolized

27. The groundnut is found in <u>moist</u> places in most parts of the eastern United States.
    (A) various
    (B) damp
    (C) fertile
    (D) sandy

28. The legendary Lady Godiva of Coventry was renowned as a <u>devout</u> noblewoman.
    (A) high-born
    (B) false
    (C) determined
    (D) pious

29. The Emancipation Proclamation, originally read to the Cabinet by Lincoln in September of 1862, <u>came into force</u> on January 1, 1983.
    (A) went into effect
    (B) received military backing
    (C) became forceful
    (D) was ratified

30. The word "Christmas," derived from the Old English for "Christ's Mass," first <u>occurred</u> in the eleventh century.
    (A) started
    (B) recurred
    (C) appeared
    (D) predominated

Part B

Directions: The rest of this section is based on a variety of reading material (single sentences, paragraphs, and the like), followed by questions about the meaning of the material. For questions 31-60, you are to choose the *one* best answer, (A), (B), (C), or (D), to each question. Then, on your answer sheet, find the number of the question and blacken the space that corresponds to the letter of the answer you have chosen.

Answer all questions following a passage on the basis of what is *stated* or *implied* in that passage.

Read the following passage.

Known in myths and legends for its slowness on land, the turtle becomes a navigational wizard when it takes to the sea. Experts on sea turtles can tell us where these creatures go and when, but they cannot explain how sea turtles guide themselves across thousands of miles of open sea to a specific spot. One example of this superb navigational instinct is the ability of female sea turtles to return to their precise place of birth, which they probably have not seen since their own birth several years previously, in order to lay their eggs.

Example I

Sample Answer
● (B) (C) (D)

The passage states that

(A) sea turtles have an uncanny sense of direction.
(B) sea turtles are used to help fishermen navigate the ocean.
(C) experts on sea turtles must guide these creatures to their nesting grounds.
(D) all sea turtles lay their eggs in the same place.

The passage describes the sea turtle as "a navigational wizard" and gives an example of its "superb navigational instinct." Therefore, you should choose (A) as the best completion of the sentence.

Example II

Sample Answer
(A) (B) (C) ●

It can be inferred that one thing the experts would like to find out is

(A) at what age sea turtles lay their eggs.
(B) the migration routes of sea turtles.
(C) how fast sea turtles can travel on land.
(D) what tells sea turtles how to get to their destinations.

The passage says that "Experts on sea turtles can tell us where these creatures go and when, but they cannot explain how sea turtles guide themselves across thousands of miles of open sea to a specific spot." Therefore, you should choose (D) as the best answer.

Questions 31-37

Curry enjoyed a degree of notoriety in the late thirties and early forties because of his controversial murals painted for the State House in his native state of Kansas. These were, however, by no means the only murals he painted, other examples of his work having already enhanced walls at the Justice Department and Interior Department buildings in the nation's capital. Nor were murals the only kind of painting Curry engaged in, for, after his return from studying at the Russian Institute in Paris in 1927, he began building a reputation as a painter of fine watercolors and oils depicting life on the Kansas farmlands. The Whitney Museum of American Art purchased his 1928 picture "Baptism in Kansas" in 1930, and it was the Whitney Studio Club that shortly afterwards put on his first one-man show. In spite of his studies in Paris, Curry is often thought of, along with Grant Wood and Thomas Hart Benson, as representing a reaction against the work of his American contemporaries who were, perhaps, over-imitative of the European modernism that enjoyed such popularity in the United States in the 1920's.

31. The author of the passage implies that Curry's paintings were most strongly influenced by
    (A) European modernism.
    (B) the Russian Institute in Paris.
    (C) the Whitney Studio Club.
    (D) his American background.

32. What type of work was the first to bring Curry some type of recognition?
    (A) paintings that represented Kansas farm life
    (B) government-sponsored murals
    (C) controversial murals painted in Kansas
    (D) paintings imitative of European modernism

33. The passage deals primarily with
    (A) Curry's life in Kansas and Paris.
    (B) American art in the 20's and 30's.
    (C) the Whitneys' influence on Curry.
    (D) Curry's artistic activity.

34. The paragraph preceding this one most probably discussed
    (A) Grant Wood and Thomas Benson.
    (B) native Kansas art.
    (C) Curry's life before 1927.
    (D) European modernism.

35. John Steuart Curry was born in
    (A) Russia.
    (B) Paris.
    (C) Kansas.
    (D) Washington, D.C.

36. Curry painted the murals at the Kansas State House
    (A) before he visited Paris.
    (B) after painting walls in government buildings in Washington, D.C.
    (C) at the time of his one-man show.
    (D) for the Whitney Museum of American Art.

37. Why does the author link John Steuart Curry with Grant Wood and Thomas Hart Benson?
    (A) because they all painted differently from the European modernists
    (B) because all three artists were Americans and contemporaries
    (C) because they all studied in Paris
    (D) because they were all Americans

Questions 38-43

Biomedical jewelry, chic accessories which monitor the wearer's vital functions or sound a warning in response to unhealthy environmental conditions, is already on the market and promises to become much more medically sophisticated and commonplace in the foreseeable future. Today, heart-monitoring devices and posture indicators can be hidden in attractive belts; necklaces may contain portable electrocardiographs, or may register body temperature or the level of pollution in the air. If the pollution level is dangerous, some necklaces open and dispense a face mask and a ten-minute supply of oxygen. One of the less serious versions of this type of necklace simply tells the wearer if his or her own breath has reached an offensive level. Still on the drawing board are designs for attractive personal ornaments which could warn of impending epileptic seizures or migraine headaches. Designers of biomedical jewelry predict that the time will come when artfully designed bracelets or necklaces will be able to diagnose, analyze, and even prescribe treatment for their wearers.

38. What is biomedical jewelry?
    (A) inexpensive medical accessories used in the most sophisticated operations
    (B) jewelry which contains devices that alert the wearer to medically dangerous conditions
    (C) non-functional pieces of equipment used to decorate medical offices
    (D) jewelry being marketed by groups interested in improving environmental conditions

39. Which of the following would be the best title for the passage?
    (A) Fashion Forecast: Accessories for the Year 2000
    (B) Jewelry for Today's Doctor
    (C) Attractive Accessories for Cleaning up the Environment
    (D) What's Wrong? Ask Your Necklace!

40. It is implied that today's biomedical jewelry
    (A) is not taken seriously by the medical community.
    (B) is still on the drawing board.
    (C) is stylish as well as functional.
    (D) is a fashion trend rather than a dependable medical device.

41. According to the passage, the biomedical necklaces mentioned can do all of the following *except*
    (A) provide oxygen.
    (B) dispense a breath freshener.
    (C) monitor the wearer's heartbeat.
    (D) indicate body temperature.

42. How does the author describe the necklace designed to monitor the wearer's breath?
    (A) less sophisticated than some others described
    (B) more for fun than some others described
    (C) simple to use
    (D) offensive

43. Designers of biomedical jewelry envisage a future in which
    (A) their designs will take over some traditional duties of a doctor.
    (B) all jewelry will contain some sort of medical device.
    (C) these artful monitors will be required by law for those suffering from epilepsy and migraines.
    (D) this type of accessory will be commonly available in sophisticated arts and crafts markets.

GO ON TO THE NEXT PAGE

Questions 44-49

It was not until a pope in the thirteenth century forbade the clergy to engage in medicine that Christian laymen in Western Europe became involved in the field. However, though medicine was taught at European universities, surgery was not, and the knife in operations came to be wielded by barber-surgeons, sometimes operating independently, sometimes under the guidance of a physician. Standards and practices among such barber-surgeons varied tremendously, but some measure of control over qualifications was introduced in Britain, at least, when the Company of Barber Surgeons of London was formed in 1540. Some two centuries later, their guild developed into the Royal College of Surgeons, and by 1800, surgery had been firmly established as part of the medical curriculum.

44. The clergy stopped practicing medicine in thirteenth century Western Europe because
    (A) there were enough laymen to do the job.
    (B) they did not have university educations.
    (C) their field of duty was moved out of Western Europe.
    (D) they were told to by the pope.

45. According to the passage, barber-surgeons in the fifteenth century
    (A) were licensed by various European universities.
    (B) operated only under the supervision of a physician.
    (C) could not be judged as a group.
    (D) offered a reliable service.

46. It can be inferred from the passage that before the sixteenth century, surgery in Britain was considered
    (A) outside the realm of trained doctors.
    (B) part of the basic education of barbers.
    (C) a university degree wholly different from one in medicine.
    (D) a tremendous business venture.

47. According to the passage, what effect did the Company of Barber Surgeons of London have on the field of surgery?
    (A) It set up standards which had to be met for qualification as a surgeon.
    (B) It provided a central location for surgical operations in England.
    (C) It offered a program of training and practice for barber-surgeons in London.
    (D) It brought barbers and physicians together to share their expertise.

48. Which of the following correctly describes surgery in the late eighteenth century?
    (A) It was no longer available to the common people.
    (B) It had become part of a physician's training.
    (C) Practitioners had formed guilds for their mutual aid and protection.
    (D) The royal family of England had replaced the popes of earlier times as its supervisors.

49. How long had elapsed between the pope's restrictions on clergymen-doctors and the establishment of the Royal College of Surgeons?
    (A) over 500 years
    (B) some 300 years
    (C) 260 years
    (D) about 200 years

GO ON TO THE NEXT PAGE

Questions 50-52

COLLEGE OF FINE ARTS
TABLE OF CONTENTS

50. Information on how much room and board will cost would most probably be found on pages
    (A) 36-38
    (B) 26-35
    (C) 17-18
    (D) 14-16

51. The best place to look for information about the requirements for a specific major in fine arts would be pages
    (A) 2-3
    (B) 36-38
    (C) 66-86
    (D) 87-151

52. Details about non-academic, college-oriented affairs for undergraduates can be found on what pages?
    (A) 4-5
    (B) 26-35
    (C) 45-47
    (D) 19-25

GO ON TO THE NEXT PAGE

Questions 53-58

One of the subjects that most mystifies astronomers lies in the Large Magellanic Cloud, a neighboring galaxy to our Milky Way, and within the Tarantula Nebula, no less than 180,000 light years from earth. Designated R136a, the object gives off so much light that some scientists have speculated that it must be a star with a mass some 3,000 times as great as our own. Other scientists, while agreeing as to the brightness, claim that, since R136a would then be at least 200 times as large as any other known star, what must be involved is a group of stars, each about 150 times the size of the sun, that is, comparable to the largest known to exist, all grouped so remarkably close together that, given their distance from earth, they cannot be separately identified with our present technology. Whichever side is right, the known facts about R136a mean that it must create stellar winds of unimaginable speed, calculated by some who support the single-star theory at eight million miles per hour. And even if those who favor the star-cluster explanation are correct, R136a would still be a thoroughly exceptional phenomenon, without parallel as far as we know in the universe.

53. How big is R136a?
    (A) 180,000 light-years across
    (B) 200 times the next largest star
    (C) 3,000 times as large as the earth
    (D) there is not enough evidence yet.

54. Where is R136a located?
    (A) in a galaxy next to earth's galaxy
    (B) within the Milky Way
    (C) not far from the Tarantula Nebula
    (D) close to the Magellanic Cloud

55. Why is R136a a mystery to astronomers?
    (A) it is in a neighboring galaxy
    (B) they are unable to determine whether it consists of one or more stars
    (C) they cannot accurately locate the Tarantula Nebula
    (D) it creates such strong stellar winds of eight million miles per hour

56. What is it about R136a that indicates to astronomers that it must be very large?
    (A) its location
    (B) its wind-velocity
    (C) its brightness
    (D) its mysteriousness

57. It may be inferred from the passage that, whichever group of scientists is right, R136a is
    (A) a star about 3,000 times the size of our sun.
    (B) a group of exceptionally large stars.
    (C) more mystifying to astronomers than anything else in the universe.
    (D) different from anything else so far encountered in the universe.

58. If the scientists who favor the star-cluster theory turn out to be right, why would R136a still be a unique phenomenon?
    (A) because the stars would be exceptionally near each other
    (B) because there are very few star clusters
    (C) because it is 180,000 light years from earth
    (D) because those who support the single-star theory would be wrong

Questions 59-60. For each of these questions, choose the answer that is *closest in meaning* to the original sentence. Note that several of the choices may be factually correct, but you should choose the one that is the *closest restatement of the given sentence*.

59. The company is ready to sell off a number of its subsidiaries in order to boost its cash position.
    - (A) Several of the company's subsidiaries are selling well and thus improving cash-flow.
    - (B) By shifting cash into some of its subsidiary companies, the parent company hopes to boost sales.
    - (C) The company is preparing to use some of its branch companies as the basis for increased sales.
    - (D) Since it is short of cash, the company is willing to get rid of some of its subsidiaries.

60. During periods of physical stress, the human body uses up more vitamins than it usually does.
    - (A) It is not unusual for periods of high vitamin use to be succeeded by others of extra physical activity.
    - (B) The human body usually requires a larger supply of vitamins than it does in periods of unusual physical effort.
    - (C) Vitamin requirements rise when the physical demands on the human body are unusually high.
    - (D) Stress can be caused by sustained periods of vitamin deficiency.

ANSWER KEY/
PRACTICE TEST VI

Section 1: Listening Comprehension

Part A	*Part B*	*Part C*
1. B	21. D	36. C
2. B	22. A	37. D
3. C	23. C	38. B
4. C	24. A	39. B
5. D	25. B	40. A
6. A	26. D	41. C
7. D	27. B	42. A
8. A	28. A	43. D
9. C	29. A	44. B
10. B	30. C	45. D
11. A	31. B	46. D
12. D	32. D	47. A
13. B	33. B	48. C
14. A	34. D	49. C
15. D	35. C	50. B
16. C		
17. D		
18. C		
19. A		
20. B		

Section 2: Structure and Written Expression

Part A

The explanations of why given answers are wrong have been kept as brief as possible. Indications of how particular incorrect answers might be made correct are provided as a stimulus to thinking about English sentence structure. The references marked FE are to the Focused Exercises which may be of help in further explaining why a particular answer is correct or incorrect and in offering more practice.

1. A Creates dependent clause, no main clause completion
   B Apposition to subject; no predicate
   C See 1-B
   D Correct (FE-6)

2. A Correct
   B "as well as" does not combine with "the only"
   C Would mean both are "the only"
   D See 2-C

3. A No "to" after "may"
   B Correct
   C Sense impossible with "last 2,000 years" (needs perfect infinitive)
   D Impossible form

4. A "that" does not relate with anything in sentence
   B Creates two main clauses unacceptably linked
   C Correct
   D See 4-B

5. A "so" requires inversion of subject and verb (FE-8)
   B Needs question-type inversion (FE-8)
   C Misplaced initial auxiliary "do"
   D Correct (FE-8)

6. A "whatever" must be followed by "the" + "noun" (FE-13)
   B Needs "the"
   C "whatever" cannot be followed by a clause
   D Correct

7. A Correct; abridged dependent clause (FE-11)
   B Creates two unacceptably linked main clauses
   C Either needs verb to make dependent clause (FE-10) or no subject to create abridged dependent clause (FE-11)
   D Illogical semantically

8. A Wrong form of conjunction
   B Correct (FE-15)
   C Conceivable if "not" in initial position, creating participial phrase (FE-12)
   D "as" wrong conjunction of comparison for two different nouns

9. A Creates dependent phrase with no main clause (FE-12)
   B Correct (FE-6)
   C Would create a subject with no predicate
   D Needs article "a" with profession

10. A Preposition incomplete (FE-28)
    B "nose" cannot "add"
    C Adverb cannot modify noun
    D Correct

11. A Correct (FE-10)
    B Repetition of subject (FE-3)
    C Missing verb (acceptable as abridged clause FE-12 without "which")
    D See 11-B

12. A Creates two unacceptably linked
    main clauses
 B Dependent clause lacks subject (FE-
    10)
 C Correct
 D Does not create clause after "which"

13. A "that" requires anticipatory "it" (FE-
    4)
 B Correct (FE-4)
 C See 13-A
 D See 13-A

14. A Wrong tense sequence (FE-29)
 B Passive not possible (FE-7)
 C Correct
 D Would create dependent participial
    phrase requiring subsequent main
    clause

15. A Finite verb would require subject
 B Creates two unacceptably linked
    main clauses
 C See 15-B, plus misplaced subject
    and verb (FE-13)
 D Correct (FE-12)

Part B

In every case the answer is given first. Where there is an FE reference,
this indicates the number of the Focused Exercise which may offer useful
further practice of the point in question. Where words in quotation marks
follow the letter of the correct answer, these show what would be needed for
the sentence to be correct. This usually occurs in cases where none of the
Focused Exercises is applicable.

16. A (FE-17)
17. C (FE-32)
18. D (FE-24)
19. D (FE-23)
20. B (FE-28)
21. A (FE-19)
22. C (FE-16)
23. B (FE-39)
24. D (FE-14, 33)
25. D (FE-19)
26. A ("sometimes")
27. D (FE-37)
28. B (FE-40)

29. A (FE-25)
30. D (FE-20)
31. C ("crustacean")
32. C (FE-23)
33. B ("average") (FE-40)
34. A (FE-25)
35. D (FE-14, 33)
36. D (FE-39)
37. A (FE-25)
38. C (FE-38)
39. B (FE-16)
40. B (FE-40)

Section 3: Reading Comprehension and Vocabulary

Part A

1. B	11. B	21. A
2. C	12. D	22. D
3. D	13. A	23. C
4. A	14. B	24. D
5. C	15. C	25. A
6. B	16. B	26. B
7. A	17. D	27. B
8. A	18. A	28. D
9. D	19. B	29. A
10. C	20. C	30. C

Part B

31. D	41. B	51. D
32. C	42. B	52. B
33. D	43. A	53. D
34. C	44. D	54. A
35. C	45. C	55. B
36. B	46. A	56. C
37. A	47. A	57. D
38. B	48. B	58. A
39. D	49. A	59. D
40. C	50. D	60. C

LISTENING COMPREHENSION TAPESCRIPTS

Tapescript/Practice Test 1

Section 1, Part A, Listening Comprehension

Example I

The teacher had already called the roll by the time I got to class.

Example II

Our new coffee table is made out of copper.

1. Unpaid parking tickets make students ineligible for receiving student activity cards.
2. Sue hasn't paid her share of the rent, so she must not have found a job yet.
3. Would it be inconvenient for you to lend me a tray of ice?
4. It doesn't seem possible that the twins are already teenagers.
5. His reaction struck me as laughable.
6. Joan inspires confidence in her co-workers.
7. Since it was so hot, we all felt overdressed.
8. The students kept writing when the bell had rung.
9. This history book is no longer up-to-date.
10. The airport was closed today so they must not have gone to Chicago.
11. If I were able to get in, that's the show I'd like to see.
12. The owner of the building assured us that there would be no rent increase this year.
13. Having quit his last job, Jeff found it difficult to get another.
14. I'm sorry, you can only buy traveler's checks at window eight.
15. Rarely have I had such a wonderful meal.
16. The least they could do is write to their parents once in a while.
17. Betting on sports events is illegal in some states.
18. The two old women had the man carry their cases.
19. You can't do it?
20. How come you don't visit us anymore?

Section 1, Part B

Example: WOMAN: Have you decided which offer to accept?

MAN: Not yet. What would you do if you were in my shoes?

What can be said about the man?

21. MAN: Are you going to dinner with us later?

WOMAN: If only I'd finished my lab report, I'd be joining you with pleasure.

What is the woman going to do?

22. WOMAN: Is this line for purchasing tickets?

MAN: Yes, but all they have left are tickets for the late performance.

What does the man mean?

23. WOMAN: The brakes on my station wagon are still not working properly.

MAN: Come over and we'll check them out.

What are these people discussing?

24. WOMAN: Let's get a bite to eat after the meeting tonight.

MAN: I'd love to, but I have to pick up my car before eight.

What does the woman suggest?

25. WOMAN: I'm off to Canada tomorrow.

MAN: You'd better take something to keep warm in. The weather there is not what you're used to.

What does the man advise the woman to do?

26. MAN: Pam was half an hour late for work this morning.

WOMAN: So, what else is new?

What can be said about Pam?

27. WOMAN: Can you pass me the potatoes?

MAN: Don't you think you've had enough?

What does the man mean?

28. MAN: We should have the lawn seen to and those bulbs transplanted.

WOMAN: Well, I haven't got the time. Why don't you call Mr. Davis?

What is Mr. Davis's occupation?

29. WOMAN: Ted, do you know how to get to the sports center from here?

TED: Why not ask that policeman?

What does Ted mean?

30. WOMAN: I don't think we'll find a better buy than this.

MAN: Let's try at least one more place.

WOMAN: Well, if you insist.

What did they decide to do?

31. MAN: Professor Miller is the best teacher I've had in the biology department.

WOMAN: I took one of his elementary courses and didn't think much of it.

What do these people think of Professor Miller's courses?

32. WOMAN: I'm sorry you had to wait for me, I ran out of gas about half way here.

    MAN: That's too bad. Unfortunately, we can't go in until intermission now.

What will these people have to do now?

33.   MAN: Can you give me a hand tomorrow? I want to re-arrange some things in our spare room.

    WOMAN: Tomorrow's impossible, but I'm free this weekend.

What does the man ask the woman to do?

34. WOMAN: I was elected president of the Explorers' Club at our meeting last night.

    MAN: Way to go!

How does the man react to the woman's news?

35. WOMAN: Congratulations. That was an inspiring commencement address.

    MAN: Thank you. Getting my degree in engineering meant a lot to me.

Where did this conversation probably take place?

Sample Talk

The Columbiana Community College would like to announce a new two-year program in Office Technology. This program of study is recommended for individuals who are interested in secretarial work but have had little or no business training or experience. Most credits earned in this program cannot be applied to a degree program, but some may. To determine which credits do apply to a B.A. or B.S. degree, the student should consult an academic adviser.

Example I

Who is the program designed for?

Example II

What will the credits earned in this program count towards?

Questions 36-39

Yesterday, we talked about the difficulties faced by the earliest settlers who came from England. Today, we move on to a figure of particular importance to those seventeenth-century farmers. As you know, most of the New England settlers were peasants who relied on the handed-down wisdom of their parents and grandparents to guide them in their farming. But this oral tradition was much more difficult to maintain in the New World with its sparse and scattered population, and so writers such as Thomas Tusser began to collect advice for farmers and publish it in farmers' handbooks. Tusser became very important in the 1600's because he gave farmers valuable information in an easy-to-read-and-remember style. In all, Tusser wrote down more than 500 points of good husbandry—from reminders of when to plant crops to how and why to preserve meat—in order to help farmers in their struggle for survival.

36. What is the main topic of the talk?

37. According to the speaker, what was one difference between farming in England and farming in the New World in the seventeenth century?

38. What farmers is the speaker referring to?

39. What did Thomas Tusser write about?

WOMAN: I've given you a corner room on the fifth floor with a nice view of the park. Shall I get a bellboy to help you with your luggage?

MAN: No, that's all right. I haven't got any. I wasn't intending to stay the night in town, but I missed my plane. By the way, do you happen to sell toilet requisites? I need a toothbrush, toothpaste, and a comb.

WOMAN: Well, sir, I have toothbrushes and paste, but I don't have any combs left.

MAN: I really need a comb, too. Is there a store anywhere that's open at this hour?

WOMAN: Certainly, that's not difficult. There's one open 24 hours. Turn right when you leave the hotel. Go to the second stoplight and turn left. You'll see the sign on the right-hand side of the road.

40. What is the woman's position?
41. What did the man need from the store?
42. Where is the store?

43. What can best be said about the man?
44. How can the woman's attitude be described?

Questions 45-50

I would like to thank the Future Farmers of America for inviting me to speak at your annual Thanksgiving banquet. Your program chairman has asked me to discuss the problem of lightning in our rural communities. Each year, more than 100 deaths in the United States are caused by lightning and usually four times as many injuries—more yearly deaths and injuries than by hurricanes, tornados, and floods combined. And, those of us living outside of cities are the most likely to be among the 400 injured by lightning. Let's begin by listing the three most dangerous places to be during a thunderstorm. First on our list is any open space where you are taller than your surroundings; therefore, leave fields or plains immediately if a thunderstorm threatens. The second largest number of people killed by lightning each year are among those who have taken refuge under a solitary tree. And, finally, nearly one-tenth of the lightning casualties have to do with water. You should avoid water in ponds or lakes, and under no circumstances swim or wade, nor remain on the water in a small open boat.

45. What is the topic of the man's speech?

46. Which of the following causes the most deaths and injuries in the United States?

47. Approximately how many people are injured by lightning annually?

48. Who is the speaker's audience?

49. According to the speaker, which of the following places would be the most dangerous in a thunderstorm?

50. What does the speaker say about being near water during a thunderstorm?

Tapescript/Practice Test II

Section 1, Part A, Listening Comprehension

Example I

My cousin makes lamps out of drift-wood.

Example II

Term papers are due a week from to-morrow.

1. If I were the chairman, I would have resigned long ago.

2. Could I borrow your notes from today's lecture?

3. Why don't we at least phone them and welcome them home?

4. Don't give me anymore, I've already had more than enough.

5. I expect you to pay attention when I'm talking.

6. Kay had changed jobs so often that she received no pension when she retired.

7. I'm not accustomed to driving on the left.

8. We can have this garage cleaned out by tomorrow, can't we?

9. While you're up, bring me the telephone.

10. Carolyn is a much better typist than Chris.

11. You really liked that movie?

12. If only I had known about Professor Baker's course.

13. This section of the library is reserved for graduate students.

14. Robert withdrew from the race at the last moment.

15. The hostess will seat you, if you wait here.

16. Because of the harsh weather, the far North is sparsely populated.

17. Phil must have failed this course last semester.

18. Sam's computer stopped working, so I lent him mine.

19. Peter intends to stay in Alaska whether he finds gold or not.

20. You must be more skillful than I had imagined.

Section 1, Part B

Example: WOMAN: Let's cook out tonight instead of going to a restaurant.

MAN: That's a great idea. Do we have any charcoal?

What are these people going to do this evening?

21. MAN: Can you tell me how many hours I have to carry to be considered full-time?

WOMAN: Yes, you must carry a courseload of at least 12 hours per term.

Where did this conversation probably take place?

22. MAN: I just can't make out this signature.

WOMAN: I certainly see what you mean.

What can be concluded from this conversation?

23. WOMAN: Is it true that they make a lot of pottery in the Ohio River valley?

MAN: Oh, yes. That's because there's an abundance of the right kind of clay.

According to the man, what is true about the Ohio River valley?

24. WOMAN: It's the next house on the left. How much will that be?

MAN: The fare's on the meter.

What kind of job does the man have?

25. MAN: At least Frank always gets here on time.

WOMAN: True enough, but his punctuality doesn't make up for his inefficiency.

What does the woman think about Frank?

26. MAN: Let's go to the park for a while.

WOMAN: Oh, I can't move. I started an exercise class at the gym this morning.

What does the woman mean?

27. MAN: I can't tell you how much this gift means to me.

WOMAN: We wanted you to have something to remember us by.

What does the man mean?

28. WOMAN: Your living room looks beautiful. Did you paint it yourself?

MAN: Of course not. I paid my younger brother to do it.

What does the man say about his living room?

29. MAN: Did you have a good time at Susan's party last night?

WOMAN: We didn't get there.

What does the woman mean?

30. WOMAN: Excuse me, how often is there a westbound express train?

MAN: Westbound? That's on the other side of the tracks. Platform six.

What does the man tell the woman?

31. MAN: This notice says that checkout time is noon. What does that mean?

WOMAN: You have to vacate your room by twelve or pay extra.

What are these people discussing?

32. WOMAN: Marsha was telling me about
        an apartment for rent in her
        building.
      MAN: Don't get your hopes up. Every-
        thing in that neighborhood is
        out of our price range.
What does the man mean?

33. WOMAN: Ted, could you mail these let-
        ters on your way to the club?
      TED: The club's closed. I'm meet-
        ing Chris at his house.
Where is Ted going now?

34.   MAN: Do you know anything about
        Professor Simpson's classes?
      WOMAN: If you're looking for an easy
        course, forget it. Simpson
        writes the trickiest exams in
        the department.
*What do you learn about Professor
Simpson?*

35.   MAN: This dish is too spicy for me.
      WOMAN: I know what you mean. My
        mouth is on fire.
What are these people talking about?

Section 1, Part C

Sample Talk

Even though it is called a weed, the goldenrod makes a very good garden plant. In the United States, this so-called weed grows especially well east of the Rockies. It thrives in fields, woodlands, prairies, swamps, on high plains—in fact, just about anywhere. In late summer and autumn, the plant produces a profusion of small, brilliant yellow flowers which are usually arranged in wandlike clusters. Because it is a weed, the goldenrod is not usually for sale in plant shops, but it is easy to find, easy to grow, and will actually improve under the care of a gardner.

Example I

Which of the following best expresses the speaker's opinion?

Example II

Where would you be most likely to find goldenrod?

MAN: How are you feeling?

WOMAN: Not too well.

MAN: I'll bet. How long do you have to stay in bed?

WOMAN: At least through the weekend. Can you bring me up-to-date with what happened in Professor Jones's class today?

MAN: He talked about Salem, Massachusetts and the trials for witchcraft held there in 1692. Did you know that those trials resulted in the hanging of nineteen people?

WOMAN: No, I didn't. I had the impression that just one or two people were found guilty of being witches.

MAN: Well, you can find out the details in our book; you should finish chapters eight and nine before Monday. And we're also supposed to think about topics for term papers. Professor Jones suggested that someone could do research on the colonial influence on present-day Salem.

WOMAN: That sounds interesting, but I'll be lucky if I get through the reading assignment *this* weekend.

36. Why did the woman miss Professor Jones's class today?

37. What subject does Professor Jones probably teach?

38. When is the woman likely to return to Professor Jones's class?

39. What do the man and woman think about the Salem witchcraft trials?

40. What will the woman probably do this weekend?

<u>**Questions 41-46**</u>

Today, we will talk about purchasing and preparing raw fish—a gourmet treat unfamiliar to most Americans. The first fish we will experiment with is the bluefin tuna. Our piece of fish is from Nova Scotia and was flown in fresh today to one of the best fish markets here in New York City. When buying bluefin tuna, you must consider four things: first, the fish should be cold, between 40 and 45 degrees F., but should not be frozen, a process which destroys some of its delicate flavor. Second, you must decide what color of meat best suits your taste. Bluefin meat ranges from bright red to pink. Third, you must know the cut that you are buying. The best cuts come from the muscle around the body cavity. And last, you should know how much to pay for this exquisite fish. What we have here cost $18.00 a pound in a retail fish market, and would cost 25 to 50 dollars a pound in a restaurant. Now, we will look at some ways to prepare this fish for the table . . .

41. Where is the speaker?

42. Where was the bluefin referred to caught?

43. What is the speaker's purpose?

44. What can be said about the speaker's opinion of bluefin tuna?

45. What color is considered to be the best in bluefin tuna?

46. What will probably happen next?

<u>**Questions 47-50**</u>

It is hardly surprising that the practice of collecting stamps began much later than that of coin collecting, which has had followers for more than 2,000 years. The fact is that, although various kinds of postal services have existed for perhaps as much as three thousands years, it was not until the adhesive, prepaid stamp (the kind we are all familiar with) was invented in 1836 in Scotland that the potential for stamp collecting emerged. After that, interest was not long in coming and there was already a considerable number of enthusiasts by the middle of the 1850's.

47. What does the speaker believe about stamp collecting?

48. According to the speaker, how long have postal services been in existence?

49. What gave the impetus for stamp collecting?

50. Once adhesive stamps were introduced, what happened to stamp collecting?

Tapescript/Practice Test III

Section 1, Part A, Listening Comprehension

Example I

Her parents tried to attract her to farming.

Example II

The major leagues hope to make the old-timers' game an annual event.

1. If I had known you had company, I wouldn't have dropped in.
2. Ben carried out his end of the deal.
3. That's the way you wanted it?
4. It's too hot to study indoors.
5. Bill chews gum constantly.
6. When Dave completed his training, he was forced to look for work.
7. The voting was heavier than expected.
8. I don't think it's a good idea to borrow money.
9. The teacher apologized for giving them the wrong solution.
10. Tracy was supposed to contact her uncle before the end of the month.
11. Allen would have proposed if he had thought Maria would accept.
12. Whatever happens, remember it's just a game.
13. If only I had studied harder last quarter.
14. How can I help you?
15. We plan to go back there because of the marvelous beaches.
16. Tony barely had time to catch his breath before his boss arrived.
17. You'd never know, but Jean made that suit herself.
18. I don't see how this map's going to help us.
19. Bill won't like this even if you show him why it's important.
20. You used to spend time at the coast every summer, didn't you?

Section 1, Part B

Example: WOMAN: Do you have time to type this letter before you leave?

MAN: I'd like to, except that I have to get to the post office before it closes.

What can be concluded from the man's reply?

21. WOMAN: Excuse me, I've been waiting for more than twenty minutes to cash my pay check.

MAN: I'm afraid everyone has had to wait today. Our computer's down.

What is the woman complaining about?

22. MAN: If you're making spaghetti sauce, could you please leave out the garlic this time?

WOMAN: Well, I could, but it won't taste very Italian without it.

What does the man ask the woman to do?

23. MAN: Did the Johnsons come to your dinner party?

WOMAN: Not only did they turn up, but they brought two strangers with them.

What does the woman mean?

24. WOMAN: Why are you returning this tie?

MAN: I got it for my birthday, but I don't wear ties.

How did the man get the tie?

25. WOMAN: I can't see how to divide up this work.

MAN: You'll have to consult with your co-workers about that.

What does the man tell the woman to do?

26. MAN: Isn't the litter in the park awful?

WOMAN: Yes. The trash has spoiled it for me.

What are these people complaining about?

27. MAN: Have you finished that article you promised to do for our magazine?

WOMAN: I won't be able to get to it until after my exams if that's okay with you.

What does the woman want to do?

28. MAN: It's a beautiful day for gardening.

WOMAN: Yes, but I wish you wouldn't trail half the garden through the living room.

What does the woman mean?

29. WOMAN: That's an interesting aroma. What is it?

MAN: I'm trying my mother's recipe for Irish stew.

What is the couple discussing?

30. MAN: I wonder what my old roommate is doing now?

WOMAN: You mean Keith? He's living out West and writing short stories.

What did the man find out?

31.   MAN: How much are you earning
           these days?
    WOMAN: I don't consider that any of
           your business.
           What does the woman mean?

32. WOMAN: We're still not satisfied with
           the reception, Mr. Gray.
    MR. GRAY: Well you can't expect to get
           a perfect picture with a five-
           year-old set.
    What is Mr. Gray's occupation?

33.   MAN: Do you know what food con-
           tains vitamin A?
    WOMAN: No, but you could look under
           "diet" in the index in your
           medical encyclopedia.
    *What does the woman suggest the man
    do?*

34. WOMAN: Jane bought some beautiful
           fabric at a factory outlet on
           her recent trip to Oregon.
       MAN: That's unusual. I thought the
           best textile mills were still in
           the South.
    *What can be concluded from this con-
    versation?*

35.   MAN: The study with all those
           bookshelves would be very
           useful.
    WOMEN: And here is the kitchen,
           which comes equipped with a
           built-in washer and dryer.
    *Where did this conversation probably
    take place?*

Section 1, Part C

Sample Talk

To all who see it, the International Peace Monument is a reminder of the long history of good will between the United States and Canada. The memorial was dedicated in 1941 to celebrate 126 years of peace and friendship between the two countries, and the inscription states the mutual desire of the two nations for continued peace and harmony. The monument was contributed by the Monument Builders of America and stands on Belle Isle, in the Detroit River, midway between the cities of Detroit in the United States and Windsor in Canada.

Example I

What does the International Peace Monument commemorate?

Example II

Where is the International Peace Monument located?

Welcome to the first meeting of the Alumni Association for this school year. Our association was founded in 1920 and presently maintains records on more than 70,000 alumni. Our aim is to provide channels of communication between the university and you, its former students. To do this, we can provide you with social and business contacts through alumni clubs and can help you solve all sorts of problems by using resources available at the university.

In turn, the Association asks its members to help the university by referring quality students for admission, advising on programs, enhancing the university's good reputation in your communities, and providing needed financial assistance.

Also, as a member, you will receive invitations to all campus-sponsored social and academic events, and you will receive the alumni bulletin nine times a year.

36. Who is the speaker addressing?

37. What is the stated purpose of the Alumni Association?

38. How long has the Alumni Association existed?

39. How do the Alumni Association members help the university?

40. Which of the following is *not* mentioned as an advantage of the Alumni Association for its members?

Questions 41-44

By comparison with fashions from earlier epochs, today's shoe styles seem boringly practical. Take the pointed toe as an example. In the tenth century, aristocrats in Western Europe began to prefer shoes with sharp points at the end. By the twelfth century, the point of a well-dressed nobleman's footwear extended two inches past the end of his toes. And by the fourteenth century, the toe of the pointed shoe reached twelve inches beyond the foot and was stuffed with moss, hay, or wool and shaped with whalebone. Even though many religious and secular leaders condemned this final example of frivolous exaggeration by the nobility, it lasted for nearly a hundred years until pointed toe shoes ended their five-century reign.

41. What is the main topic of the talk?

42. According to the speaker, how do today's footwear fashions compare with those of six or seven centuries ago?

43. According to the speaker, for approximately how long were pointed-toe shoes in fashion?

44. According to the passage, who wore the pointed toe footwear referred to?

PATIENT: Well, doctor, what have I got?

DOCTOR: The results of the skin test indicate that you have what is commonly known as hay fever.

PATIENT: But how can that be possible? I'm not a farmer! I work in the public library.

DOCTOR: First of all, hay fever is not usually caused by hay-producing grasses in this part of the state. And as you've noticed, your illness is not characterized by fever, but by sneezing, a runny nose, and itching eyes. And, in the second place, the pollen which usually causes a condition likes yours is microscopic in size and, at this time of the year, is in very high concentrations throughout our environment.

PATIENT: But then why doesn't everyone have hay fever?

DOCTOR: It is the same as with most allergies. To be a sufferer, you must have a hereditary sensitivity to something, in this case to pollens.

PATIENT: Well, I can't change my ancestors. Is there anything I *can* do?

DOCTOR: Of course. I'll write you a prescription for some medicine which will almost totally relieve your symptoms.

45. Why is the man at the doctor's office?
46. How can hay fever be diagnosed?
47. What kind of work does the man do?
48. What causes hay fever?
49. According to the doctor, who is most likely to suffer from hay fever?
50. Where will the man probably go now?

Tapescript/Practice Test IV

Section 1, Part A, Listening Comprehension

Example I

The French teacher usually has the students practice conversation in small groups.

Example II

My attorney needs to arrange the details with the court.

1. Not until the last moment did I realize who she was.
2. Are you sure you can get along without your car this afternoon?
3. The news took their breath away.
4. The little theater held auditions the month before last.
5. If you hadn't called, I would have slept through the examination.
6. Because of fire damage, the mall was closed for repairs for a month.
7. Nancy was proud of her tan.
8. The children were taught to be well-behaved.
9. When he got off the bus, he left his briefcase behind.
10. Jane changed her mind about having her hair cut.
11. Chemistry majors are required to take at least two math courses.
12. Cynthia isn't nearly as bright as Paul.
13. Richard waved to us as he boarded his plane.
14. The report talks about the recent jump in local food prices.
15. Would you mind delivering this message to Mr. Alexander?
16. He'd better give up fast cars and late nights.
17. The president made several wrong decisions, so his country is now badly off.
18. Please concentrate on your lines.
19. Mark let them talk him into selling his boat.
20. I would've taken your picture if it hadn't been so cloudy out.

Example: WOMAN: Is Amy really quitting school?

MAN: Probably. She doesn't have enough money for next semester's tuition.

What will Amy do?

21. MAN: That was a wonderful meal. Every course was beautifully prepared.

WOMAN: I had no complaints—except for the size of the bill.

What do these people agree on?

22. MAN: Do you have anything on the history of baseball cards?

WOMAN: I believe so. Look in the card catalogue under baseball and also under hobbies.

Where did this conversation take place?

23. WOMAN: Just a second. I want to leave a message for Bill.

MAN: Don't bother. We'll be back in less than an hour.

What can be concluded from this conversation?

24. MAN: What did your accountant say about the mix-up?

WOMAN: He thinks it's my fault, but I'd certainly value your opinion.

What does the woman mean?

25. WOMAN: I really should have done better. I was ahead for the first three laps.

MAN: There'll be other races.

Why was the woman disappointed?

26. WOMAN: Could you change a fifty-dollar bill?

MAN: Fifty? That would take all the change I've got.

What does the man mean?

27. MAN: Aren't you going to apologize for breaking that window?

WOMAN: Why should I? I didn't throw the ball.

How does the woman feel about the situation?

28. MAN: Would it help if I looked after the baby?

WOMAN: That would give me time to get everything else ready.

What is the man going to do?

29. WOMAN: This package was returned to me.

MAN: That's because you didn't put enough postage on it.

What did the man tell the woman about the package?

30. WOMAN: How did you find New Orleans?

MAN: I had a great time. It's a city full of contrasts with everything from the French Quarter to the Superdome.

What are these people discussing?

31. MAN: Didn't you say you'd drive me to the airport?

WOMAN: Right. We'll leave immediately after the news.

What are these people going to do now?

32.   MAN: Paula, have you seen my navy blue blazer? I can't find it anywhere.

WOMAN: I sent it to the cleaner's. It should be ready this afternoon.

Why can't the man find what he's looking for?

33.   MAN: I'd better get going if I want to get home before dark.

WOMAN: Give my best to Ann and the kids.

What do we learn from this conversation?

34. WOMAN: The mailman just delivered Mr. Marshall's bill. I think he overcharged us for our car stereo.

MAN: I'll ask him about it when I stop to pick up that toaster we bought for your mother.

What does Mr. Marshall do?

35.   MAN: Why don't we go to Las Vegas this summer?

WOMAN: We can't go through Death Valley in our old car. We'll have to save some money and go by plane.

What are they going to do this summer?

Sample Talk

Melford College is now accepting applications for the position of director of its freshmen residence halls. The responsibilities of the director will include supervising maintenance, room assignments, the social programs, and the cafeteria of all four on-campus dormitories for first-year students. Applicants must have a minimum of five years experience working in a similar facility. Apartment and meals are included. Salary will be based on the applicant's training and experience.

Example I

What is Melford College looking for?

Example II

According to the announcement, which of the following will probably be a duty of the new director?

Questions 36-40

MAN: What is that?

WOMAN: It's a picture of a Komodo dragon that Walter sent me from the island of Komodo when he was vacationing in the South Pacific.

MAN: Wow! It's really ugly! How did he get a photograph? Isn't that thing extinct?

WOMAN: No. As a matter of fact, there are believed to be between 5,000 and 7,000 of them on Komodo and nearby islands. Walter took this picture himself.

MAN: Aren't they dangerous? This one looks ferocious.

WOMAN: Walter says they can be quite dangerous because they are erratic in their behavior. I looked them up in the encyclopedia. Sometimes they are as curious and gentle as a housecat, but they have also been known to eat live human beings, although they are more likely to go for goats or water buffaloes.

MAN: Really? How big are they?

WOMAN: A big dragon can weigh several hundred pounds. It's the largest of forty-two species of monitor lizards found in the Pacific, Asia, and Africa. They have *one* Komodo dragon in the San Diego Zoo. Why don't we drive down and have a look at it this weekend?

MAN: Great idea!

36. What are these people talking about?
37. Why did Walter go to the South Pacific?
38. What is a Komodo dragon most likely to eat?

39. Why are Komodo dragons considered dangerous?
40. Where do Komodo dragons occur naturally?

<u>Questions 41-48</u>

The same purpose has always guided the Chautauqua Institute, now in its second century of existence: the combining of daily study with healthful recreation. Founded on Chautauqua Lake, in New York, in 1874 by John H. Vincent and Lewis Miller, the institute has always sought to provide a summer vacation spot that offers the benefits of both social and educational activities. Summer visitors may choose from, among other activities, lectures, concerts, readings, and dramatic entertainments. At one time, there were as many as fifty chautauqua-type organizations scattered throughout the country as well as a few traveling chautauquas. The latter attempted to provide the same type of program as that presented in the stationary chautauquas for about a week at a time to residents of various small towns and villages throughout the summer season. The traveling groups and most of the smaller organizations disappeared with the coming of radio, movies, and the mass production of the automobile. The original Chautauqua Institute, on the other hand, has continued to attract thousands of participants each summer up to the present time.

41. Where is the Chautauqua Institute located?

42. For what purpose was the Chautauqua Institute founded?

43. For how long has the Chautauqua Institute existed?

44. How did the traveling chautauquas differ from the original Chautauqua Institute?

45. How extensive is the usual program at the Chautauqua Institute?

46. According to the speaker, what contributed to the disappearance of the smaller chautauquas?

Questions 47-50

WOMAN: I won't be able to go to the movie with you tonight. I must have my presentation for the Beauty Bar Soap account ready for a nine o'clock meeting tomorrow morning.

MAN: I thought you finished that last weekend.

WOMAN: I did, but my boss wants a series of ads that will appeal to men as well as women. My original treatment was aimed at the female consumer.

MAN: Well, I think your boss is right. Men have recently become just as concerned as women about skin care.

47. What is the woman's presentation to be about?

48. According to her boss, what was the problem with the presentation the woman completed last weekend?

49. According to the man, how have men changed recently?

50. What will the woman probably do now?

Tapescript/Practice Test V

Section 1, Part A, Listening Comprehension

Example I

They missed the exit and ended up thirty miles past their destination.

Example II

The family sadly watched as their home went up in smoke.

1. I wanted to catch the early train, but I couldn't get a ride to the station.
2. Finding a parking place near the university is such a nuisance now.
3. If they'd made Bill a better offer, he would have willingly relocated.
4. By the time the game was over, most of the fans had left.
5. I'm fed up with this weather.
6. I wish she'd drop the subject—her remarks are more offensive than she realizes.
7. Jogging is a great way to keep fit.
8. After the storm, we had to replace part of our roof.
9. Economists predict an off year for the auto industry.
10. They must've gotten lost or they would have been here by this time.
11. Did you *hear*, Fred?
12. Even if the final exam is postponed, you should still begin to study for it now.
13. Take your time, there's no big hurry.
14. I've never lived abroad and neither has Cathy.
15. With all of your deductions, you should have an expert help you with your tax return.
16. The race will begin as soon as the contestants reach the starting line.
17. The nominees will meet after classes on Thursday.
18. The physicists resumed their discussion after the bomb scare.
19. The orchestra was brilliant, but the soloist spoiled the performance for me.
20. You should have waited for the light to change.

Example: WOMAN: It's difficult to shift into reverse and the right turn signal doesn't work.

MAN: We'll take care of those things and give it a tune-up.

What are these people discussing?

21. WOMAN: How long have you worked for an insurance company?

MAN: I've only been here for two years, but I worked for our southern branch for six years before being transferred.

How long has the man worked for his present employer?

22. MAN: JoAnn, we were wondering if we could have our next club meeting at your house.

JOANN: I wish I could say yes, but we're in the process of having all of the downstairs re-decorated.

Will the next club meeting be at JoAnn's house?

23. MAN: I thought I was prepared for that exam, but I couldn't answer more than half of the questions.

WOMAN: Me neither. I don't think we covered some of that material in class.

What did these students think about the test?

24. WOMAN: Ted and I saw that movie last week, but we'd like to see you *after* the show.

MAN: Great. Let's get together at my house at ten.

When will they see each other?

25. MAN: Can you tell me how to find out about a painting by Winslow Homer?

WOMAN: You'll find several books about Homer in the section near the telephone booth.

What is the man looking for?

26. MAN: Unfortunately, you haven't had enough basic courses to take an advanced course in physics.

WOMAN: Can't I persuade you to bend the rules this once?

What does the woman mean?

27. WOMAN: The play should have begun ten minutes ago. What's holding things up?

MAN: The leading man is caught in a traffic jam.

What is the problem?

28. MAN: Have you decided who you're going to have take care of the graduation banquet?

WOMAN: Yes, Mrs. Talbott has agreed to organize the whole operation—she's a professional, you know.

What does Mrs. Talbott do?

29. WOMAN: Mr. Perkins, I wonder if you could give me Friday afternoon off. My sister is getting married.

MR. P: I really shouldn't. You're two weeks behind with the accounts, but I guess you've got a good reason.

What can be concluded from this conversation?

30. WOMAN: Have you seen the price of gasoline lately?

MAN: Yes. It's enough to make me sell my car and get a bicycle.

What are these people talking about?

31. MRS. B.: Hello Jane. This is Mrs. Brown. Has your mother gotten back from Texas yet?

JANE: She got here early this morning Mrs. Brown, but she's over at my grandmother's at the moment.

Where is Jane's mother?

32. MAN: I'd like to place a help wanted ad.

WOMAN: I'm sorry, the person in charge of classified ads is out to lunch. Could you come back later?

Where did this conversation probably take place?

33. WOMAN: I'm very sorry. I've spilled my coffee on your magazine.

MAN: It's easy for you to say you're sorry. *My* magazine is ruined.

How does the man feel?

34. WOMAN: Did you know that most of Australia's population lives along the coast?

MAN: Yes, that's because the interior is one big desert which offers very few ways for people to earn a living.

According to the man, what accounts for Australia's population distribution?

35. MAN: Was your trip to the Orient a success?

WOMAN: I'm afraid not. I guess selling is just not my cup of tea.

What can be said about the woman?

Section 1, Part C

Sample Talk

On our right, across from the world renowned Hotel del Coronado, is the Glorietta Bay Inn. The main lobby, offices, meeting rooms, and some suites are located in the famous Spreckels Mansion, built by John D. Spreckels in 1908. In 1977 the Mansion acquired the status of Historical Landmark. On either side of this elegant mansion, are modern wings bringing the total of guest rooms to one hundred. In addition, the inn regularly receives the blue ribbon prize from the Coronado Floral Society for its beautiful landscaping and gardens.

Example I

What is this talk about?

Example II

Where are the guest rooms located in this hotel?

Questions 36-41

FEMALE STUDENT: Excuse me, Professor Burnham, may I talk to you for a moment?

PROFESSOR BURNHAM: Yes, of course. What can I do for you?

FEMALE STUDENT: I'll be graduating next month, and then I'm going to look for a job in business administration. Since I took two management courses with you, I was wondering if you would write a letter of recommendation for me.

PROFESSOR BURNHAM: Well, you see, I'm very particular about who I write letters of recommendation for. In your case, I could certainly state that you made excellent grades in my courses, but I would also have to point out what I observed to be your limitations.

FEMALE STUDENT: Could you tell me what you see those to be?

PROFESSOR BURNHAM: Even though your performance on exams was excellent, you seemed to find it difficult to work with your classmates on projects which were supposed to represent a group effort. And probably of most importance, you did not take advantage of any of the opportunities the department offered for business majors to gain hands-on experience. The ability to work in a group, even as the leader, and, especially, initiative are too essential in the job of an administrator to be ignored.

FEMALE STUDENT: Well, I see what I need to work on. Thank you for pointing these things out to me, Professor Burnham.

36. What does the student ask Professor Burnham for?

37. How can Professor Burnham's attitude toward the student be described?

38. What was the student's greatest strength?

39. How can Business Administration majors gain practical experience in management?

40. What characteristic does Professor Burnham consider essential for an administrator?

41. What is one thing the student will probably do now?

To begin our study of the North American armadillo, I want you, first of all, to forget everything you think you know about this astonishing animal and look at the observable facts.

Firstly, the armadillo's armor-like covering does not protect it from the teeth of medium-sized carnivores such as dogs. And, the armadillo, contrary to what many people believe, cannot protect itself by rolling into a ball. So, is there any reason for the armadillo's armor? Of course. The armor allows the armadillo to escape into thick brush and thorns that its unarmored enemies, such as dogs and humans cannot enter safely.

Secondly, the armadillo is not simply a 55-million-year-old oddity. The armadillo is useful to us in many ways. Some people consider armadillo meat a delicacy, and others value this odd animal for the insect pests it consumes.

42. What is the main idea of this talk?

43. According to the speaker, what is an advantage of the armadillo's armor?

44. For how long has the armadillo survived?

45. According to the speaker, what is one way that the armadillo is useful to human beings?

The following is brought to you as a public service announcement by this station.

The Professional Examination administered by the Kansas State Board of Examiners of Architects will be given on Saturday, May 24 from 9AM to 4PM. An architect may practice professionally in this state upon successful completion of this examination.

To qualify for the exam, you must be in one of the following categories:

Category #1: You must have a professional degree, that is a B.A. or an M.A., from an accredited school of architecture.

Category #2: You must have a total of eight years of education and/or experience in architecture acceptable to the Board, *and* you must have passed the qualifying test.

The deadline for registration for the Professional Examination is April 10. You can register in Room 10 of the Memorial Building. For more information about the test or about qualifications, please call 321-8341, extension 13.

46. Who sponsored this announcement?

47. What is the announcement about?

48. Who must take a qualifying test?

49. When can an applicant register for this test?

50. How can one get more information about this examination?

Tapescript/Practice Test VI

Section 1, Part A, Listening Comprehension

Example I

When Tom made the reservations, he didn't know that they couldn't be changed.

Example II

Keith has never been as good at bowling as his wife is.

1. What is Craig like?
2. Tim is the fourth doctor in his family, but only the second surgeon.
3. When the deficit was discovered, the accountant was forced to resign.
4. It was a bargain, but I couldn't come up with the cash.
5. Watch out for the traffic in this kind of weather.
6. Barely a month had passed before their new restaurant folded.
7. You'll find that information under "house plants."
8. Ken objected to having the meeting in his study.
9. How do you account for your victory?
10. Off-campus housing tends to be expensive.
11. We were almost out of gas just as we found a service station.
12. If I could afford it, I would subscribe to that particular journal.
13. Barbara won't be able to see the doctor until the end of next week.
14. His heart attack was brought on by tension and a poor diet.
15. Sally must either cash a check or borrow some money before she goes shopping.
16. Carry-on luggage must fit under your seat.
17. The tickets for the benefit were sold out this morning.
18. It's too late to correct all of the test papers tonight.
19. To think Harvey is all of thirteen years old.
20. You should look up that word.

Section 1, Part B

Example   MAN: These power failures are causing a lot of trouble at the plant.
WOMAN: I don't think the situation's likely to get better.
What does the woman mean?

21. WOMAN: Well, make-up, costumes and sets have all been taken care of.
MAN: Yes and the lighting's all settled. I guess we're ready for opening night.
Where do these people work?

22. WOMAN: I can't see how to connect these new speakers to my stereo.
MAN: Let me show you. I have the same model.
What does the man mean?

23. MAN: I refuse to ride with David again.
WOMAN: I'm on your side. From now on, I'll take the bus rather than risk my life.
What are these people discussing?

24. WOMAN: How is Dan doing in medical school?
MAN: At first, he found the schedule very rigorous, but now he's learned to plan his time and accomplish more.
What do you learn about Dan?

25. WOMAN: Are you still planning to hire a new salesman?
MAN: Yes, but not until I get back from my vacation.
What will the man do first?

26. MAN: I thought you didn't like working eight-hour days.
WOMAN: At first I didn't, but everyone here is so much fun to work with that I don't mind the hours.
What does the woman mean?

27. MAN: I've been waiting for at least ten minutes to buy this one lousy shirt.
WOMAN: I'm very sorry sir. I'll take care of it right away.
What is the man complaining about?

28. WOMAN: I really think you should've cleaned up that mess by now.
MAN: You're right. There's no excuse for my having put it off so long.
What is the man doing?

29. MAN: Did you see the movie on channel eight last night?
WOMAN: No, I turned in early instead.
What does the woman mean?

30. MAN: I'm afraid something didn't agree with me. I think I'm going to be sick.
WOMAN: Why don't you get a breath of fresh air?
What's the man's problem?

31. WOMAN: The chapel is on this side of the campus, isn't it?
MAN: I believe you're right.
What is the woman trying to find out about?

32.   MAN: Jack's not coming in today. His cab broke down out near the airport last night.
    WOMAN: Yeah, he borrowed five hundred dollars from me to pay for a new transmission.
What does Jack do?

33. WOMAN: I'll get someone to help you carry your lamp to your car.
    MAN: If you don't mind, I'd like to have it delivered.
What does the man mean?

34. WOMAN: Jack and Maria were the last couple I expected to break up.
    MAN: I guess their problems started when Jack was promoted to assistant production manager.
What are these people talking about?

35.   KEVIN: I'm exhausted after that board meeting.
    WOMAN: I'm not surprised, Kevin, it went on for four hours.
Why is Kevin tired?

Section 1, Part C

<u>Sample Talk</u>

The Carnegie Public Library will open its annual Anthropology Film Festival on Tuesday, August 30, at 7:30 P.M. with "A Trip to Morocco." This beautifully photographed film takes the viewer through Moroccan cities and countryside to visit the famous medieval city of Fes, the souks of the Marrakech, and camel markets at Rissani. Mr. Paul Talbott, professor of anthropology from the State University, will be on hand to answer questions and lead a discussion about the film at its conclusion.

Example I

What is the film about?

Example II

What is Paul Talbott's profession?

Questions 36-40

The Office of Computer Services has been set up to help all members of the university community. Our primary activities include implementing student and faculty research and providing instruction in computer and information sciences. If you are interested in making extensive use of our services which, by the way, are free for full-time students and faculty members, please observe the following procedure:

1. Submit a written summary of your project to us with a detailed description of the computer help you will need.
2. Make an appointment with one of our staff members to discuss your project and to set up a work schedule for your project. One staff member will be assigned to your project and work on it with you until completion.

36. What does the Office of Computer Services do?

37. How is the cost of using the computer services determined?

38. According to the speaker, why was the Computer Services Office set up?

39. What is one of the jobs of staff members at the Office of Computer Services?

40. What can best be said about the procedure described for using the Office of Computer Services?

WOMAN: We've been in this apartment for over two years now. I think we should consider redecorating some of the rooms.

MAN: But it's just beginning to feel like home! Why would you want to change anything?

WOMAN: Well, for one thing, we both have good jobs now, so we can afford to have the kind of furniture we've always wanted. We can finally get rid of the secondhand things.

MAN: I think just the opposite—every piece of our old furniture has a story. Throwing it out would be like tossing out our memories.

41. How does the man feel?
42. What does the woman want to do?
43. How has the couple's life changed in the last two years?
44. What does the man say about their old furniture?

Questions 45-50

Since 1975, when John Moody of Milwaukee mounted a twelve-horsepower motor on his hang glider, the more adventurous among us have had the opportunity to try something approaching pure flight. Moody's idea led to the production of ultralights which consist of a wing, a single seat for the pilot, and a small motor. Most ultralight enthusiasts are simply interested in the pleasure of controlled flight exposed to the air, but these fragile-looking vehicles—in appearance similar to hang gliders—have also been used for crop-dusting as well as for military and police surveillance. At present, there are few restrictions on the use of ultralights. They may not exceed 254 pounds or carry more than five gallons of fuel. Their speed limit is 63 miles per hour, and ultralights must not fly after dark or in restricted airspace.

45. What is the topic of the talk?
46. Which of the following is the best description of an ultralight?
47. Who is John Moody?
48. What causes most enthusiasts' interest in ultralights?
49. According to the speaker, which of the following is illegal in an ultralight?
50. Which of the following is not mentioned as a practical use for the ultralight?

PRACTICE TEST ANSWER SHEETS I-VI

HOW TO MARK THE ANSWER SHEET

When you mark your answers on the answer sheet, you should:

1. Use a medium-soft (#2 or HB) black lead pencil.

2. Mark *only one* answer to each question.

3. Be sure to mark your answer in the row with the same number as the number of the question you are answering.

4. Carefully and completely blacken the oval corresponding to the answer you choose for each question. If you change your mind about an answer after you have marked it on your answer sheet, completely erase your old answer and then mark your new answer.

The examples below show you the *correct* way and *wrong* ways of marking an answer sheet. Be sure to fill in the ovals on your answer sheet the *correct* way.

CORRECT	WRONG	WRONG	WRONG	WRONG
Ⓐ Ⓑ ● Ⓓ	Ⓐ Ⓑ Ⓒ Ⓓ	Ⓐ Ⓑ Ⓒ Ⓓ	Ⓐ Ⓑ Ⓒ Ⓓ	Ⓐ Ⓑ Ⓒ Ⓓ

Answer Sheet for Practice Test I

(Remove This Sheet and Use it to Mark Your Answers)

SECTION 1
LISTENING COMPREHENSION

SECTION 2
STRUCTURE AND WRITTEN EXPRESSION

SECTION 3
READING COMPREHENSION AND VOCABULARY

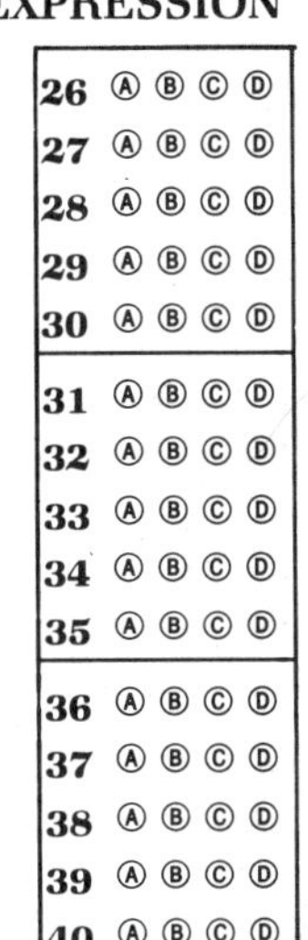

Answer Sheet for Practice Test II

(Remove This Sheet and Use it to Mark Your Answers)

SECTION 1
LISTENING COMPREHENSION

SECTION 2
STRUCTURE AND WRITTEN EXPRESSION

SECTION 3
READING COMPREHENSION AND VOCABULARY

Answer Sheet for Practice Test III

(Remove This Sheet and Use it to Mark Your Answers)

SECTION 1
LISTENING COMPREHENSION

SECTION 2
STRUCTURE AND WRITTEN EXPRESSION

SECTION 3
READING COMPREHENSION AND VOCABULARY

Answer Sheet for Practice Test IV

(Remove This Sheet and Use it to Mark Your Answers)

SECTION 1
LISTENING COMPREHENSION

SECTION 2
STRUCTURE AND WRITTEN EXPRESSION

SECTION 3
READING COMPREHENSION AND VOCABULARY

Answer Sheet for Practice Test V

(Remove This Sheet and Use it to Mark Your Answers)

SECTION 1
LISTENING COMPREHENSION

SECTION 2
STRUCTURE AND WRITTEN EXPRESSION

SECTION 3
READING COMPREHENSION AND VOCABULARY

Answer Sheet for Practice Test VI

(Remove This Sheet and Use it to Mark Your Answers)

SECTION 1
LISTENING COMPREHENSION

1 Ⓐ Ⓑ Ⓒ Ⓓ	26 Ⓐ Ⓑ Ⓒ Ⓓ	
2 Ⓐ Ⓑ Ⓒ Ⓓ	27 Ⓐ Ⓑ Ⓒ Ⓓ	
3 Ⓐ Ⓑ Ⓒ Ⓓ	28 Ⓐ Ⓑ Ⓒ Ⓓ	
4 Ⓐ Ⓑ Ⓒ Ⓓ	29 Ⓐ Ⓑ Ⓒ Ⓓ	
5 Ⓐ Ⓑ Ⓒ Ⓓ	30 Ⓐ Ⓑ Ⓒ Ⓓ	
6 Ⓐ Ⓑ Ⓒ Ⓓ	31 Ⓐ Ⓑ Ⓒ Ⓓ	
7 Ⓐ Ⓑ Ⓒ Ⓓ	32 Ⓐ Ⓑ Ⓒ Ⓓ	
8 Ⓐ Ⓑ Ⓒ Ⓓ	33 Ⓐ Ⓑ Ⓒ Ⓓ	
9 Ⓐ Ⓑ Ⓒ Ⓓ	34 Ⓐ Ⓑ Ⓒ Ⓓ	
10 Ⓐ Ⓑ Ⓒ Ⓓ	35 Ⓐ Ⓑ Ⓒ Ⓓ	
11 Ⓐ Ⓑ Ⓒ Ⓓ	36 Ⓐ Ⓑ Ⓒ Ⓓ	
12 Ⓐ Ⓑ Ⓒ Ⓓ	37 Ⓐ Ⓑ Ⓒ Ⓓ	
13 Ⓐ Ⓑ Ⓒ Ⓓ	38 Ⓐ Ⓑ Ⓒ Ⓓ	
14 Ⓐ Ⓑ Ⓒ Ⓓ	39 Ⓐ Ⓑ Ⓒ Ⓓ	
15 Ⓐ Ⓑ Ⓒ Ⓓ	40 Ⓐ Ⓑ Ⓒ Ⓓ	
16 Ⓐ Ⓑ Ⓒ Ⓓ	41 Ⓐ Ⓑ Ⓒ Ⓓ	
17 Ⓐ Ⓑ Ⓒ Ⓓ	42 Ⓐ Ⓑ Ⓒ Ⓓ	
18 Ⓐ Ⓑ Ⓒ Ⓓ	43 Ⓐ Ⓑ Ⓒ Ⓓ	
19 Ⓐ Ⓑ Ⓒ Ⓓ	44 Ⓐ Ⓑ Ⓒ Ⓓ	
20 Ⓐ Ⓑ Ⓒ Ⓓ	45 Ⓐ Ⓑ Ⓒ Ⓓ	
21 Ⓐ Ⓑ Ⓒ Ⓓ	46 Ⓐ Ⓑ Ⓒ Ⓓ	
22 Ⓐ Ⓑ Ⓒ Ⓓ	47 Ⓐ Ⓑ Ⓒ Ⓓ	
23 Ⓐ Ⓑ Ⓒ Ⓓ	48 Ⓐ Ⓑ Ⓒ Ⓓ	
24 Ⓐ Ⓑ Ⓒ Ⓓ	49 Ⓐ Ⓑ Ⓒ Ⓓ	
25 Ⓐ Ⓑ Ⓒ Ⓓ	50 Ⓐ Ⓑ Ⓒ Ⓓ	

SECTION 2
STRUCTURE AND WRITTEN EXPRESSION

1 Ⓐ Ⓑ Ⓒ Ⓓ	26 Ⓐ Ⓑ Ⓒ Ⓓ
2 Ⓐ Ⓑ Ⓒ Ⓓ	27 Ⓐ Ⓑ Ⓒ Ⓓ
3 Ⓐ Ⓑ Ⓒ Ⓓ	28 Ⓐ Ⓑ Ⓒ Ⓓ
4 Ⓐ Ⓑ Ⓒ Ⓓ	29 Ⓐ Ⓑ Ⓒ Ⓓ
5 Ⓐ Ⓑ Ⓒ Ⓓ	30 Ⓐ Ⓑ Ⓒ Ⓓ
6 Ⓐ Ⓑ Ⓒ Ⓓ	31 Ⓐ Ⓑ Ⓒ Ⓓ
7 Ⓐ Ⓑ Ⓒ Ⓓ	32 Ⓐ Ⓑ Ⓒ Ⓓ
8 Ⓐ Ⓑ Ⓒ Ⓓ	33 Ⓐ Ⓑ Ⓒ Ⓓ
9 Ⓐ Ⓑ Ⓒ Ⓓ	34 Ⓐ Ⓑ Ⓒ Ⓓ
10 Ⓐ Ⓑ Ⓒ Ⓓ	35 Ⓐ Ⓑ Ⓒ Ⓓ
11 Ⓐ Ⓑ Ⓒ Ⓓ	36 Ⓐ Ⓑ Ⓒ Ⓓ
12 Ⓐ Ⓑ Ⓒ Ⓓ	37 Ⓐ Ⓑ Ⓒ Ⓓ
13 Ⓐ Ⓑ Ⓒ Ⓓ	38 Ⓐ Ⓑ Ⓒ Ⓓ
14 Ⓐ Ⓑ Ⓒ Ⓓ	39 Ⓐ Ⓑ Ⓒ Ⓓ
15 Ⓐ Ⓑ Ⓒ Ⓓ	40 Ⓐ Ⓑ Ⓒ Ⓓ
16 Ⓐ Ⓑ Ⓒ Ⓓ	
17 Ⓐ Ⓑ Ⓒ Ⓓ	
18 Ⓐ Ⓑ Ⓒ Ⓓ	
19 Ⓐ Ⓑ Ⓒ Ⓓ	
20 Ⓐ Ⓑ Ⓒ Ⓓ	
21 Ⓐ Ⓑ Ⓒ Ⓓ	
22 Ⓐ Ⓑ Ⓒ Ⓓ	
23 Ⓐ Ⓑ Ⓒ Ⓓ	
24 Ⓐ Ⓑ Ⓒ Ⓓ	
25 Ⓐ Ⓑ Ⓒ Ⓓ	

SECTION 3
READING COMPREHENSION AND VOCABULARY

1 Ⓐ Ⓑ Ⓒ Ⓓ	26 Ⓐ Ⓑ Ⓒ Ⓓ	51 Ⓐ Ⓑ Ⓒ Ⓓ
2 Ⓐ Ⓑ Ⓒ Ⓓ	27 Ⓐ Ⓑ Ⓒ Ⓓ	52 Ⓐ Ⓑ Ⓒ Ⓓ
3 Ⓐ Ⓑ Ⓒ Ⓓ	28 Ⓐ Ⓑ Ⓒ Ⓓ	53 Ⓐ Ⓑ Ⓒ Ⓓ
4 Ⓐ Ⓑ Ⓒ Ⓓ	29 Ⓐ Ⓑ Ⓒ Ⓓ	54 Ⓐ Ⓑ Ⓒ Ⓓ
5 Ⓐ Ⓑ Ⓒ Ⓓ	30 Ⓐ Ⓑ Ⓒ Ⓓ	55 Ⓐ Ⓑ Ⓒ Ⓓ
6 Ⓐ Ⓑ Ⓒ Ⓓ	31 Ⓐ Ⓑ Ⓒ Ⓓ	56 Ⓐ Ⓑ Ⓒ Ⓓ
7 Ⓐ Ⓑ Ⓒ Ⓓ	32 Ⓐ Ⓑ Ⓒ Ⓓ	57 Ⓐ Ⓑ Ⓒ Ⓓ
8 Ⓐ Ⓑ Ⓒ Ⓓ	33 Ⓐ Ⓑ Ⓒ Ⓓ	58 Ⓐ Ⓑ Ⓒ Ⓓ
9 Ⓐ Ⓑ Ⓒ Ⓓ	34 Ⓐ Ⓑ Ⓒ Ⓓ	59 Ⓐ Ⓑ Ⓒ Ⓓ
10 Ⓐ Ⓑ Ⓒ Ⓓ	35 Ⓐ Ⓑ Ⓒ Ⓓ	60 Ⓐ Ⓑ Ⓒ Ⓓ
11 Ⓐ Ⓑ Ⓒ Ⓓ	36 Ⓐ Ⓑ Ⓒ Ⓓ	
12 Ⓐ Ⓑ Ⓒ Ⓓ	37 Ⓐ Ⓑ Ⓒ Ⓓ	
13 Ⓐ Ⓑ Ⓒ Ⓓ	38 Ⓐ Ⓑ Ⓒ Ⓓ	
14 Ⓐ Ⓑ Ⓒ Ⓓ	39 Ⓐ Ⓑ Ⓒ Ⓓ	
15 Ⓐ Ⓑ Ⓒ Ⓓ	40 Ⓐ Ⓑ Ⓒ Ⓓ	
16 Ⓐ Ⓑ Ⓒ Ⓓ	41 Ⓐ Ⓑ Ⓒ Ⓓ	
17 Ⓐ Ⓑ Ⓒ Ⓓ	42 Ⓐ Ⓑ Ⓒ Ⓓ	
18 Ⓐ Ⓑ Ⓒ Ⓓ	43 Ⓐ Ⓑ Ⓒ Ⓓ	
19 Ⓐ Ⓑ Ⓒ Ⓓ	44 Ⓐ Ⓑ Ⓒ Ⓓ	
20 Ⓐ Ⓑ Ⓒ Ⓓ	45 Ⓐ Ⓑ Ⓒ Ⓓ	
21 Ⓐ Ⓑ Ⓒ Ⓓ	46 Ⓐ Ⓑ Ⓒ Ⓓ	
22 Ⓐ Ⓑ Ⓒ Ⓓ	47 Ⓐ Ⓑ Ⓒ Ⓓ	
23 Ⓐ Ⓑ Ⓒ Ⓓ	48 Ⓐ Ⓑ Ⓒ Ⓓ	
24 Ⓐ Ⓑ Ⓒ Ⓓ	49 Ⓐ Ⓑ Ⓒ Ⓓ	
25 Ⓐ Ⓑ Ⓒ Ⓓ	50 Ⓐ Ⓑ Ⓒ Ⓓ	

ESSAY PRACTICE SECTION

This section provides a straightforward approach to writing the 200-300 word essay required by the TOEFL Writing Section. In general, in order to answer the writing question, you are required to deal with two sides of an issue, express an opinion (either personal or in relation to some specific consideration, e.g., someone your age, your country, etc.), and provide support for this opinion.

The ideal essay will . . .

1) be well organized and well developed.

2) effectively deal with the writing task.

3) support its thesis or illustrate its ideas with appropriate detail.

4) show unity, coherence and progression.

5) display consistent facility in the use of language.

6) demonstrate syntactic variety and appropriate word choice.

The final two considerations depend fundamentally on your general level of English and your written English in particular. Those points are only briefly touched on here (see *Stage Ten*). The first four points depend on an understanding of what Americans judge to be good expository writing. By following the guidelines given here in *Stages One—Nine*, by completing the exercises, by examining the model paragraphs given, and by practicing the whole process with the 10 extra questions given in Appendix I, you will be able to improve your score on the Essay Section, whatever your level of English.

Stages One—Five deal with organizing your ideas on the subject. Stage One asks you to identify the issue; Stage Two, to list the things you are asked to do in relation to the issue; Stages Three and Four, to arrange, select and order the specific points you think of on one side or other of the issue; and Stage Five, to decide which side to support—as a function of the points you have been able to make rather than by simply following your personal sentiments. Going systematically through each of these stages will constitute a very positive step in the direction of achieving each of the goals enumerated in points 1–4 made above to describe the ideal essay.

Stages Six—Nine provide you with guidelines for writing a well-organized, well-developed essay that shows unity, coherence and progression. Stages Six and Seven are concerned with the relationship between topic sentences and the specific supporting points you wish to make. Stages Eight and Nine offer suggestions for, and practice in, linking together your ideas more tightly and effectively through appropriate use of connectors and reference words.

Stage Ten contains a checklist of what you might profitably keep in mind while writing your essay and might review in any time you have left after completing your essay. Among other things, this covers certain common grammatical errors.

Time is a critical factor, which must be taken into consideration in the Essay Section. Clear indications are given as to how much time you should ideally spend on each stage. While working through the practice exercises, you may find you need more time at first. but your aim should be eventually to do each stage within the recommended time-frames. THE PRACTICE QUESTIONS IN APPENDIX I ARE OFFERED TO HELP YOU GET THE TIMING RIGHT!

You will have a total of 30 minutes to produce your essay, and it is essential to make full and efficient use of the whole time available. In general, you should be working toward the following time-frames:

Stages One—Five:	10-12 minutes
	(The work done in Stages One–Five will appear as your rough notes on the exam paper.)
Writing Your Essay:	15 minutes
	(This time period will include dealing with the considerations in Stages Eight—Nine, which you should aim to make part of your essay-writing routine.)
Stage Ten:	3–5 minutes
	(Check for errors.)

Appendix I contains ten additional questions for you to practice on after you have worked through the ten stages given here. You should try to answer those questions one by one under examination time conditions.

Appendix II offers practice in questions which are accompanied by information expressed in the form of charts and graphs. YOU MAY WELL ENCOUNTER INFORMATION IN THIS FORM IN THE EXAM, AND YOU SHOULD WORK THROUGH THIS APPENDIX TO PREPARE YOURSELF FOR SUCH AN EVENTUALITY.

The three-paragraph (thesis, antithesis, synthesis) approach you are recommended to follow in Stages One—Nine is the one most likely to correspond to the type of question you will be asked. The first two paragraphs deal with one side of the issue, then the other, while the third paragraph brings in any specific considerations you are asked to make, contains your opinion, and supports this with reasons. However, this is not, of course, the only approach possible. APPENDIX II OFFERS ALTERNATIVES.

Stage One: What is the issue?

In the Essay Section of the TOEFL, you will almost always be asked to compare and/or contrast two things (attitudes, options, approaches). It is very important to answer the question which is asked—and not some other, related question which perhaps might interest you more. It is essential, therefore, to identify the issue and focus your attention on it. One way of doing this is to summarize for yourself in a single phrase the essence of the question asked.

Two exercises providing practice for this crucial first step are offered in Stage One. Once you have identified the issue, you will need to examine the question again to determine how you are expected to relate to it, for example, by giving your opinion, by discussing it in terms of your own country, etc. This problem will be dealt with in Stage Two.

Exercise A:

Check (✔) the answer you think best reflects the essence of the question. Explain what you think is wrong with the other answers.

Question 1:   Complaints are frequently heard regarding the role and cost of advertising in society; defenders of advertising, meanwhile claim benefits for it ranging from the economic to the aesthetic. Examine the two sides of the argument, providing concrete examples. Say which point of view you agree with, and why.

________ **a.** Benefits of advertising

________ **b.** The high cost of advertising

________ **c.** Advertising: Good or bad?

Question 2:   Some people argue that capital punishment is necessary to deter certain crimes; others say that the state should never resort to such an extreme method whatever the circumstances. Outline the major arguments of both positions. What is your opinion and why?

________ **a.** Serious crimes: What will stop them?

________ **b.** Crime deterrents: The state's responsibility?

________ **c.** Capital punishment: For or against?

Question 3:   Many people believe that the traditional nuclear family with a father as the provider, a mother as the homemaker, and several children under one roof is the best arrangement for human beings. Other people have rejected this lifestyle and have found alternative living arrangements, such as communes, more satisfactory. Describe one or two benefits of living in a traditional nuclear family and one or two benefits of living in a commune. Compare the two lifestyles and explain which you think might be more beneficial for young children.

________ **a.** Nuclear family vs. commune

________ **b.** Father's role vs. mother's role

________ **c.** Traditional vs. revolutionary lifestyles

Question 4:   It is sometimes argued that countries should protect their own industries from foreign competition. Other people, by contrast, say that everyone benefits if countries freely import and export their products. Explain some of the arguments for each side. Which do you think is more appropriate for your country? Give reasons for your answer.

________ **a.** Importing vs. exporting

________ **b.** Foreign goods vs. national goods

________ **c.** Free trade vs. protectionism

Question 5:   The expression "Life begins at 40" suggests that young people do not enjoy all the advantages in life. "You're only young once," on the other hand, tends to suggest the opposite idea. Give specific claims which might be made in support of each argument. Which are you in favor of, and why?

_________ **a.** Advantages vs. disadvantages of youth

_________ **b.** Youth vs. maturity

_________ **c.** After 40: The best years

Exercise B:

Read Questions 6–10 carefully. Then summarize the essence of each question in a single phrase.

Question 6:   It is sometimes said that people should have the right to read, listen to or look at anything they choose, free from the censorship of any individual or group. The opposing point of view holds that both individuals and society are better off if some works are banned and, therefore, not available to the public. Discuss the benefits of each of these two ways of thinking. In your opinion, which is more appropriate for people your age?

____

Question 7:   Industrialization has contributed enormously to a general improvement in living standards. Many people today, however, protest that the cost of this industrialization is too high in environmental terms. Do you agree? Provide specific evidence for each side of the controversy and say where you think leaders of your country should stand on the issue and why.

____

Question 8:   Some educators believe that children in public schools should be separated according to their academic ability and then educated in different groups with each group moving ahead at its own pace. Others say that there are greater benefits for all students if all children in the same age group are educated together. Suggest one or two benefits of each approach and explain which you think more appropriate for students in your country.

____

Question 9:   Many sociologists claim that the violence in modern American society is partly, or even largely, the result of the excessive amount of violence portrayed on TV. Others deny this, arguing that there is no cause-and-effect relationship between watching TV violence and committing violent acts. Discuss these positions with specific examples, state your own point of view, and explain your reasons.

____

Question 10:   There are advantages to inheriting wealth and social prestige from one's parents; different kinds of advantages may accompany the achievement of influence and/or wealth by one's own efforts. Outline some of the pros and cons of each position and explain which you think would be preferable for a leader in your country. Give reasons for your choice.

Stage Two: How are you asked to relate to the issue?

Having established the issue, you should also take careful note of precisely how you are asked to relate to it. You may be specifically required to do one or more things:

First, you may be asked to
>> provide concrete examples
>> describe some pros and cons
>> compare and contrast.

Secondly, you may need to
>> give your personal opinion
>> say what/which you think is better for someone your age, someone from your country, etc.

Finally, you will be required to
>> say why you hold a certain opinion.

Write down each requirement separately so that you can check, as you write, that you do not ignore any.

Exercise C:

Look at the ten questions in Stage One and list for each the specific things you are asked to do.

Examples:

<u>**Question 4:**</u> 1) Advantages—both sides
2) Which better for my country?
3) Reasons for #2

<u>**Question 5:**</u> 1) Concrete examples—both sides
2) Personal opinion
3) Reasons for #2

Stage Three: What points can you make for each side?

Your TOEFL essay will be graded according to how you organize and express your thoughts. But, before you can produce a well-organized, clearly-written essay, you need to bring together your ideas about the issue you have been asked to write about.

In Stages One and Two, you established what the issue was and how you were asked to relate to it. Now, you must brainstorm about the topic—listing all the relevant points you can think of to support the two sides of the issue. As you practice this essential step, keep the following hints in mind.

1) **Make two lists of supporting ideas—one for each side of the issue.** (See how this has been done in Exercise E.)

2) **Write down all relevant points.** You will see how to choose the best points for your essay in Stage Four.

3) **Do not worry about the order of your supporting points.** Ordering will also be dealt with in Stage Four.

4) **Do not worry about coming up with brilliant ideas.** Your essay will be judged on its organization, development, and coherence and on how clearly the ideas are expressed—not on its originality.

5) **Do not be discouraged if the topic does not interest you.** Remember, you will not have a choice of topics, so get on with your work. Note: You will improve with practice! Also, if you have difficulty in thinking of sufficient points for your argument, the exercises in Appendix II will help.

6) **Complete your brainstorming in 5-6 minutes.** This stage represents essential preparation for writing a well-organized essay, but you will need most of the 30 minutes allotted to the Essay Section for the actual writing of your essay.

Stage Three offers two exercises to prepare you for brainstorming (Exercises D and E) and one exercise which lets you practice this skill just as you will need to apply it during the TOEFL (Exercise F). You will find a total of 20 questions to practice brainstorming with (ten questions in Stage One and ten in Appendix I). REMEMBER: PRACTICE HELPS!

Exercise D:

In each of the following, mark the points *A* or *B* to indicate which side of the argument they would fit under. (There will not necessarily be an equal number of points on the two sides.)

1. What is the issue? *Advertising: Good or bad?* (Question 1)

> How are you asked to relate to the issue?
> Discuss both sides—with concrete examples
> My point of view—with reasons
> Supporting ideas: *A*—Advertising/good
>   *B*—Advertising/bad

1. Informs people of what is available, what's new, cost, content, components, etc.

2. Creates needs rather than meeting them.

3. Creates demand and, therefore, makes mass production, lower prices possible.

4. Emphasizes image over substance (name brands over quality).

5. Adds to cost of merchandise.

6. Billboards all over countryside.

7. Livelier cityscapes (compare East and West Berlin).

8. Representative of free market forces vs. centralized decisions.

9. Desires standardized away from individual preferences by mass media ads.

10. Creates jobs by selling products.

11. Uses valuable economic, human resources.

12. State-of-the-art ads entertain as well as inform.

2. What is the issue? *Capital punishment: For or against?* (Question 2)

How are you asked to relate to the issue?
        Outline arguments on both sides
        My opinion—with reasons
Supporting ideas: *A*—For capital punishment
                B—Against capital punishment

________ **1.** No statistical evidence of deterrent effect.

________ **2.** Cost of long prison sentences—a burden on society.

________ **3.** "Eye for an eye, tooth for a tooth."

________ **4.** Morbid interest in executions.

________ **5.** Possibility of irreversible mistake.

________ **6.** Not applied equitably—only to some classes, races, etc. (poor, blacks, etc.).

________ **7.** Some people cannot be rehabilitated—society is better off without them.

________ **8.** Society should not descend to criminal's level.

________ **9.** Many murderers would kill anyway because they are mentally unstable.

________ **10.** Stops other people committing capital crimes.

________ **11.** Some crimes (mass murders, etc.) are so inhuman that this is the only appropriate response.

________ **12.** In past centuries used as punishment for minor crimes.

After you have listed supporting ideas for both sides of the issue, make a quick check to see that each point really will back up the heading under which it is listed. Cross out any items which are inappropriate or irrelevant.

The following criteria may help you recognize points which do *not* belong in your lists.

A. An idea that argues against what you are trying to prove or explain. (Sometimes these ideas are appropriate for the other side of the issue.)

B. Personal details which do not prove or explain the issue.

C. Ideas or facts related to the topic but unconnected to the issue.

D. Ideas or facts that have nothing to do with the topic or the issue.

Exercise E:

Some of the points included in the following lists suggested for Questions 3 and 4 are NOT suitable for inclusion. (i) Circle the number of those items which are unsuitable. (ii) Mark each unsuitable point with a letter (A, B, C, or D) corresponding to a reason from the box above.

1. What is the issue? *Nuclear family vs. communal living* (Question 3)

How are you asked to relate to the issue?
Describe one or two benefits of each side.
Compare the two lifestyles.
Which do you think more beneficial for young children?

NUCLEAR FAMILY	COMMUNAL LIVING
1. Financial security—a father who accepts responsibility for providing for his own children.	**1.** Communes were very popular in the US in the 1850s and 1960s.
2. Socially acceptable, respectable lifestyle.	**2.** Varied experience/many opinions and points of view.
3. Most adults don't want more than two children.	**3.** Opportunity for all to experiment with different roles—not just as parents or sons/daughters—leads to greater chance of self fulfillment.
4. Mother at home to give care, nurturing, etc.	**4.** If parents are sick or incompetent, others can fill in and care for children.
5. Living in a large group of non-relatives is exciting.	**5.** My best friend wants to live in a commune someday.
6. Children are special to their own parents.	**6.** Children see people cooperating.
7. I was raised in a nuclear family.	**7.** Flexible, creative problem-solving.
8. Emotional security/automatic love from parents and siblings.	**8.** Probably better systems than either nuclear family or communal living are around.

2. What is the issue? *Free trade vs. protectionism* (Question 4)

How are you asked to relate to the issue?
Advantages of each approach
Which approach is good for your country?
Reasons

<table>
<tr><th style="text-align:center">FREE TRADE</th><th style="text-align:center">PROTECTIONISM</th></tr>
</table>

FREE TRADE	PROTECTIONISM
_______ **1.** Means more trade.	_______ **1.** Provides local employment.
_______ **2.** More trade leads to more prosperity for everyone.	_______ **2.** To become a manufacturer, you must obtain the necessary permits.
_______ **3.** I prefer foreign-made clothes.	_______ **3.** Helps local industry to develop.
_______ **4.** Lower prices lead to better living standards.	_______ **4.** Improves balance of trade.
_______ **5.** George Bernard Shaw was in favor of free trade.	_______ **5.** Free trade only makes some people rich.
_______ **6.** Every country produces what it can make the best and the most efficiently.	_______ **6.** My father is convinced that buying foreign products hurts our country.
_______ **7.** Protectionism leads to inefficient, expensive production.	_______ **7.** Protectionism reduces the variety of products available.
_______ **8.** Many people don't understand exactly what free trade is.	_______ **8.** Means less dependence of raw-materials producers on manufacturing nations.
	_______ **9.** All countries want free trade for what they produce cheaply, and protection for what they don't.

Exercise F:

Look at Questions 5—10 given in Stage One (pages 273–275) and write down all the *relevant* points you can think of for each question. Divide the points according to the way you formulated the issue (Exercises A and B). (Note: Set out your supporting points as indicated for Questions 3 and 4 in Exercise E.)

TIME: Allow yourself 5-6 minutes for making your lists for each question.

Stage Four: How can your points be made into an outline?

When you come to turn your list of points into an outline, you will probably find that you have too many unconnected points. At this stage you should

1) Cross out any items which are inappropriate or irrelevant.

2) Choose three or four of the remaining points for each side.

3) Try to see some connecting links between the points you have chosen for each side.

4) Decide in which sequence you can best introduce the points, first from one side and then the other.

There is no need, and probably no time, to write out the supporting points you have selected all over again. Much better, indicate to yourself on your rough notes which points you have decided on and the order. There are many ways of doing this. The way suggested here is to circle the numbers chosen and write new numbers beside the circles to indicate the sequence. What is important is for you to decide on a system and use it every time you practice answering a question in the Essay Section. Do not wait until the day of the exam to decide! (*Note:* There are no "right" answers here. Choose the three or four points on each side which *you* feel *you* can make into the most coherent argument.)

Exercise G:

Look at the list of supporting points you made for Questions 6–10, Stage 3, Exercise F. For each set of points, do the folllowing:

i) Cross out any inappropriate or irrelevant points.

ii) Choose three or four of the remaining points for each side.

iii) Order the points you have chosen for each side.

Stage Five: Which side will you support and why?

Now you must decide which side to support and, therefore, the basic content and direction of your third paragraph. Again, there are things to remember:

1) There is no "right" side of the issue. You will be graded on the structure and content of your essay and on how well you defend your opinion, but it absolutely does not matter which side of the issue you choose to support.

2) Remember two criteria for choosing the side of the issue you will support.

A) For which side can you produce the most coherent argument, based on what you did in Stages Three and Four?

B) For which side can you produce some "extra" point in paragraph 3 to tip the balance?

3) Your decision about which side to support will directly affect the structure of your first two paragraphs. Paragraph 1 of your essay will contain the argument of the side you decide NOT to support. Paragraph 2 will contain the argument of the side you choose to support.

Exercise H:

Based on the points you have made (Stage Three), selected and ordered (Stage Four), decide which side you are going to support in each of the ten questions introduced in Stage One.

Stage Six: Making your outline into paragraphs

In the first five stages you practiced coming up with and organizing the IDEAS you will need to have in response to the Essay Question on the TOEFL. Obviously, the ideas depend on you (but remember, PRACTICE in answering TOEFL-type questions will help you to come up with ideas quickly). Now you must think about how to EXPRESS these ideas.

In this stage you will examine an aspect of the rhetorical development of paragraphs: The relationship between general and specific, that is, between TOPIC SENTENCES and SUPPORTING SENTENCES, respectively. At this stage you will write topic sentences for the first two paragraphs of your essay, and in Stage Seven you will look at the same task in relation to your concluding paragraph.

Before you try to write your topic sentences, think about the following:

1. **The topic sentence covers or summarizes the specific supporting points in the paragraph.** You have already made a list of the supporting points you want to use for both sides of the issue (Stages Three and Four). How can you introduce/summarize the two or three points you want to make in each of the first two paragraphs?

2. **The topic sentence usually comes first in a paragraph.** This is a good rule to follow for your first paragraph, and the same is generally true of the second paragraph, too, but sometimes the connection you make between the first and second paragraphs may occupy a whole sentence. In that case, your topic sentence would normally move to the second position.

3. **The kind of topic sentence you write will depend on the kind of specific points you intend to make.** The most common types of specifics are (a) examples, (b) analysis, and (c) reasons (this type of specific is likely to be used in your concluding paragraph). General types of topic sentences suggest themselves in relation to each of these types of specifics:

   A) EXAMPLES: A large number of *attitudes/factors/examples* may be *identified/mentioned* on *behalf of/in support of/which offer support to* the *idea/view/opinion* that . . .

   B) ANALYSIS: The fundamental belief of those who support . . .
   In a nutshell, the argument of people who claim . . .
   Basically, the argument on behalf of . . .

   C) REASONS: It is my belief that . . .
   The best approach for my country is to . . .
   Someone my age should preferably . . .

4. **Write a topic sentence.** Do not write a simple title or heading, such as "Why some people think capital punishment is wrong," "Some attitudes associated with the idea that life begins at 40," or even "What is the position of people who support free trade?"

5. **Vary the form of the topic sentences in your first two paragraphs.** For example, do NOT write:

   Paragraph 1: There are many reasons why . . .
   Paragraph 2: On the other hand, there are also many reasons why . . .

Instead, try, for example, the following:

Paragraph 1: There are many reasons why . . .
Paragraph 2: On the other hand, a convincing case can be made for . . .

In this stage, you will find two exercises (I and J) which require you to relate general and specific sentences, one exercise (K) which asks you to produce topic sentences for your lists of specifics, and a final exercise (L) in which you must analyze the relationship between topic sentences and supporting points in model paragraphs.

Exercise I:

For each topic sentence given, suggest the most appropriate type of specific points (*examples, reasons, analysis*), and then suggest some appropriate specifics of that type. (Write the supporting points in note form if you prefer.)

1. What is the issue? *Advertising: Good or bad?* (Question 1)

   Topic sentence: Most people who complain about today's advertising agree that it is, in general, harmful to society.

   Type of specifics: ____

   Examples of specifics: i) _______________________________________
          ii) _______________________________________
          iii) ______________________________________
          iv) ______________________________________

2. What is the issue? *Capital punishment: For or against?* (Question 2)

   Topic sentence: People who support capital punishment generally claim two principal benefits for it: Its deterrent effect and its suitability for certain crimes.

   Type of specifics: ____

   Examples of specifics: i) _______________________________________
          ii) _______________________________________
          iii) ______________________________________
          iv) ______________________________________

3. What is the issue? *Nuclear family vs. commune* (Question 3)

   Topic sentence: There can be little doubt that the nuclear family as a unit is so widespread throughout the world because it provides members with a series of important benefits.

   Type of specifics: ____

   Examples of specifics: i) _______________________________________
          ii) _______________________________________
          iii) ______________________________________
          iv) ______________________________________

4. What is the issue? *Free trade vs. protectionism* (Question 4)

    Topic sentence: The crux of the argument of economists who support the concept of free trade is that free trade means more trade and that more trade is better for everyone.

Type of specifics: _______________________________

Examples of specifics: i) _______________________________
                  ii) _______________________________
                iii) _______________________________
                iv) _______________________________

5. What is the issue? *Youth vs. maturity* (Question 5)

    Topic sentence: There are a number of attitudes which it is possible to associate with the saying "You're only young once."

Type of specifics: _______________________________

Examples of specifics: i) _______________________________
                  ii) _______________________________
                iii) _______________________________
                iv) _______________________________

Exercise J:

For each of the following lists of specifics, write an appropriate topic sentence. (Two topic sentences for each question.)

Note: The specifics given in this exercise are probably in more complete sentences than you would write (your list of supporting points may not even be in English) because here you need to understand someone else's rather than your own ideas.

1. What is the issue? *Censorship: For or against?* (Question 6)

    How are you asked to relate to the issue?
      Discuss benefits of both sides
      Give your opinion about which is more appropriate for people your age
    Specific supporting points:

CENSORSHIP	
FOR	**AGAINST**
1. Countries should be allowed to ban works which are ideologically counter to the standards of the nation.	**1.** Leads to suppression of ideas (e.g. censorship of textbooks which discuss evolution).

(continued)

2. Adults may be able to recognize and reject obscene works, but if they exist, children will be exposed to them—and they will not be able to understand/deal with them maturely.

3. Some works are generally agreed to be obscene—therefore, should not be seen by anyone.

4. Artists and writers should be encouraged to produce works that emphasize the positive side of life.

Topic Sentence: ________________________
____
____

2. Censors do not reflect everyone's view of what is obscene. Whose point of view should prevail?

3. What was once considered obscene is now considered inoffensive, e.g. *Lady Chatterley's Lover.*

4. Individual censorship is more effective. Let the public reject artists and writers whose works have a bad effect on society.

5. It doesn't work. Censored works are more sought after.

Topic Sentence: ________________________
____
____

2. What is the issue? *Benefits of industrialization vs. environmental cost* (Question 7)

How are you asked to relate to the issue?
   Specific examples for each side
   Which side for leaders of your country and why?
Specific supporting points:

BENEFITS OF INDUSTRIALIZATION	**ENVIRONMENTAL COST**

1. Greater number of jobs
2. Improved living standards
   Transportation
   Sanitation
   Housing (heating, etc.)
   Appliances
   Cheaper clothing, shoes, etc.
	1. Polluted air
	2. Dangerous factories (asbestos, etc.)
	3. Poisoned water supplies
	4. Noise
	5. Dying forests
	6. Disappearing farmland—produces urbanization, population needed for factories
	7. Psychological impact of factory-generated city center living

Topic Sentence: ________________	Topic Sentence: ________________

3. What is the issue? *Track system vs. Comprehensive education system* (Question 8)

How are you asked to relate to the issue?

One or two benefits of each side
Explain which is better for students in your country.
Specific supporting points:

TRACK SYSTEM	COMPREHENSIVE EDUCATION SYSTEM
1. Bright students are allowed to move ahead at their own pace. **2.** Slow students receive the extra help they need to understand their basic subjects. **3.** Specially prepared teachers for the needs of each group. **4.** Real life requires people to be educated to different levels and in different directions for different jobs.	**1.** Students and not labeled "slow" or "fast" so they don't get stuck in one category and simply perform to that expected level. **2.** Bright students help slower classmates. **3.** Some slow starters prove themselves to be very capable over the long run. **4.** Students benefit from socializing with all types of students. **5.** Students learn to treat each other as equals since no one is labeled as "good" or "bad."
Topic Sentence: ________________ ________________________________ ________________________________	Topic Sentence: ________________ ________________________________ ________________________________

4. What is the issue? *TV: Does/Doesn't cause violence* (Question 9)

How are you asked to relate to the issue?
  Discuss both sides with examples
  Your point of view—explain reasons
Specific supporting points:

TV CAUSES VIOLENCE	TV DOESN'T CAUSE VIOLENCE
1. TV viewers become desensitized to violence; begin to think violent acts don't really hurt or cause harm. **2.** TV shows people solving everyday problems with violence. **3.** Violence on TV is identified with law-abiding, respectable characters as well as with the bad guys. **4.** TV overemphasizes sensational aspects of society—people then decide to arm themselves because the world is full of danger.	**1.** Adults and children can distinguish between reality and TV shows. **2.** Children generally follow examples of parents, teachers, etc., not examples set by TV characters. **3.** There were violent people before the days of TV. **4.** People say that TV violence leads to real violence, so does it follow that TV virtues also lead to real-life virtues?

(continued)

5. Children spend so much time watching
TV that it becomes reality for them.

Topic Sentence: _________________   Topic Sentence: _________________

___________________________   ___________________________

___________________________   ___________________________

5. What is the issue? *Inherited money and position vs. Earned money and position* (Question 10)

How are you asked to relate to the issue?
Pros and cons of each position
Which preferable for leader of your country—give reasons
Specific supporting points:

INHERITED MONEY AND POSITION	**EARNED MONEY AND POSITION**
1. Understanding—through example of parents—of how to deal with money and position	**1.** Development of character through hard work
2. Time to devote to study and politics without worry of how to make money and gain position	**2.** Understanding of the common man/woman because he/she has been there
3. Access to other people in high positions—important political contacts	**3.** Satisfaction in knowing that he/she has earned what he/she has
4. Public, in general, prefers and trusts leaders with well-known names, e.g. Kennedy, Rockefeller, etc. in US	**4.** Better equipped to recognize talent and hard work in others
Topic Sentence: _________________	Topic Sentence: _________________

Exercise K:

Write a topic sentence for each list of specific supporting points which you wrote for Questions 6–10 at Stages Three and Four.

Exercise L:

Look at the following models (first two paragraphs only, in each case) and analyze the kind of specific support provided.

i) Identify the topic sentence in each paragraph.

ii) Say why the topic sentence in each paragraph is appropriate.

Note: You are *not* asked to agree or disagree with the points which are made.

Question 3   (Nuclear family vs. communal living)

Many children derive numerous benefits from the secure, close-knit lifestyle provided by their nuclear families. They enjoy for instance, freedom from financial worries because they have a father who provides them with their material needs. In addition, they have the emotional security provided by a mother who is always at home when they need her, caring for the house and for her children's day-to-day needs. Finally, there is the consideration that the nuclear family has proved quite successful over the centuries and throughout much of the world in maintaining the kind of society we are familiar with.

What happens, however, when the father has no job or the mother becomes desperately ill, when one or more members of a nuclear family fails to do his or her part? For some people, a commune may offer an alternative that is different in a number of ways. The first and most obvious is that no one's role is rigidly fixed, each person finding how his or her talents can contribute to the success of the community. A natural concomitant of this is that women are not limited to mothering and housekeeping, nor are men barred from these activities. Additionally, children have the opportunity to learn from many adults who offer different points of view and role models. Finally, adults are able to shift responsibilities from one person to another if the need arises without affecting the order and continuity of the lives of the commune's children.

Question 4   (Free trade vs. protectionism)

Those who argue for free trade say that when international tariffs are eliminated, the total amount of trade increases, and that this benefits everyone. For example, they often quote the 1930s, when the introduction of tariff barriers coincided with less prosperity for almost everyone. By contrast, they point to the 1960s, where freer trade coincided with increasing prosperity. Furthermore, these people claim that free trade means better living standards since everyone can buy what they want as cheaply as possible.

On the other hand, people who favor protectionist measures generally insist that, among other reasons, they are necessary to protect local jobs. Obvious examples in the United States include jobs in the steel, auto and textile industries, which are threatened by cheap imports. Nevertheless, every country, even big exporters like Japan, has its special cases (Japanese farm products, which are heavily protected, are the most expensive in the world). In developing countries, another argument for maintaining protectionism is that local industries need it initially to grow and compete. In addition, it is said that this approach helps the balance of trade by reducing imports.

Stage Seven: How can your conclusion be made into a paragraph?

In Stages Three—Six you planned paragraphs 1 and 2 of your essay. In this stage, you will see how to plan paragraph 3. The following table shows how paragraph 3 differs from paragraphs 1 and 2.

	Paragraphs 1 and 2	**Paragraph 3**
1. Focus	Specific arguments to be made on either side of the issue (see Stages One, Three and Four).	The point of view from which you are asked to consider the issue, your opinion, and reasons for your choice (see Stages Two and Five).
2. Topic Sentence	In paragraphs 1 and 2, the topic sentence covers the specific supporting arguments in a general, introductory way.	In paragraph 3, the topic sentence does not have the generalizing function in relation to the rest of the paragraph as it did in the first 2 paragraphs. Here, the topic sentence will contain *your* opinion.

Exercise M contains two model third paragraphs for you to analyze in relation to what you are asked to do in the TOEFL-type question. These paragraphs include the writer's point of view and answer all the points established in Stage Two (How are you asked to relate to the issue?). Note that in paragraph 3 for Question 3 (Nuclear Family vs. Communal Living), the writer's opinion is combined with a reference to the point of view he/she was asked to consider. Alternatively, in paragraph 3 for Question 4 (Free trade vs. Protectionism), the writer's reference to the point of view he/she was asked to consider is given separately. Equally your opinion may be expressed in the first sentence (see Capital punishment: For or against?—Question 2; Youth vs. Maturity—Question 5; or Advertising: For or against?—Question 1 in Stage Eight) with your reasons following, or the reasons may come first, followed by the topic sentence combining your opinion (see Question 3 again).

Exercise N asks you to write two concluding paragraphs. Again, remember that in your final paragraph, it should be very clear that all remaining elements of the question (apart from the issue itself which you dealt with in the first 2 paragraphs) have been taken into consideration.

Exercise M:

Look at the two model concluding paragraphs below (third paragraphs for the model answers in Stage Six) and identify the following:

i) The sentence in which the writer gives his/her opinion.

ii) The manner in which the writer refers to the "considerations" in the question (see Stage Two).

iii) The reasons given in support of the conclusion.

Question 3   (Nuclear family vs. communal living)

If the world were a perfect place, with all parents playing their parts responsibly, the nuclear family would probably offer the ideal arrangement. However, this is not the case and, therefore, I believe that the commune, with many adults working together, offers young children
20   a better chance of dealing with the inevitable ups and downs of family life.

Question 4   (Free trade vs. protectionism)

15   My own country is a third-world nation with a large foreign debt. I believe it needs protection to help its developing industries and, thus, to provide jobs to its fast-growing population. At present, it is too dependent on importing manufactured articles at high prices, while its exports of raw materials are at prices which apparently always go down and which are controlled by the rich countries. Unfortunately, in this discussion, it appears that every country wants free
20   trade for things it produces cheaply (in the case of my country, oil and textiles), but protection for other products. To sum up my own country's situation, it needs to produce manufactured articles, and it needs protection to develop the industries involved.

Exercise N:

Write concluding paragraphs for Questions 1 and 2 (see Stage One) assuming two first paragraphs in each case based on some of the specifics given in Stage Three. Make sure you include references to all the appropriate considerations you noted for these questions at Stage Two.

Stage Eight: Connecting your ideas

This stage and the next are both concerned with ways of ensuring that your essay is clearly and tightly argued and developed. Here in Stage Eight you will look at overt ways to link together the different parts of your essay, especially the specific supporting points you thought of in Stages Three and Four, by means of connectors. In Stage Nine, you will see how appropriate use of reference can further tighten up the style of what you write.

The important thing to remember is that by including some expressions of this type in your essay, you indicate that YOU know where you are going, and that each of your sentences has a purpose (just as your topic sentences, examined in the previous stages, indicate that your paragraphs have a purpose). Though it may not be desirable to include connectors between all of your sentences (the effect would be heavy and mechanical), it is a good idea to ask yourself in each case what the connector *would be* since this will focus your attention on making sure each sentence has a function.

This stage offers five exercises aimed at making you more conscious of the function and use of connectors. The first two (Exercises O and P) ask you to complete sentences or paragraphs by choosing suitable connectors. The remaining three (Exercises Q—S) are based on model essays to Questions 1 and 5 (see Stage 1), and ask you to identify and categorize the connectors used and, finally, to write a model essay based on a plan that you have examined for one of the models.

The connectors examined here have a function similar to signposts along a road. They tell the reader where you (the writer) are going by indicating what direction you are taking in a particular sentence.

You should be familiar with the following five types of connectors:

Type	Simple Example	Sample Sentence
1. LISTING OR SEQUENCE	also	People who support capital punishment say it deters criminals, and it *also* is appropriate punishment for some crimes.
2. CONTRAST	but	The arguments for advertising are strong, *but* the arguments against it are even stronger.
3. CAUSE	as	The deterrent argument is questionable *as* statistics from a number of countries indicate little change in murder rates if capital punishment is abolished.
4. EFFECT	so	Statistics from a number of countries indicate little change in murder rates if capital punishment is abolished *so* the deterrent argument is questionable.
5. EXEMPLIFICATION	such as	There are a number of typical arguments against TV advertising, *such as* its poor quality, its encouragement of consumerism and its effect on the attitudes of young children.

Note that each of these ideas (sequence, contrast, etc.) can be expressed in a number of ways. For example, instead of *also*, you might say *in addition, furthermore, moreover, on top of this*, etc.—all with fundamentally the same effect, though some might involve changes in the grammatical structure of the sentence. The following table lists some of the possibilities. (*Note:* All the expressions in a single column have the same basic rhetorical function. Some may be more appropriate in certain cases than others.)

1. Listing or Sequence	2. Contrast	3. Cause	4. Effect	5. Exemplification
also	but	because of	so	for instance
in addition	however	as a result of	therefore	for example
(to)	nevertheless	due to	thus	to take one
further-	on the other	thanks to	consequently	example
more	hand	attributable to	as a result	an obvious instance
similarly	by contrast			of this
likewise	although			such as
moreover	whereas			
first(ly)				
second(ly),				
etc.				
finally				
in the first				
place				

Exercise O:

Complete each of the following paragraphs with appropriate connectors from the respective boxes.

i)

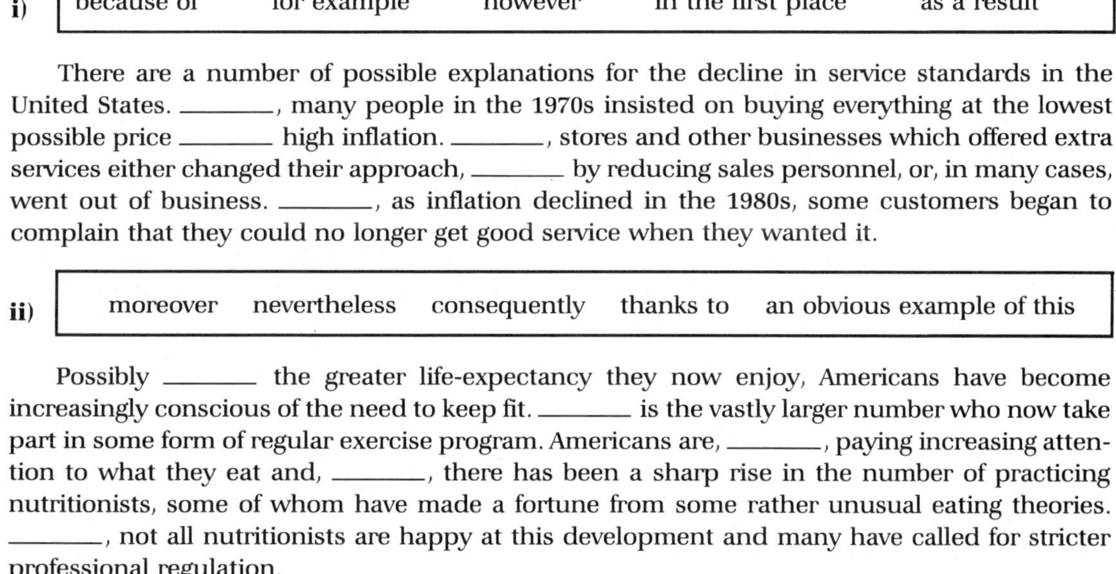

because of	for example	however	in the first place	as a result

There are a number of possible explanations for the decline in service standards in the United States. _______, many people in the 1970s insisted on buying everything at the lowest possible price _______ high inflation. _______, stores and other businesses which offered extra services either changed their approach, _______ by reducing sales personnel, or, in many cases, went out of business. _______, as inflation declined in the 1980s, some customers began to complain that they could no longer get good service when they wanted it.

ii)

moreover	nevertheless	consequently	thanks to	an obvious example of this

Possibly _______ the greater life-expectancy they now enjoy, Americans have become increasingly conscious of the need to keep fit. _______ is the vastly larger number who now take part in some form of regular exercise program. Americans are, _______, paying increasing attention to what they eat and, _______, there has been a sharp rise in the number of practicing nutritionists, some of whom have made a fortune from some rather unusual eating theories. _______, not all nutritionists are happy at this development and many have called for stricter professional regulation.

<table>
<tr><td>iii)</td><td>finally   for instance   due to   whereas   thus</td></tr>
</table>

Some educators encourage children to take part in team games _________ others prefer them to try individual sports. The former say that team games encourage attitudes valuable to society, cooperation, _________; the latter claim that sports like tennis or swimming develop self reliance and _________ prepare the children for the rigors of adult life. My own opinion is that individual sports are preferable since they usually avoid the frequent injuries _________ the physical contact characteristic of team games; they prepare one better for the individual sports one can more easily take part in in later life and, _________, they allow each individual to develop his abilities at his own pace, without worries about letting the team down.

<table>
<tr><td>iv)</td><td>therefore   such as   by contrast   likewise   attributable to</td></tr>
</table>

The advantages _________ to mass-transit systems _________ buses, subways and trains involve a number of factors: They require far fewer vehicles and, _________ cause little congestion and little pollution of the environment. _________, transportation in individual cars causes both congestion and pollution. _________, mass-transit systems, when efficiently organized, have proved to be considerably cheaper than cars.

Exercise P:

The aim of this exercise is to get you to practice using connectors. In a few cases, the structures involved may demand a particular connector, but in most cases, a number are possible. Try, however, to use the one you feel is most appropriate.

Part i:

For this exercise, use connectors introducing *CONTRAST* given in the table.

1. For many people the nuclear family remains the ideal lifestyle _________, some prefer the relative unpredictability of communal life.

2. _________ most countries speak in favor of the principle of free trade, in practice they often introduce protectionist measures.

3. TV advertising is costly, often insulting to people's intelligence and frequently irritating because it interrupts programs at crucial moments. _________, it may be argued that it makes many of the programs possible, may reduce prices by creating mass markets and is sometimes informative and entertaining.

4. Many people say capital punishment deters criminals, _________ statistics suggest otherwise.

5. It is usually young people who say "You're only young once;" _________, those who claim that "Life begins at forty" are very rarely under thirty-five.

Part ii:

For this exercise, use connectors introducing *LISTING OR SEQUENCE given in the table.*

1. The deterrent effect of capital punishment is an obvious reason for retaining it. There are, ________, some crimes which are so serious or horrifying that no other punishment is adequate.

2. ________the reasons suggested above, there is the biblical justification of "An eye for an eye, a tooth for a tooth."

3. The Americans require such anti-free-trade actions as "voluntary restrictions" on car exports ________, the European Common Market countries impose a variety of measures on imports which are effectively protectionist.

4. There are several complaints which might be made against individual advertisements. ________, many of them are an insult to the intelligence of those they are directed toward ________ there is the fact that they are endlessly repetitive and ________ (though only for lack of space to include more) they have the undesirable effect of developing consumerist attitudes among highly susceptible young children.

5. Communes offer children a variety of roles they can adopt, and they ________ provide a wide range of contacts with generally well-disposed adults.

Part iii:

For this exercise, use connectors introducing *CAUSE AND EFFECT* given in the table.

1. There was a series of negative effects directly ________ the protectionist measures taken in the 1930s.

2. The Japanese are clearly superior at producing certain electronic goods ________ they are naturally in favor of free trade in these categories.

3. There are many disadvantages associated with advertising, but, in my opinion, the advantages far outweigh them. ________, I would certainly not be in favor of a generalized ban on advertising, even if I would be against TV advertising for certain products.

4. When I was quite young I was deeply impressed by the case of a man who was executed and later proved innocent of the crime he was supposed to have committed. ________, I have always been strongly opposed to capital punishment.

5. The virtues of respect for authority, cooperation and fraternal love are the very basis of a healthy society. ________ the family unit, these virtues still exist in my country.

Part iv:

For this exercise, use connectors introducing *EXAMPLES* given in the table.

1. Many examples of the beneficial effects of advertising may be cited. ________, they provide potential buyers with information concerning the many competing products available.

2. Most of the benefits of the nuclear family, _______ warmth, affection and protection, are also offered, often to a greater degree, by a commune.

3. There are a number of circumstances in which one may hear the phrase "You're only young once." _______ would be a mother excusing the exaggerated behavior of her children when faced with complaints by their father.

4. Capital punishment is shockingly final and mistakes are sometimes made. _______, there is a cross on a gravestone in Arizona which says "George Johnson. Hanged by mistake." Nothing else really needs to be said.

5. Some so-called "third-world" countries, in Africa and South America _______, may require protectionist measures in order to build up local industries.

Exercise Q:

Read the following model essays and

i) Underline the connectors.

ii) Mark each connector 1, 2, 3, 4 or 5 according to the types of connectors identified in the table on page 291.

1. Advertising: Good or bad?

It is quite easy to find reasons for attacking advertising. First, it tends to be extremely costly (TV advertising during Super Bowl XXI cost more than $1,000,000 per minute!), and this cost must eventually be paid by the consumer. Second, it uses up valuable human resources: The advertising profession occupies many of the best brains in any country. In addition, from the
5 social standpoint, advertising promotes image over substance (a typical example of this is the fascination with designer names which advertising has created, with people paying extra for such a name, not for better quality) and a standardization of taste, especially among children (each Christmas in the United States there is a crazy impulse to buy particular toys made popular by advertising—one year Cabbage Patch dolls, another Masters of the Universe, another GI
10 Joe, etc.).

However, there are also a number of cogent arguments which may be advanced in defense of advertising, principally, but not exclusively, economic ones. In the first place, it has a valuable informative function, helping potential customers know about the characteristics and prices of products or where they can buy a particular product cheaply. Then, by stimulating demand for
15 successful products, advertising creates jobs in the manufacturing and service sectors. Finally, it can reduce prices by making mass-production possible.

The discussion can, of course, go on forever, but my preference is clear: I would naturally like all advertising to be honest, intelligent, amusing, and informative, but if I must choose between living in a society with typical advertising or without advertising, personally I prefer the
20 former. West Berlin, for example, symbolizes the former, East Berlin the latter. I have visited both places. I would certainly prefer to live in West Berlin, where the city, its TV programs and its magazines are full of advertisements—and, as a result, full of life, interest and, especially, variety.

2. Youth vs. maturity

There are many attitudes intrinsically associated with the view that "You're only young once." For example, there is the idea that a young person may be excused if his or her behavior is not up to normal standards, if he or she is, in fact self-indulgent, because later, life will be hard. There is, moreover, the idea that time is passing by and can never be recovered: "Gather ye rosebuds while ye may," says Herrick. Such attitudes may undoubtedly be connected with the shorter life-expectancy that was characteristic of bygone days. Finally, however, it must be said that the fundamental attitude reflected in the phrase is a pessimistic one: The good part of life is short, make the most of what you can; don't expect much further down the road.

By contrast, the attitude implicit in "Life begins at forty" is notably more optimistic, though not necessarily less potentially selfish. The first thing to say, of course, is that it is a phrase usually uttered only by those about to reach, or who have already attained, the age mentioned. It is their way of declaring that they are not giving up. Naturally, too, the phrase suggests that the wisdom and judgment, the patience and experience age is said to bring are more than adequate compensation for the loss of youthful passion and vigor.

My own attitude to life naturally inclines me more towards the second phrase. "You're only young once" may sound fine, but it is, in fact, full of self-pity and fear for the future, of apprehensions about a hard later life, and ultimately, of the grave. Far better, I think, the refusal to concede defeat, the determination to make the most of things, to think of beginnings rather than ends contained in "Life begins at forty" even if, admittedly, this phrase these days tends to connote a certain selfishness.

Exercise R:

Look at the following "skeleton outline" which shows the plan for ONE of the model essays given in Stage Six, page 287 (first 2 paragraphs only). Decide which model essay this plan describes, and then write in the actual connectors which have been used in the essay.

What is the issue ? ____

1st Paragraph	**1.** General statement (one side of the argument)	
	2. Exemplification ______________________________	
	3. Contrast (within exemplification) ________________	
	4. Additional argument ________________________	
	5. Cause (basis) for this argument ________________	
2nd Paragraph	**6.** General statement (other side of the argument) preceded by contrast __________________________________	
	7. Exemplification ____________________________	
	8. Contrast (within exemplification) ________________	
	9. Additional argument ________________________	
	10. Additional argument ________________________	

Exercise S:

Look at the "skeleton outline" below, corresponding to the model essay on *Advertising: Good or bad?* (page 294).

What is the issue? *Advertising: Good or bad?*

1st Paragraph	**1.**	General statement (one side of the argument)
	2.	Listing (to exemplify general statement)
	3.	Listing (to exemplify general statement)
	4.	Sequence (to exemplify general statement)
2nd Paragraph	**5.**	General statement (other side of the argument) introduced by . . . contrast
	6.	Listing (to exemplify general statement)
	7.	Sequence (to exemplify general statement)
	8.	Sequence (to exemplify general statement)

i) Note what specific connectors have been used in the model essay on advertising.

ii) Write the first two paragraphs of a 3-paragraph essay, following the same outline. (You may, of course, choose different connectors from the same categories, if you wish.) Assume that you are working on the following question and have made the notes given below.

<u>**Question:**</u> Many teachers emphasize the value of team sports in developing certain desirable characteristics among the participants; others, however, prefer to emphasize individual sports. Discuss both approaches and say which you think more desirable. Give reasons for your opinion.

What is the issue? *Team sports vs. individual sports*
How are you asked to relate to the issue:
         Discuss both sides
         Say which side you prefer and why

TEAM SPORTS	**INDIVIDUAL SPORTS**
1. Teaches spirit of cooperation.	**1.** Everyone can participate.
2. Individual puts team (and so company? community? nation?) first.	**2.** Performance level may be secondary.
3. Comradeship.	**3.** Self-reliance.
	4. Easier to practice in later life (swimming, ping-pong, tennis, golf, etc.).

Stage Nine: Tightening the connections

One way of ensuring that your essay has cohesion and direction was examined in Stage Eight. The present stage examines the question of reference, and thus ways of tightening up relationships between the words you use.

The use of reference words saves unnecessary repetition and ties one sentence—or even paragraph—in with another, or one part of a sentence with another part. "When did Susan marry George?" is unlikely to receive the answer: "Susan married George in 1986," but "She married him in 1986" is certainly a possible response. Since in good expository writing the content of one sentence will certainly bear some relationship with that of the one(s) before and the one(s) following, it would be surprising indeed if reference words did not play an important part.

This stage offers five exercises. In the first (Exercise T), you are asked to identify referents for words and expressions in a model essay in answer to Question 2 (see Stage One), while the next two (Exercises U and V) require you to do the same with model essays offered in earlier stages. The final two exercises (W and X) invite you to rewrite sentences making use of reference words to tighten them up.

Exercise T:

Read the following model essay and answer the reference questions which follow it.

Capital punishment: For and against?

Those who support capital punishment generally claim that it deters criminals from committing crimes for fear of execution and, furthermore, that some crimes are so terrible that the only appropriate punishment for them is death. Others also point out that alternative punishments, such as extremely long prison terms, are a great expense to society and rarely result in
5 rehabilitation, so that the criminal would be a danger to the community if he was ever freed.

While there is some truth in these arguments, opponents say that statistical evidence, for example from both Great Britain and the United States, clearly shows that capital punishment does not affect murder rates, but only arouses morbid interest in executions. They add that civilized society should not descend to the barbarous level of the criminals themselves, and that
10 many of the most horrible crimes are committed by deranged persons whom nothing would deter. Finally, they argue that if a mistake is made and the wrong person is executed, nothing can be done to right that wrong.

The arguments on both sides are persuasive but certain other factors incline me to vote against capital punishment. These are related to both the present-day world and historical
15 precedents. Firstly, I am horrified by the extremely selective application of the penalty among qualified criminals these days. More important, though, is the historical parallel: In the Middle Ages in Europe, and much later in many places, capital punishment was imposed for minor crimes and executions were public. Hardly anyone today would agree with this, but, in those days, exactly the same arguments were used to support capital punishment as are used by pro-
20 ponents today.

What do the following refer to?

<table>
<tr><td>1. it (line 1) ___________________</td><td>6. these (line 14) ___________________</td></tr>
<tr><td>2. others (line 3) ___________________</td><td>7. this (line 18) ___________________</td></tr>
<tr><td>3. he (line 5) ___________________</td><td>8. alternative punishments (lines 3–4) ______</td></tr>
<tr><td>4. they (line 8) ___________________</td><td>9. that wrong (line 12) ___________________</td></tr>
<tr><td>5. whom (line 10) ___________________</td><td>10. those days (lines 18–19) ___________________</td></tr>
</table>

Exercise U:

What do the following refer to?

1. *Nuclear family vs. communal living* (See page 287.)

a. their (line 2) ______________________

b. them (line 3) ______________________

c. her (line 5) ______________________

d. his or her (line 9) __________________

e. his or her (line 11) __________________

f. this (line 12) ______________________

2. *Free trade vs. protectionism* (See page 287.)

a. this (line 2) ______________________

b. they (line 2) ______________________

c. they (line 4) ______________________

d. they (line 6) ______________________

e. which (line 9) ______________________

f. its (line 10) ______________________

g. which (line 11) ______________________

h. it (line 12) ______________________

3. *Advertising: Good or bad?* (See page 294.)

a. it (line 1) ______________________

b. this (line 5) ______________________

c. another (line 9) ______________________

d. ones (line 12) ______________________

e. it (line 15) ______________________

f. the former (line 20) __________________

g. the latter (line 20) __________________

h. its (line 21) ______________________

4. *Youth vs. maturity* (See page 295.)

a. his or her (line 2) __________________

b. one (line 7) ______________________

c. it (line 10) ______________________

d. it (line 11) ______________________

e. their (line 12) ______________________

f. it (line 16) ______________________

Exercise V:

What do the following refer to? Trace the referent as far back as possible.

1. *Free trade vs. protectionism* (See page 287 for paragraphs 1 and 2; see page 289 for paragraph 3.)

a. these people (line 5) ________________

b. another argument (line 12) _________

c. this approach (line 13) ______________

d. this discussion (line 19) ______________

e. other products (line 21) ______________

f. the industries involved (line 22)__________

2. *Advertising: Good or Bad?* (See page 294.)

    a. this cost (line 2) _______________

    b. a name (line 7) _______________

    c. cogent arguments (line 11) _______________

    d. both places (lines 20–21) _______________

3. Youth vs. maturity (See pages 295.)

    a. the idea (line 2) _______________

    b. attitude (line 7) _______________

    c. the age mentioned (line 11) _______

    d. the phrase (line 12) _______________

    e. the second phrase (line (lines 15) _______

____

Exercise W:

Rewrite the following sentences by replacing the underlined words with reference words. In 9 and 10, also change the two sentences into one.

1-2. Just as other countries seek to protect <u>these other countries'</u> own interests, so <u>Japan</u> must look after <u>Japan's</u> own interests in the field of international trade.

____

____

3-4. Opponents of free trade usually claim that protection is needed to preserve local jobs. <u>Opponents</u> also frequently claim that everyone wants free trade for some products but protection for <u>some different products</u>.

____

____

5. A great variety of new products was marketed in 1987. <u>The great variety of new products</u> was due to a change in company policy.

____

____

6-8. In the nuclear family, other roles must be understood in relation to <u>the roles</u> of the mother and father, with <u>the mother</u> offering care and emotional security and <u>the father</u> traditionally providing financial security.

____

____

9. There are some very strong arguments for this point of view. <u>Some of the arguments</u> are outlined above.

____

____

10. Most of the large advertising agencies have their headquarters in New York City. <u>In New York City</u> Madison Avenue symbolizes the advertising profession.

____

____

Exercise X:

Fill in each blank with (i) a demonstrative adjective from the box and (ii) one of the nouns indicated for each sentence.

	this	that	these	those

1-2. punishment/arguments
Some people insisted that if hanging were abolished, civilized people would all be killed in their beds, and so on. _______ were demonstrated to be without foundation when _______ was indeed abolished without the civilized world expiring.

3-4. belief/prohibitions
In medieval Europe it was thought that lending money at interest was immoral. However, with the rise of capitalism, _______ disappeared along with concerns regarding such things as cornering markets and tampering with products, which had also been forbidden. _______ would have been out of place in the free-for-all atmosphere of early laissez-faire capitalism.

5-6. attitude/determination
"Life begins at 40" is clearly positive and optimistic in tone, but it must be admitted that _______ is also tinged with the selfishness of someone who intends to get everything he/she can for himself/herself out of future opportunities. _______ may not bode well for a society in which an ever-increasing proportion will be well over not only 40, but 65 too!

7-8. costs/prices
Reports that the 1987 Superbowl advertising rates reached $1 million per minute rarely included any comment on the obvious fact that it is the purchasing public that must bear _______, since the companies paying for such valuable advertising minutes charge economic amounts for their products and _______ clearly include a certain percentage to cover advertising.

9-10. approach/institutions
The church, the government, even corporations tend to automatically favor the nuclear family, for _______, like the nuclear family itself, tend to be hierarchic rather than anarchic. Communes, on the other hand, emphasize freedom of choice and a flexible structure, and _______ may represent a threat not only to a particular type of family organization but to a particular model of society as well.

Stage Ten: Proofreading your essay

After you have finished writing your essay, you should still have the final three-five minutes for correcting mistakes. As you go through your work, look for three types of problems:

a) Composition problems

b) "English" problems

c) Form problems

     Essay Practice Section

A) Composition problems

In five minutes you will not be able to *think about* the following list of questions, but, by practicing ahead of time (that is, by asking yourself these questions about your practice essays), you should have a clear understanding of the types of problems you are looking for. Ask yourself the following questions about your essay:

1. Have I answered the question that was asked? (See Stage One.)
2. Have I addressed all of the parts of the question? (See Stage Two.)
3. Does each paragraph have a main idea? (See Stage Six.)
4. Does everything else in each paragraph support or explain the main idea? (See Stage Four.)
5. Does each paragraph have sufficient and appropriate supporting points? (See Stages Three and Four.)
6. Does the final paragraph make it clear which side of the argument I support and why? (See Stages Five and Seven.)
7. Have I used connecting words and reference words to make my essay clearly and tightly argued? (See Stages Eight and Nine.)

B) "English" problems

Many of the common grammatical problems non-native speaekers have in their written English are the same types you looked at in the Focused Exercises at the beginning of this book (see pages 1-39). Before doing your practice work on the Essay Section, it would be a good idea to review the Focused Exercises. An awareness of these common mistakes should help you avoid them in your TOEFL essay.

Obviously, you will not be able to run through a 40-point checklist after you have completed your TOEFL essay, but, as with the *Composition problems*, by checking your practice essays carefully for the problems discussed on pages 1-39, you will develop a more automatic response to errors in your written work.

C) Form problems

Form problems should be the easiest for you to correct in any extra time you may have. If you are not confident about the rules for punctuation and capitalization in English, consult a style book written for U.S. college students before you write the practice essays suggested in Appendix I. It is also a good idea to have your English instructor or a native speaker of English check your practice essay for the following problems:

1. Have I indented the first line to indicate the beginning of each paragraph?
2. Have I used capital letters where necessary?
3. Are there any spelling mistakes?
4. Are there any punctuation mistakes?
5. Are there any sentence fragments?

APPENDIX I

Use the following ten questions for TOEFL-type practice. Allow yourself 30 minutes to write a 200-300-word essay for each question. Each time you do a practice essay, try to follow the ten stages you have practiced on pages 272-301. **Before you take the TOEFL you must get used to completing this section in 30 minutes.**

Question 1:   Some educational systems emphasize general subjects for teenagers; others put a premium on developing specialized technical skills. Summarize the advantages of each approach and say which you think more appropriate for your country. Explain the reasons for your decision.

Question 2:   Some people insist that careful grooming and appropriate clothes are very important if a person wants to get ahead in the world. Others take a different position and believe that a person's performance is the only factor that leads to success. Discuss these two points of view and explain which you think might be more useful for someone your age.

Question 3:   Billions of dollars are spent each year by the superpowers on various aspects of the conquest of space. Defenders of such expenditure claim it is money well spent, but some others insist that there are more important priorities to which the money should be devoted. Specify some of the principal arguments on either side and give your own opinion, with reasons.

Question 4:   No-smoking areas have now been provided in many public places in response to demands that non-smokers be allowed to enjoy smoke-free environments. Many smokers, on the other hand, claim that they have the right to smoke in any public area or facility they please. Outline the major arguments put forward on each side. Which side do you agree with and why?

Question 5:   For many years, researchers have made use of live animals in scientific experiments, which are frequently fatal for the animals involved. They defend these experiments since in some cases, they have resulted in significant discoveries being made. Those who oppose such experiments sometimes protest vigorously, even violently, against them. Summarize the main arguments, say which side you support, and give reasons for your position.

Question 6:   In the industrialized countries, people in many jobs are obliged to retire when they reach a certain age (65 in a large number of cases). Some people protest against such regulations, while others believe that they are necessary and beneficial. Explain the major arguments and say whether you think compulsory retirement is appropriate in your country. Give reasons for your choice.

<u>**Question 7:**</u> In every age, there are people who suffer from horrible, incurable diseases or painful, irreversible physical handicaps. Many people believe that such people should be able to ask a medical doctor or a relative to end their lives painlessly. Others believe that, under no circumstances, must a person be allowed to end the life of another person on purpose. Compare these two positions, giving concrete examples of both. Which position do you agree with? Why?

<u>**Question 8:**</u> In some countries, the state takes a leading, sometimes dominant role in the economy; in other countries, the state plays no more than a minimal part. In almost every country, the government claims that its particular level of participation is the ideal. Describe some of the arguments for and against state participation and say, with reasons, what level you think appropriate for your own country.

<u>**Question 9:**</u> While some people claim that a person's essential quantities are inherited at birth, others insist that the circumstances in which a person grows up are principally responsible for the kind of person he/she becomes. Discuss and exemplify both points of view. Which do you agree with and why?

<u>**Question 10:**</u> A number of fans have become disenchanted with professional sports because of the astronomical salaries that some of the best athletes receive. Others feel that high salaries for the top stars are well-deserved. Give one or two reasons why athletes should not earn extraordinarily high salaries and one or two reasons why they should. Discuss the two sides to this controversy and explain which you think is better for the future of professional sports.

APPENDIX II

Writing a Graph-based Essay

Should you have to write an essay based on information offered in a graph, or other form, the same basic principles apply that we have examined in detail previously.

The clearest difference is that, instead of having to think of ideas to use, you will be given the information necessary. Another way of saying this is: In the other type of essay you are given the argument and you must give the details and; here, you are given the details and you must formulate an argument.

The following are particularly important considerations in writing a graph-based essay:

(1) Make sure you UNDERSTAND the information.

The information may appear in a graph (there are a variety of kinds—two of which are exemplified in this section); or in a table, or in both. It is clearly important for you to practice extracting information from sources of these types if you are not already accustomed to doing so.

(2) As discussed in Stage One for the other kind of essay, make sure you UNDERSTAND THE QUESTION.

Here this may not mean precisely understanding the issue. It may involve role-playing. For example, the instruction may say "Imagine you are writing a report"/ "Imagine you have been requested to evaluate . . . ", etc. Understanding the question here means taking account of such instructions and also identifying clearly WHAT you are asked to report on, evaluate, etc. Trends? Differences? Relationships? Or is there simply an open invitation to comment as you wish on the information given?

(3) Make sure you understand the IMPLICATIONS of the question.

Whatever form the question takes, you cannot simply describe the information contained in the graph, table, etc. You must SELECT the information which strikes you as significant after first getting a general overview of the basic themes, trends, differences or relationships that the information demonstrates. (Such information, after all, is usually presented not in a vacuum but with the PURPOSE of showing or proving something; if you feel you can identify this purpose, so much the better). Note the information which you think is significant (as in Stage Three) because you will need to develop an issue which in some way relates to this information.

Organizing a Graph-based essay (See Stage Two).

1) In this type of essay, you will probably want to present a point of view relating to the information offered in an introductory paragraph.

2) The body of the essay in this type of question will consist of a pargraph, or paragraphs, which support the point of view you have already stated. Each paragraph will have a topic sentence and supporting evidence just as we have practiced earlier, except that these will relate to the information you have selected rather than to the supporting ideas you have thought of.

3) The concluding paragraph must once again take up the theme of the opening paragraph. It should not, however, be a mere repetition of what you wrote there, but should examine how the information in the body of the essay confirms your point of view. This should be done in the first sentence, and the essay should conclude by widening the theme (drawing more general, if tentative, conclusions or relating it in some other way to a wider context.)

Note that the differences between this type of essay and the type discussed in Stages One-Ten should not be seen as drastic ones. The general principles of "good expository writing", which we carefully practiced for the other type of essay, will be equally applicable for this type. You should keep them in mind as you practice answering both types of TOEFL writing questions.

Analyzing a Model Essay (based on a graph)

The following model essay exemplifies the process described above. Read it and then write essays in answer to the remaining questions, always basing yourself on these preliminary steps in planning your essay:

1) Read and understand the question.

2) Take note of how you are asked to relate to the information (evaulate it; write a report; comment on it, etc.).

3) Write down information which strikes you as important.

4) Make these points into an outline.

5) Decide on a point of view to adopt.

Question: Surveys carried out among large groups of 25 to 40-year-olds in 1960 and 1985 asked respondents to indicate what proportion of their leisure time they spent on different activities. Imagine you are writing a report on changes in leisure time activities. Discuss the trends suggested by the information in the graphs below.

PERCENTAGE OF FREE TIME SPENT ON DIFFERENT ACTIVITIES

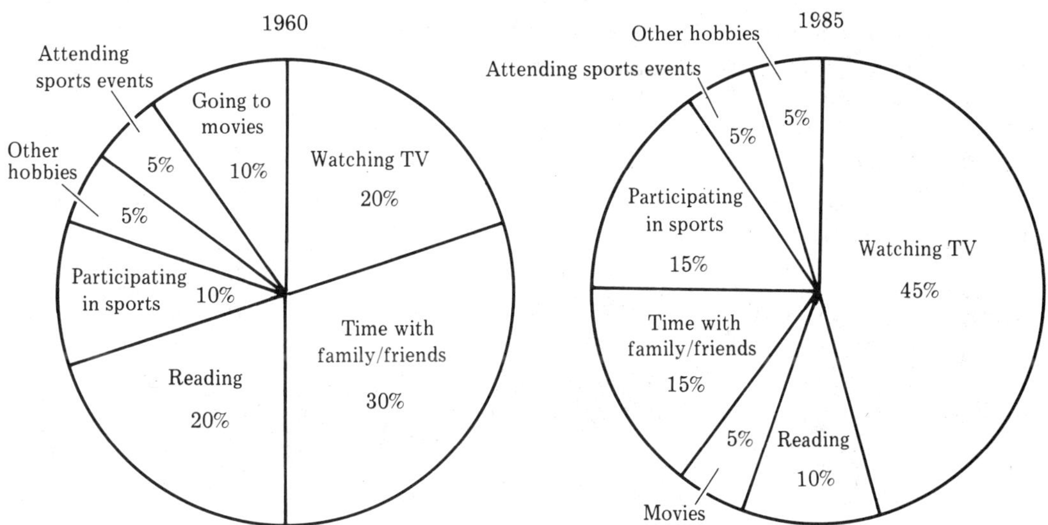

Model Essay

Probably the first thing which should be said about any survey of large groups of people, and especially about a matter so obviously subject to personal inclination as leisure time activities, is that average percentages hide enormous individual differences. Nevertheless, there are a number of clear trends which can be extracted from the graphs. Without any doubt the most outstanding is the increasing amount of time taken up by watching TV, and a corresponding decrease in the time spent with family or friends and on reading.

The increase in the time spent watching TV is astonishing since it has more than doubled, from one-fifth to almost one-half. Even more disturbing than the increase, however, is the amount of time spent on this passive activity. It is probably no coincidence that the time spent on reading—a much more participatory activity whatever the kind of reading involved—had fallen by half over the 25-year period. Family and friends, too, seem to have been pushed into the background by the television, with its often isolating effect on people. It is more understandable that movie-going, which is in some ways in direct competition with TV, has dropped by half.

The three factors discussed in the previous paragraph occupy such a large percentage of the total (80 and 75 percent, respectively, in 1960 and 1985) that the other figures are difficult to comment on. Attending sports events and other hobbies evidence no change, while participation in sports rose by 50%. This last may perhaps be explained by the fitness revolution in the eighties, which certainly involved even older people in jogging, running, tennis, and so on.

The general impression created by these figures is a worrying one. Activities which involve socializing or using the brain are declining while a completely unproductive, unimproving activity (watching TV) is coming to dominate people's leisure time. Even if this is partially offset by an increasing participation in physical activities, it must be hoped that the next survey, presumably in 2010, will provide more encouraging news, especially since people will probably have a lot more leisure time to occupy.

Practice Questions

Question 1:   Imagine you are writing a report on the development of long-term trends in American imports and exports. Look at the two graphs below, which show the composition of U.S. imports and exports at different points in time, and compare and contrast the relative importance of the different categories for both imports and exports.

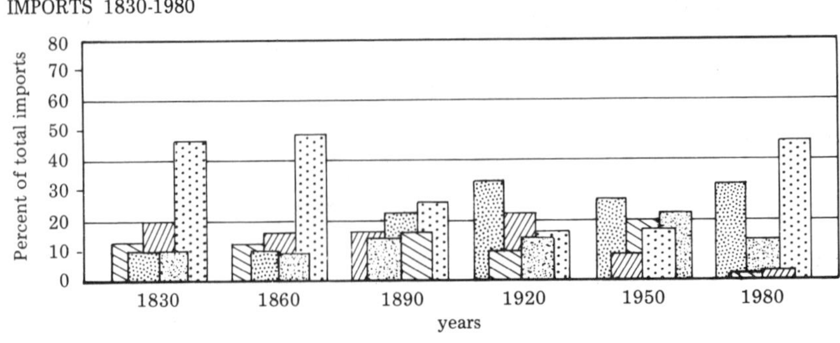

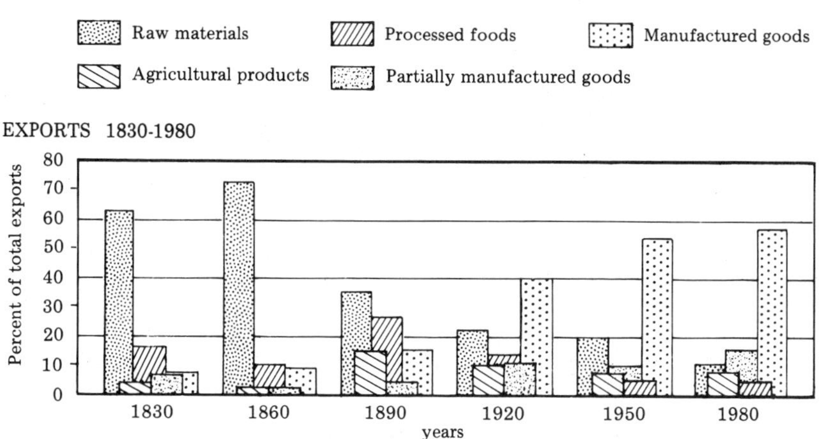

Question 2: Imagine you have been asked to write a short report on the dietary habits of the two 25-year-olds whose food intake is indicated in the graphs below. Include your own observations on the apparent effects produced.

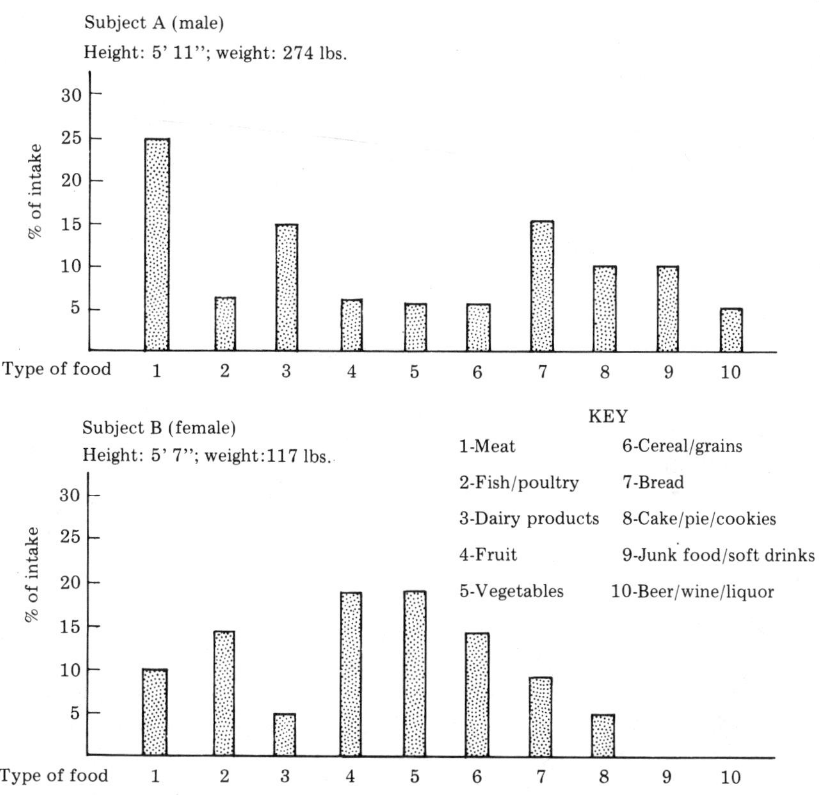

STUDYING FOR THE TOEFL? ━━━━

Critical Listening Practice for THE BEST TOEFL TEST BOOK . . .

Two additional cassettes are available to help you master the listening comprehension section of the TOEFL.

    Cassette 1 (#16472) includes recorded material for Tests 1, 2, and 3.
    Cassette 2 (#16473) includes recorded material for Tests 4, 5, and 6.

Don't delay! Order today.

$16.00 each plus $1.00 postage (U.S. only)

To order, enclose your check or money order, payable to ADDISON-WESLEY PUBLISHING COMPANY, in an envelope. Address it to:

World Language Division
Addison-Wesley Publishing Company
Jacob Way
Reading, MA 01867

For other materials to practice and polish your TOEFL skills, see reverse of this page.